GULF OIL IN THE AFTERMATH
OF THE IRAQ WAR
STRATEGIES AND POLICIES

THE EMIRATES CENTER FOR STRATEGIC
STUDIES AND RESEARCH

THE EMIRATES CENTER FOR STRATEGIC STUDIES AND RESEARCH

The Emirates Center for Strategic Studies and Research (ECSSR) is an independent research institution dedicated to the promotion of professional studies and educational excellence in the UAE, the Gulf and the Arab world. Since its establishment in Abu Dhabi in 1994, ECSSR has served as a focal point for scholarship on political, economic and social matters. Indeed, ECSSR is at the forefront of analysis and commentary on Arab affairs.

The Center seeks to provide a forum for the scholarly exchange of ideas by hosting conferences and symposia, organizing workshops, sponsoring a lecture series and publishing original and translated books and research papers. ECSSR also has an active fellowship and grant program for the writing of scholarly books and for the translation into Arabic of work relevant to the Center's mission. Moreover, ECSSR has a large library including rare and specialized holdings, and a state-of-the-art technology center, which has developed an award-winning website that is a unique and comprehensive source of information on the Gulf.

Through these and other activities, ECSSR aspires to engage in mutually beneficial professional endeavors with comparable institutions worldwide, and to contribute to the general educational and academic development of the UAE.

The views expressed in this book do not necessarily reflect those of the ECSSR.

First published in 2005 by
The Emirates Center for Strategic Studies and Research
PO Box 4567, Abu Dhabi, United Arab Emirates

E-mail: pubdis@ecssr.ae
Website: http://www.ecssr.ae

ISBN 9948-00-753-0 hardback edition

ISBN 9948-00-752-2 paperback edition

CONTENTS

Oil Market Restructuring

Diversification of Energy Supply

Gulf Oil: Outlook and Options

FIGURES AND TABLES

FIGURES

TABLES

ABBREVIATIONS AND ACRONYMS

ADGAS	Abu Dhabi Gas Liquefaction Company
ADMA–OPCO	Abu Dhabi Marine Operating Company
ADNOC	Abu Dhabi National Oil Company
AHF	Al Haramain Foundation
AOC	Arabian Oil Company
API	American Petroleum Institute
APR	Asia–Pacific Region
ASEAN	Association of South East Asian Nations
bpd	barrels per day
CEO	Chief Executive Officer
CBE	Commander of the Order of the British Empire
CEPMLP	Centre for Energy, Petroleum and Mineral Law and Policy
CCGT	combined cycle gas turbine
CDU	crude distillation unit
CGES	Centre for Global Energy Studies
CIF	cost, insurance and freight
CIS	Commonwealth of Independent States
CITIC	China International Trust and Investment Corporation
CNG	compressed natural gas
CNPC	Chinese National Petroleum Corporation
CNOOC	China National Offshore Oil Corporation
CSIS	Center for Strategic and International Studies
DWT	deadweight tons
ENOC	Emirates National Oil Company
EPSA	exploration and production sharing agreement
EU	European Union
FACTS	Fesharaki Associates Consulting and Technical Services Inc.
FDI	foreign direct investment
FSU	Former Soviet Union
GCC	Gulf Co-operation Council
GDP	gross domestic product
GTL	gas-to-liquids

GW	gigawatt
HFO	heavy fuel oil
HPCL	Hindustan Petroleum Corporation Limited
HSK	Hydroskimming
IAEE	International Association for Energy Economics
ICEED	International Research Center for Energy and Economic Development
IDC	Iraq Drilling Company
IEA	International Energy Agency
IEA	International Energy Associates, Inc
IMEMO	Institute of the World Economy and International Relations
IMF	International Monetary Fund
INOC	Iraq National Oil Company
IOC	Indian Oil Corporation
IOC	international oil company
IPC	Iraq Petroleum Company
IPIC	International Petroleum Investment Company
ISODC	Iraq State Oil Drilling Company
JAPEX	Japan Petroleum Exploration Company
JNOC	Japan National Oil Company
JODCO	Japan Oil Development Company
KBR	Kellogg Brown & Root
KGOC	Kuwait Gulf Oil Company
KPC	Kuwait Petroleum Company
KOGAS	Korea Gas Corporation
KPC	Kuwait Petroleum Corporation
LNG	liquefied natural gas
LPG	liquefied petroleum gas
LHG	liquefied hazardous gas
MAP	Ministry on Anti-Monopoly Policy
MEES	Middle East Economic Survey
MDHDS	middle distillate hydro-desulfurization
mbpd	million barrels per day
MPS	Murmansk Pipeline System

MPGC	Middle East Petroleum and Gas Conference
NATO	North Atlantic Treaty Organization
NGL	natural gas liquids
NOC	national oil company
NOC	Northern Oil Company
OECD	Organization for Economic Cooperation and Development
ONGC	Oil and Natural Gas Corporation
OPEC	Organization of Petroleum Exporting Countries
PDO	Petroleum Development Oman
PEL	Petroleum Economics Ltd.
PEMEX	Petróleos Mexicanos
PDVSA	Petróleos de Venezuela, SA
ppm	parts per million
PSA	production sharing agreements
PSO	Pakistan State Oil
PTTEP	PTT Exploration and Production Public Company Ltd.
RCC	Residue Catalytic Cracking
SCOP	State Company for Oil Projects
SOMO	State Oil Marketing Company
SARS	Severe Acute Respiratory Syndrome
SOAS	School of Oriental and African Studies
SOC	Southern Oil Company
SPR	Strategic Petroleum Reserve
UAE	United Arab Emirates
UES	United Economic Space
USSR	Union of Soviet Socialist Republics
WEIO	World Energy Investment Outlook
WTO	World Trade Organization
ZADCO	Zakum Development Company

Geopolitical upheavals in strategic regions of the world often lead to global economic turmoil. The US-led invasion of Iraq in 2003 not only disrupted international oil supplies but created price and market fluctuations that continue to have a deep impact on the global economy and to pose particular challenges for the world's energy producers. As a founding member of the Organization of Petroleum Exporting Countries (OPEC) with reserves that are second only to those of Saudi Arabia, Iraq has always been a major force in the oil market, despite the constraints imposed by UN sanctions and the weakened infrastructure of its industry. The dwindling of Iraqi oil supply in the aftermath of the invasion and the manner and time-frame for its resumption have important implications for Iraq, the Arabian Gulf producers, OPEC, international oil companies and the world oil market. Following the invasion, OPEC had to grapple with a volatile market situation and moved decisively to stabilize oil supply and prices. However, such geopolitical crises continue to create major hurdles for OPEC in regulating the oil market.

Other challenges are also emerging for OPEC producers. In the new oil map of the world, exploration and production is shifting from traditional areas such as the Arabian Gulf to locations such as Russia, the Caspian basin, Venezuela and the West African rim. With global energy demand growing phenomenally, especially in Asia, and with oil-importing nations diversifying their future oil supplies, non-OPEC sources are gaining in importance, challenging OPEC's dominant position. To meet future supply imperatives and to retain respective market shares, both OPEC and non-OPEC countries must make strategic choices to boost investment in production capacity as well as in refining and transportation facilities.

In this context, the ECSSR Ninth Annual Energy Conference, held from October 19-20, 2003 in Abu Dhabi, UAE, focused on the theme: *Gulf Oil in the Aftermath of the Iraq War: Strategies and Policies*. The conference presentations in this book examine the determinants shaping the future of Gulf oil in the wake of the Iraq war, with all its repercussions. While analyzing the new challenges and opportunities for the Gulf oil industry, the book also explores strategies and policies for Gulf oil producers to successfully manage the long-term implications of changing market realities. The book covers five main areas of interest: the realities for Gulf oil producers following regional developments, Iraq's role in the future global energy scenario, issues of oil market restructuring, diversification of energy supplies from emerging non-OPEC suppliers, including Russia; and the strategic outlook and policy options for Gulf oil producers in the new global energy market.

ECSSR would like to express its appreciation to the distinguished scholars and industry experts for their conference participation and for sharing their insight on these energy issues. A word of thanks is also due to ECSSR editor Mary Abraham for coordinating the publication of this book.

Jamal S. Al-Suwaidi Ph.D.
Director General
ECSSR

INTRODUCTION

Gulf Oil in the Aftermath
of the Iraq War

The US-led invasion of Iraq in 2003 dramatically altered the future of the country, changed the dynamics of the global energy market and created new realities for the Gulf oil producers. Against the backdrop of evolving regional geopolitics and continuing economic uncertainties, ECSSR's Ninth Annual Energy Conference, held from October 19-20, 2003 in Abu Dhabi, UAE, focused on the subject of *Gulf Oil in the Aftermath of the Iraq War: Strategies and Policies.* The conference examined key energy issues stemming from the invasion, the resulting long term challenges and the emerging opportunities for the Gulf oil industry. It also pinpointed effective strategies and policies for the Gulf oil sector to deal with the broader implications of an altered energy scenario.

Divided into five main segments, the conference presentations in this book focus on: the changing realities for Gulf oil producers; Iraq's prospective role in the global energy scenario; issues of oil market restructuring; diversification of energy supplies from non-OPEC nations, including Russia; and the strategic outlook and policy options for Gulf producers in the changing energy market. Some of the short term assessments and projections in these papers have been overtaken by actual events in Iraq and even overridden by the unexpectedly dramatic surge in world oil demand in 2004. However, they collectively offer a valuable long-term perspective on the wider repercussions of the Iraq invasion and its resulting impact on global energy markets. The highlights of these conference presentations as summarized below provide a general overview.

Continuity and Change

Despite turbulent geopolitical changes such as the Iraq invasion, there are strong forces for continuity in the energy market. In his keynote address, Richard Paniguian highlights these contrasting themes of continuity and change. The first element of continuity is the abiding importance of oil— hydrocarbons are expected to remain the predominant source of energy for the foreseeable future. While much attention has been focused on developing renewable energy, logistical and economic factors will tend to limit its impact for the next few decades. Hydrogen has also been the subject of considerable discussion and research but its widespread commercial use will inevitably take decades to achieve.

Clearly, oil and gas production and consumption will peak at some point, but this will be driven more by the evolving forces of economics and technology, rather than just the laws of physics and geology. Thus, while Gulf oil will continue to be crucial to world supplies, oil-producing states in the region cannot afford to be complacent. In an increasingly inter-connected world, countries such as Russia recognize the global significance of their hydrocarbon resources and their potential for fuelling national economic growth.

Since supply is essentially irrelevant without the corresponding demand, the question that arises is whether the world will continue to use oil as it has been doing over the past century. The general consensus is that oil will make up the largest share of world energy consumption – and even consumption growth – over the next 20 years, with a growth trajectory between 1-2 percent a year. The key factor underlying this growth is transport, which is literally a driving force. Around half the global oil consumption is in the field of transportation and this demand continues to surge as the world becomes increasingly wealthier.

Yet beneath all this continuity, some significant changes are taking place, particularly the growth of gas, supported by a number of factors. First, environmental problems dictate the need for cleaner energy and gas is almost sulfur-free. Second, combined cycle gas turbine (CCGT) power stations are more efficient to build and run, giving gas a definite advantage in power generation. Third, one kilowatt hour of electricity generated from natural gas emits only about half the amount of carbon dioxide as the same kilowatt hour generated from coal. All these factors will contribute towards the growth of gas in the decades to come.

The second significant shift is that although oil growth is projected to continue, there is ongoing diversification both in terms of the locations where oil is produced and the extent to which it is traded internationally. The same trend applies to gas but to a lesser extent. Dependency on a single country or region is no longer the norm and strengthening supply security through diversity of sources has become an important consideration for many governments. Such diversity can help to generate further growth in demand.

The resilience of oil supplies despite periodic turbulence points to the strength of the system and its underlying relationships and reveals the interconnectedness of the energy market as part of a single, global system. Both oil and gas markets are more open and competition is more intense, avoiding duplication, shedding inefficiencies and creating a more streamlined supply chain.

Technology is one of the keys to unlocking future reserves as it raises efficiency levels and enhances the ability to discover and extract more oil and gas. It remains a critical element in shaping the future, representing both a force for continuity as well as change.

Investment Climate for Oil Companies

While technological change generally brings positive effects in its wake, political and economic uncertainties tend to have a negative impact on the markets. The world lives in a climate of political uncertainty—with particular concerns about terrorism and security threats. The global economic outlook remains hazy with growth slowing down in many regions. In addition, there are regional uncertainties, the most obvious of these being the future role of Iraq.

Against this backdrop, governments in the Gulf region need to address several long term economic and social challenges, stresses Walter van de

Vijver. The region's population is expected to grow phenomenally from 280 million to 400 million by 2020. This will put increasing demands on government budgets to provide more jobs, education, health care and other public services. These pressures could widen budget deficits, a trend that can already be witnessed in some parts of the Arab world.

Many Gulf countries have identified these challenges and taken constructive steps to provide a more attractive environment for business and investment. These include progress in free trade area negotiations between the Gulf Co-operation Council (GCC), the European Union and the United States; the GCC's aspiration to create a common currency and free trade area, the positive approach to business in the new Qatari constitution and the creation of a dynamic business climate in the UAE.

Progress in Saudi Arabia's privatization program and its negotiations to join the WTO are very welcome developments. The *Shura* council's debates on proposed government legislation also reveal increasing openness, which helps to build up investor confidence. For instance, the performance of the Saudi stock market was one of the best in the world during the first half of 2003.

These positive moves will help to increase international investment, thereby easing some of the pressure on government budgets, bringing in additional revenue and creating more jobs and opportunities. However, the momentum on energy investment by international oil companies must be maintained by creating a stable investment climate and rewarding economic performance with suitable returns.

There are some particular areas where international oil companies can make a substantial contribution. The first is their ability to make the significant capital investment needed by energy projects, provided there is some assurance of future income and a supportive contractual framework. One possible model is the greater use of production sharing agreements (PSAs), which have proved very effective in achieving an appropriate balance of incentives between Governments and oil companies. Another key area for international oil companies is in applying cutting-edge technology, which assumes increasing importance as several oil fields in the region reach maturity levels.

[6]

Middle East Oil Investment Outlook

For the Middle East oil sector to retain and even boost its market share, massive investment is an obvious necessity. Fatih Birol analyzes the investment needs of the Middle East oil sector through 2030 based on the IEA's *World Energy Investment Outlook* (WEIO) of November 2003. Attention is also focused on the main obstacles to capital mobilization and on the global implications likely to stem from lower-than-projected levels of investments occurring in the region.

The level of investment in expanding oil production capacity in the Middle East will be vital in determining the prospects for the global energy market in the medium to long term period. Mobilizing such investment will depend on the production and investment policies of key producers, particularly Saudi Arabia. The costs of developing the region's vast reserves are lower than anywhere else but restrictions on foreign participation and dependence on national oil companies for a large share of state revenues might constrain the amount of investment actually channeled into new production capacity. Of course, investment prospects in Iraq are particularly uncertain.

Projected growth in Middle East oil production would require capital spending of around $523 billion in exploration and development over the next three decades. Investment will need to rise substantially from an average of $12 billion a year in the current decade to around $23 billion a year in the last decade of the projection period. Almost half of this investment will be geared towards supplying OECD countries.

Exploration and development costs for new supplies are assumed to be broadly constant for both low-cost onshore and higher-cost offshore fields over the projection period, but a gradual shift towards offshore drilling in some countries will raise average costs slightly in the region. Nonetheless, costs in the Middle East are likely to remain the lowest in the world, well below assumed price levels.

Downstream oil investment needs will also be considerable, with refining capacity expected to rise from just over 6 mbpd in 2002 to 10 mbpd in 2010 and 15.6 mbpd in 2030—equivalent to one large new refinery a year.

This will involve capital outlays of around $99 billion, or $3.3 billion a year. Investment in gas-to-liquids (GTL) capacity, mostly in Qatar and Iran, will amount to $12.7 billion, more than 30% of the world total.

The principal uncertainties clouding future Middle East supply and consequently investment needs are the rate of growth of global oil demand, the resulting call on OPEC supply and the supply policies of producers. A slightly lower rate of demand growth than that projected in *WEO-2002* would have a marked impact on investment needs in the Middle East as the main residual supplier of oil to the international market.

There are also supply side uncertainties. The policies of host countries on opening up oil industries to private and foreign investment, the fiscal regime and investment conditions, and government revenue needs may reduce capital flows. Regional instability stemming from the US-led occupation of Iraq, interminable negotiations over an Israeli-Palestinian peace deal, and social and political tensions across the Gulf region compound the political and economic unpredictability.

Future trends in the natural decline rates of Middle East oilfields will also determine the level of investment that will be needed. Much of the Middle East oil comes from giant fields that have been in operation for several decades and therefore face the likelihood of rising rates of natural decline.

Stabilizing the Oil Market

Declining production from established oilfields is only one of several factors contributing to oil market instability. Thomas E. Wallin examines the issue of instability from both political and economic perspectives. After tracing the energy market trends over the last 15 years, key episodes of extreme instability are analyzed to illustrate the critical factors influencing oil prices. This is followed by a review of government policies intended to influence oil markets and their effectiveness. By projecting the way these policies and oil market dynamics might develop, some predictions are made about the future prospects for oil price stability. Ideas are also offered to forge a sounder commercial and corporate basis for future oil markets that would lead to a reintegration of the international oil business and more market stability.

The international oil market took its current form in the late 1980s, following the price crash of 1986. Since then, price volatility has been a fixture in the international oil business. Price fluctuations stem from the market structure, which involves multiple actors and therefore makes it difficult for OPEC or any other actor or group to impose their own will. Given the unexpected convulsions in supply and demand caused by political disruptions and other external influences, price instability seems intrinsic to the market. Futures and other derivatives markets have developed to hedge the price risk caused by volatility and support speculation. Whether dealing with refinery margins or long-term upstream investments, the international oil companies (IOCs) have developed strategies for managing price instability. At a certain level, the commercial world has adjusted and accepted the commoditization of oil and the attendant price fluctuations.

Nevertheless, for both oil producers and consumers, market instability remains a serious economic problem. Obviously, oil-producing and oil-exporting nations that lack a diversified economic base are particularly vulnerable. However, even consuming countries suffer significant effects. It may be noted that high oil prices have played a contributory role in every US economic recession over the last 40 years. High gasoline prices are not only economically damaging but politically contentious in the United States and Europe. Governments in both oil exporting and oil importing countries have thus pursued policies to deal with the dislocations created by oil market instability.

Stable oil prices are universally favored but the term "price stability" is not an objective term and carries different connotations for producers and consumers. For oil producers and for OPEC the term "stable" connotes fair or equitable oil prices—implying steady prices above a certain minimum acceptable level. On the other hand, for oil consumers and importers "stable prices" denote reasonable or attractive oil prices that are steady but low enough to encourage economic growth and restrain inflation. Thus, the entire discussion on oil market stability is closely linked to the interests and perspectives of producers and consumers about broader issues of oil security and economic vulnerability.

[9]

The Future of Iraqi Oil

Doubts over the prospects for Iraqi oil fuels uncertainty and further undermines oil market stability. Herman T. Franssen underscores the importance of Iraq's oil reserves, which are considered second only to those of Saudi Arabia. The country also has significant natural gas prospects. Moreover, except for Kirkuk and Rumaila (North and South), Iraqi oil fields are among the least developed in the world. Iraq thus has the potential to equal Saudi Arabia in terms of future oil production. However, the crucial question remains: when will this potential be realized?

Optimists in Iraq believed that after a period of slow oil production recovery following the US invasion, security and stability would be restored and oil production would reach pre-war capacity as early as 2004. Optimists also assume the early reentry of IOCs into Iraq's upstream oil industry and expect that Iraq may reach its pre-war goal of 6 mbpd by 2010 or 2012.

On the other hand, pessimists believe that security will not be restored quickly, that violence will continue and restoration to pre-war capacity and steady production of 2.4 mbpd will go beyond 2004. In a worst-case scenario, the Balkanization of Iraqi society may keep production low and volatile for years to come. Without a legitimate and stable Iraqi government, IOCs will delay any plans for re-entry into Iraq and in the absence of internal stability, the desired pre-war goal of 6 mbpd will remain an unrealized dream for years. Under this scenario, Iraq's oil production may still be below 4 mbpd by 2015.

Both scenarios are possible. The early optimism following the US military success in April 2003 and the collapse of Saddam Hussein's regime was replaced by increasing concern about the US failure to bring security and order to Iraq. A return to full and unfettered Iraqi sovereignty is necessary for stability and there is growing fear that the domestic situation could deteriorate into internal chaos similar to Lebanon in the 1980s.

However, if major progress is made in restoring security and basic services to Iraqi society in the months ahead; if there are signs of economic improvement; if there is early internationalization of the effort to maintain internal stability; if Iraqi political forces reach a quick consensus on the political structure of the country and, if there is timely transfer of full power to Iraqi nationals, the political outcome may still be positive. Moreover, if the democratic model were to work successfully in Iraq, it will probably have far-reaching repercussions throughout the entire region.

IOCs are a politically sensitive issue and if foreign companies enter prematurely without a clear legal and fiscal regime regulating investments, the result could be chaotic. A new petroleum law and other laws governing foreign investment, taxation and foreign exchange repatriation are essential for the successful entry of IOCs. Only a legitimate, duly elected Iraqi government can define the long-term relationships between the host country and IOCs. An elected government is due to take office in 2005 as part of the unfolding constitutional process. Since it would take a few years to develop a legal regime for the petroleum industry in a host country, the interim Iraqi government can do the groundwork with possible help from the World Bank and internationally known consultants.

Post-War Iraq and OPEC

Iraq's re-entry into the world energy market and its membership status will have a considerable impact on OPEC's future. In sketching the future Iraqi-OPEC relationship, Dorothea El Mallakh envisages two possible scenarios. If Iraq opts to participate in price-setting, then it will remain within OPEC and use its leverage to support a policy that maximizes revenue flows while ensuring a vigorous longer-term demand for oil. On the other hand, Iraq could become a "price taker" along with ex-OPEC members and non-OPEC suppliers.

However, it is worth noting that Iraq's historical ties to OPEC are deep-rooted and solid, being one of the founding members of the organization. The Iraqi oil sector is among the oldest in the Gulf. Reconstruction and development demands create an enormous capacity for Iraq to absorb revenue and capital. With its large reserves and heavy revenue requirements, Iraq shares the interest of other OPEC members in maximizing revenue flows but keeping the oil price competitive with other energy sources, thereby sustaining vigorous, long-term demand for petroleum.

Moreover, with the easing of the political friction that existed earlier between Iraq and fellow OPEC states – Iran, Kuwait and Saudi Arabia – the shared interest in production and pricing should further enhance the

[11]

core role of the Gulf members. Therefore, it is not surprising that Iraq's Oil Minister announced at the September 24, 2003 OPEC meeting that his country expects to remain within this grouping. In the medium-to-longer term and with expected additions to non-OPEC volumes, staying within the organization would allow Iraq to participate actively in setting output levels in order to influence the supply balance and prices. An assessment of reserves and reservoirs is expected to be a top priority of the Iraqi oil sector in the aftermath of the war.

Changing Dynamics of OPEC and Non-OPEC Relations

The resumption of Iraqi oil supplies and the country's status vis-à-vis OPEC could change the dynamics of OPEC and non-OPEC relations, which have historically been based on competition and rivalry. Paul Stevens explains that since OPEC has been the residual supplier to the market, its role has been geared largely towards defending the economic rent inherent in oil prices.

A look at OPEC history is revealing. Prior to 1973, strong oil demand had allowed OPEC to increase its market share and the non-OPEC sector was largely irrelevant. The real issue over OPEC and non-OPEC relations emerged after the second oil shock of 1979-1981 when OPEC had to cut back to make room for non-OPEC production. The non-OPEC sector's willingness and ability to free ride upon OPEC stoked considerable resentment. After the 1986 price collapse, oil demand began to recover as did OPEC's market share. However, between 1991 and 2000, the call on OPEC production remained flat as non-OPEC production continued to strengthen. This trend occurred despite a dramatic collapse in FSU production although collapsing domestic consumption permitted FSU exports to remain relatively buoyant.

During the post-1986 period, there have been occasional instances of non-OPEC support for OPEC's defense of prices—generally grudging, half-hearted and frequently not implemented. Invariably, this quasi-support came during periods of price crisis, most obviously following the price collapse of 1998. From these experiences an important lesson may be drawn for the future. It appears that the better the relations between OPEC and non-OPEC, the less likely that such good relations will be sustained. Good relations imply relatively high oil prices, which sow the seeds for greater non-OPEC supply, which in turn, undermines OPEC's market share. This fundamental truth underpins the nature of the relationship.

The key to future OPEC and non-OPEC relations is the expected call on OPEC. This in turn will depend on future global oil demand, the level of non-OPEC supply and the countries actually constituting OPEC. Conventional wisdom indicates that rising oil demand and faltering non-OPEC supply would mean a rising call on OPEC and less mutual hostility. However, an alternative view gaining ground is that the call on OPEC could remain flat in the foreseeable future due to greater inhibitions on the growth of oil and the non-OPEC sector maintaining its market position. Should such a situation arise, OPEC and non-OPEC relations will be strained as OPEC members are trying to expand production capacity by encouraging the entry of multinationals. With excess capacity, OPEC members will tend to follow the non-OPEC suppliers and free ride outside the constraints of the quota system.

Although Iraq has remained in OPEC, its status and future production role is extremely uncertain. How the country chooses to act in relation to OPEC membership will be crucial in shaping future relations between OPEC and non-OPEC producers.

New Opportunities in Asian Energy Markets

Both OPEC and non-OPEC producers are eyeing future market growth in the Asian continent—particularly in oil and gas. Asia's oil product consumption is poised to grow at an annual rate of over 3% and natural gas consumption is projected to grow at annualized rates exceeding 5% in the years to come. Fereidun Fesharaki and Hassan Vahidy consider these to be conservative estimates which could be significantly higher with stronger economic growth and improved political stability.

Given its low level of energy resources, the region is heavily dependent on the Middle East for its supplies of oil and increasingly, natural gas. Currently the Gulf region exports over 60% of its oil to the Asia–Pacific region and Asian countries import 73% of their oil from the Gulf. This supplier–consumer link is poised to strengthen as Asia's growing need for

[13]

crude and refined products coupled with its own depleting energy reserves will make it increasingly reliant on imports from the Gulf. This is corroborated by the fact that all of the new refining capacity coming up in Asia is configured around medium-heavy gravity and sour crude and even the existing refineries are gearing up to a similar crude slate.

At the same time Asian energy markets have been undergoing a gradual transformation. Some major consumer nations are starting to open up their energy markets—posing both challenges and opportunities for the market players. Every Asian country is unique—faced with special conditions and often behaving in an isolated manner, which further complicates the market situation. Therefore, it is necessry to understand the different drivers for the growth of energy demand and supply in individual Asian markets.

As Asian markets deregulate, both challenges and opportunities are created for the national oil companies of the Middle East. Opportunities arise in the form of potential investment in the key growth markets of the region: China, India and Indonesia. Challenges include the heightened sensitivity of oil prices in the Asian countries and changing product specifications. In the meantime, there has been a two-way flow of investments between the two regions. Gulf oil companies have invested in Asia's downstream oil sector and the Asian oil companies have been investing in the Gulf's upstream sector. This will further reinforce the buyer-seller relationship between the two regions in the years to come.

Despite the aggressive thrust of the national oil companies of India and China, the Middle East will be dominated by its own national oil companies and Western companies for the foreseeable future. However, the participation of giant Asian companies could affect the playing field and perhaps force Western companies to offer better terms to the Gulf countries than they might otherwise have done.

Oil Prospects in the Atlantic Basin

Oil giants, including Asian companies are turning their attention away from traditional oil producing areas to promising new areas. Christophe de Margerie focuses on oil and gas prospects in West-Central Africa and the Atlantic Basin and its likely impact on the Middle East. The Atlantic Basin is not a wholly new supplier since the region has been producing oil for

[14]

several years and is now producing gas as well. Much of the success of this region is due to the positive role played by OPEC.

Renewed interest in the Atlantic Basin is triggered by the region's huge reserves of more than 180 billion barrels of oil, which represents 17% of the world total. In terms of gas, the reserves are less important, accounting for around 13% of the world total. However, production in the Atlantic Basin is much more significant in terms of world share—35% for both oil and gas. There are not only existing reserves, but also a lot of potential for new production.

There are three main drivers here. First, there are considerable reserves in the ultra-deep offshore region, mostly in Brazil, in the Gulf of Guinea, the offshore areas of Venezuela, Trinidad, in the Gulf of Mexico, and also Norway. Second, there are large heavy-oil reserve prospects, mainly in Canada, Alaska and in Venezuela serving the same markets—meaning the United States and Europe. The third driver is LNG, which enhances the value of gas reserves that are hard to valorize without a local market. Several LNG projects are now under way, some new and others existing, the biggest of these being Nigeria LNG. This project took more than 30 years to become a reality but it is now in production. Apart from current projects in Trinidad and Tobago, as well as Norway, there are also many new projects such as the one in Angola.

The impact of the Atlantic Basin on future world supply could well be quite important, but much depends also on Middle East and OPEC policy. Most Atlantic Basin countries, with the exception of Nigeria, are not OPEC members but are benefiting from "OPEC protection." Hence, it is important to consider the size of the reserves in question. It is true that most oil and gas reserves are in the Middle East and that the gas reserves of the former Soviet republics are roughly the size of Middle East reserves. In the Atlantic Basin, the oil and gas figures are far more modest. Gas accounts for a large share of reserves but the greatest potential of this region lies in its deep offshore oil resources.

Russian Hydrocarbons in the World Market

Among the energy producers currently gaining prominence is Russia, which has great potential due to its considerable reserves. Russian gas reserves of

47 trillion cubic meters constitute 29% of the world total and the country produces 26% of the world output. Its proven oil reserves are estimated to range from 48.6 to 120 billion barrels. Vitaly V. Naumkin explains that Russia's new Energy Strategy views the sector as an engine for economic growth and the country recognizes the need to boost its oil and gas exports.

Moscow harbors great expectations regarding the growth of oil exports to the United States and energy cooperation remains a major focus of US-Russian dialogue. In 2002, Lukoil and Yukos started deliveries to the US oil market. With the scheduled building of a new port in Murmansk, Russian oil will be able to meet 10% of US oil imports.

The country also envisages projects to develop exports to the European and Asian markets. However, there is a need for massive investments and new technologies. Russian oil companies are seeking to increase exports and trying to boost their productivity to achieve this end. Investment is mainly directed towards export infrastructure, including pipelines and ports. A comparison of the oil prospecting and exploitation costs of Russia's best oil companies with those of world leaders reveals that Russian companies are competitive in terms of the prime cost of oil. If these companies can find effective transportation and also secure guarantees for their oil refinement, Russia's share in the world oil market will surely grow.

Cooperation between Russia and the Asian region is viewed as a priority of Moscow's external energy policy in the twenty-first century. Interest in Asia as a new and promising avenue is conditioned by the continent's geographical proximity to Russia's eastern regions (Siberia and the Far East), which possess substantial energy resources, as well as by predictions of Asia's greater dependence on outside energy supplies.

However, the expansion of Russian supplies is not expected to seriously undermine the predominance of the Arabian Gulf region. There is a possibility of competition as well as coordination between Russia and the OPEC states. However, it must be remembered that almost all Russian companies are private and the government cannot therefore exercise full control over them.

The proposed technical overhaul of the Russian oil industry and the reform of the housing and public utilities sectors will decrease internal oil consumption and allow the country to further increase its share of oil exports.

Long Term Prospects for Gulf Oil

An increased level of oil supply from Russia must be seen not as an isolated development but part of ongoing changes in the global energy scenario. Robert Mabro CBE, envisages that oil developments over the next 20 or 30 years will be in three phases: a period of surplus production some time during this decade; a gradual tightening of the oil market towards the end of the next decade; and a drive in research and development for new transport fuels and engines gaining strong momentum in the 2020s.

These are the broad features of the scenario but the unfolding of these cycles will not be smooth. Price volatility will characterize the path of the oil market. Unforeseen events, ranging from accidents, political events, financial or economic shocks and policy changes are all likely to have an impact on prices, supply and demand.

Turmoil in the world petroleum market may lead to more successful co-operation between oil-exporting countries than in the past. It may even persuade the major oil-importing countries of the Organization for Economic Cooperation and Development (OECD), to agree on some international scheme of market stabilization. However, these are only hopes and history does not provide us with much cause for optimism.

The Gulf states need to address urgently the two major issues currently confronting them: the instability of their oil revenues in the short and medium term and the long term risk of an economic demise of oil.

The first issue calls for financial policies that balance budgets over a cycle so that public expenditures are not increased when revenues are temporarily buoyant and are not decreased when they are temporarily depressed. It also calls for a much greater governmental attention to matters of oil policy. Ministries and national oil companies require an injection of talent in order to ensure that the world oil situation is appraised continually and that market behavior is well understood. Furthermore, oil is not only a matter for geologists, engineers and economists, but involves diplomacy and international relations and relates to many vital interests of the exporting country. Oil expertise should be prominent in the fields of finance and foreign affairs, planning and industry ministries, in national assemblies, in the universities and in the media.

The long-term issue – the risks attached to the possible economic demise of oil – raises the question of economic development. Although much has been achieved by the Gulf states in the past 20 or 30 years, particularly in development of infrastructure, heavy industry, services, health and social welfare, an enormous task lies ahead. Economic development is not only about natural resources but also about building human resources and human capital. The task is to mould generations of men and women who are capable of analytical and critical thought. Economic development begins with a reform of syllabuses and of teaching methods. It also requires labor market policies that provide the right incentives for the jobs and skills on which economic development critically depends. These tasks have to be tackled gradually, and gestation periods can be very long. Oil countries may have a breathing space of some 30 years, which is barely sufficient to accomplish the required tasks and to ensure continuing prosperity even after the oil era comes to a close.

Energy Policy and Strategies for the Gulf

Given this global oil scenario, it is imperative for the Gulf energy sector to shed its traditional outlook and formulate new strategic policies and effective long term plans that take into account changing regional and international realities.

Traditionally, in the last 20 to 25 years, the hydrocarbon sector has played two basic roles for the major Gulf producers—first, as an exogenous "cash cow" that provides all the revenue needs of the state, and second, in some cases, as an instrument of foreign policy. It is exogenous because it has no real, operational links with the rest of the economy. The only input for the economy is the oil and gas revenue. It is a "cash cow" because it is the sole source for financing all government activities, and it often serves as an instrument of foreign policy because it has become the key resource of strategic significance for the producers.

Vahan Zanoyan warns that these two roles are no longer adequate. The exogeneity is no longer affordable, because of the high cost of keeping the oil and gas sector exogenous to the rest of the economy. The "cash cow" role is no longer adequate—not because of any deficiency in cash generation

[18]

but because it fails to address the real problems unless it translates into actual economic development rather than just financial well-being. As an instrument of foreign policy, this function is no longer effective simply because it is no longer an adequate means to secure the strategic importance of this region and other factors need to be taken into consideration.

Securing the present and meeting the national short-term financial requirements together constitutes the key driver of the price defense and market share defense strategy. This has been the major preoccupation of governments, whether in or out of OPEC, and this is being addressed adequately. Regional decision-makers have done extremely well and improved their grasp of the tools of supply response to existing market conditions. The term often used to describe this is "market management," but supply management describes what OPEC does much better. However, these issues, which dominate the agendas of the oil and gas ministries in most of these countries, fail to address the true strategic issues.

What are the real strategic issues for oil exporting countries? These may be regarded from two distinct perspectives: First, securing the present—maintaining the status quo. This, in turn, has two parts: first, prolonging the importance of oil as a source of energy and second, prolonging the importance of the producers as a source of oil. If an oil producing country can manage these two aspects, then its importance can be secured. This has been the main focus of policy-makers and therefore the record here is very good.

However, little thought has been given to the second major strategic issue, which is securing the future. This also involves two elements. First, it is necessary to substantially reduce dependence on oil revenues in this part of the world. This is an oft-repeated point and although several five-year plans have announced it as an objective, it does not seem to have been implemented seriously anywhere. Second, investing in the global energy sector of the future, and not just extracting hydrocarbon resources from the ground and handing it over to the market.

As stressed earlier, the challenge of reducing dependence on oil revenues may be further subdivided into three parts: macroeconomic reform, energy-intensive economic development and efficient energy clusters.

The second dimension of securing the future involves investment in the global energy business of the future. The global energy industry has evolved considerably in the past two decades. New technologies have transformed the supply side of the business, and could be on the verge of transforming the demand side as well. This process is driven by the large multinational oil and gas companies, and the main producing countries and their NOCs are not significant players in these trends. However, the national oil companies can play an important role as the main operating link between the producing countries and the international oil companies.

It may be concluded from the foregoing discussion that the Gulf energy sector needs to reorient its traditional outlook in the light of changed global realities and take decisive steps to secure its future prospects through strategic planning and forward-looking policies.

KEYNOTE ADDRESS

The Vital Role of Energy in the New Global Geopolitical Framework

Richard Paniguian

There has been a long-standing but constantly evolving relationship between BP and Abu Dhabi, which reflects many of the themes in the energy industry and the world at large. Today some of those themes will be addressed in the course of discussing what may be called the "new geopolitical framework."

Certainly, the world has recently seen some major, dramatic events. There are many forces that are working to create change, although there are also some strong forces that favor continuity.

The challenge is to distinguish the one from the other and to understand what has really changed. This region remains the key to the future of the industry based on reserves, even though the desire for supply diversification and indeed for alternatives continues. I will attempt to highlight a few salient points on these issues.

War, 9/11 and Ongoing Tension

It is easy to understand that the world today is one where "*Dawam Al Hal min Al Mohal*" (maintaining the situation or status quo is impossible).

The hope of a new kind of society emerging has remained a distant and elusive dream in the first few years of the 21st century. In reality, this has been a difficult period for many people, traumatic at times, and tragic at other times. Crucial events have given us all pause for thought: September

11, 2001; the war in Afghanistan; the war in Iraq in 2003; and the continued failure to find a solution to the Palestinian issue.

What will be the long term impact of the events in Iraq? How will Iraq's oil production develop in the future? What will be the effect of Iraqi production recovering to levels above 2 million barrels per day (mbpd) within the near future, and perhaps as much as 6 mbpd over a much longer time frame?

Russia is re-emerging as a major source of world energy. Will this undermine the leading position currently held by the countries of the Gulf? What will be the impact of this development?

All of these issues have raised fundamental questions about the relationship between the Gulf region and the rest of the world. These are questions that are given a higher profile by round-the-clock media coverage—just one dimension of what has come to be known as globalization.

Frankly, no one has the answers to these questions. There are many imponderables here and there seems limited value in continuing to guess outcomes through speculation and hypothesis. It is more worthwhile to focus first on what is known, rather than what is unknown, and second, to spend time preparing for the future, rather than attempting to predict it.

So I would like to examine what is known about the market—what has changed, and what has not changed. And I will conclude by asking what can be done to prepare for the unknown—for whatever the future may hold.

Though these changes have been profound, and despite the dramatic events the world has witnessed, it would be an exaggeration to think that *everything* has changed *forever*. From past experience it may well be concluded that "new world orders" are frequently announced but rarely sustained.

Despite massive turmoil, many of the underlying certainties remain the same. For the energy sector, the geological reality – the existence of oil and gas – will remain unchanged in the foreseeable future. At the same time, the technological developments that allow oil to be extracted at lower cost, as well as the shifts in the fundamental economics of the industry, remain steady and progressive, rather than sudden and cataclysmic.

[24]

The energy industry has witnessed many changes, but many underlying principles have endured. So I will try to sketch these enduring principles—and the genuinely significant changes in the energy business and markets. Thereafter, I will briefly explain what those factors signify for BP and its relationship with the Gulf region.

Supply and Demand: Continuity and Change

The first element of continuity is the continuing importance of oil—hydrocarbons will continue to be the predominant source of energy for the foreseeable future. Renewable energy is being researched, developed and installed all over the world, but the logistical and economic factors involved mean that its impact will be limited for the next few decades. Hydrogen is much discussed and researched but any lead time will inevitably be in terms of decades rather than years.

Clearly, oil and gas production and consumption will peak at some point. Obviously, these are exhaustible resources, and as Mark Twain once remarked about the finite nature of land: "They are not making it any more."

However, the timing of the peak cannot be known with certainty. A major reason for this is that the peak will actually be driven by the evolving forces of economics and technology, rather than just the laws of physics and geology. Indeed, the history of natural resource-based industries shows that any eventual decline is usually driven more by economics rather than by resource shortage. For example, the United Kingdom still has coal deposits that will never be extracted.

However, based on reasonable estimates of technology development, and taking into account the economics of commercializing new technology, it can be asserted fairly safely, that oil will still be a significant energy force during the lifetime of even the youngest person present here today.

In terms of "proved" reserves, there are over 1148 billion barrels waiting to be produced. At current rates of production, that oil alone will last for 40 years. However, by that time, new exploration and new technology will ensure that there is still a huge but inestimable amount of oil "yet to be found."

In addition to oil, there are proved reserves of 6.2 thousand trillion cubic feet of natural gas worldwide. At current rates of production, today's proved gas reserves will last for more than 67 years.

It is worth pointing out that today's proved reserves of oil and gas are more than half as large again as the proved reserves of 20 years ago. As the world needs more energy, we keep finding more hydrocarbons. For more than a century, the world has continued to replace reserve and has ultimately added more to reserves than to production. Technology and cost management has continually overwhelmed the natural depletion of hydrocarbons worldwide.

Within such a global scenario, Gulf oil will continue to be essential to world supplies. Although the world has sufficient hydrocarbons for many years to come, proved reserves are not evenly distributed around the globe. In terms of oil, two thirds of proved reserves are here in the Middle-East— although the challenge will continually be to access sustainable demand. In terms of gas, one third of the reserves are in the Gulf region, mechanisms for exploitation, including pipelines, LNG and even GTL, are growing and new markets are being accessed.

However, there is no room for complacency! The world is increasingly connected, and countries such as Russia, among others, are viewing their hydrocarbon inheritance as one of the vehicles for their own economic development.

Since supply is essentially irrelevant without demand, the next question therefore is: Will the world continue to use oil in the way it has done for the past century? Again there is a temptation to focus on the short term because in the past year oil consumption has been strong as a result of rapid economic growth.

It is easy to believe that the world has changed forever, when in fact it may have simply been witnessing a relatively short-lived economic upturn.

Looking at the consensus of predictions, oil is expected to continue to make up by far the largest share of world energy consumption – and even consumption growth – over the next 20 years. Its growth trajectory is projected to be between one and two per cent a year for the foreseeable future.[1]

The key factor in the continued importance of oil is transport, which is literally a driving force. Today, around half the world's consumption of oil

[26]

is used for transport. Furthermore, the demand for transport continues to grow as the world becomes increasingly wealthier. In China, for example, demand for saloon cars has been growing at 50% per year, and is likely to exceed 4 million this year.[2]

Yet it would be foolish not to note that beneath this headline of continuity, some significant stories of change are unfolding. In particular, there is very real change occurring in respect of the other two major energy sources. According to BP sources, in 1973, gas comprised 18.5% of world energy consumption and coal 27.5% while in 2003, the two fuels were at about 20% and 30% market share respectively.

The growth of gas has a number of drivers. First it reflects the environmental imperative. People are demanding cleaner energy and gas is almost sulfur-free. This has been a critical driver. Also combined cycle gas turbine (CCGT) power stations are more efficient to build and run, giving gas a win-win advantage in power generation. Moreover, one kilowatt hour of electricity generated from natural gas emits about half the amount of carbon dioxide as the same kilowatt hour generated from coal.[3] This will be a key driver in the decades to come. The growth of gas is also a positive trend for the Gulf region. Natural gas reserves are predominantly shared between the Middle East and Eurasia, mainly Russia.

The second significant shift in the pattern is that while the growth of oil is projected to continue for the immediate future, there is a diversification in progress, both in the number of places where oil is produced and in the degree to which it is traded internationally. The same is becoming true for gas, albeit on a somewhat smaller scale today.

Oil is increasingly a globally traded commodity. Traded crude and its related products is now almost 60 percent of total crude production while ten years ago, it was only just over 50 percent. Over one quarter of natural gas today passes over an international border before it is consumed.

One reason for the diversification is the very same concern that is reflected in this conference. National leaders tend to fear the loss of energy more than almost anything else. Concerns that the oil would suddenly "run out" have proved unfounded, but there remain concerns that conflict or crisis in one part of the world or another could still cut off supplies.

Security of supply has therefore been a powerful theme for many governments over this period and will continue to be so. Dependency on a single area now belongs to history.

However the events of 2001 and 2003 demonstrate just how strong the forces for continuity are, when faced with a major challenge. World oil markets continued to work, not only during the War in Iraq and after 9/11, but through supply problems in Venezuela and Nigeria, and through an economic downturn. No oil consumer faced a lack of availability and oil stocks remained untouched.

The resilience of oil supplies, when faced with the various shocks of recent years, has been a testament to the strength of the system and the relationships that underpin it. I pay tribute to the Arabian Gulf states – Abu Dhabi included – which were able to maintain oil supplies, calm markets and "cushion" the impact of successive shocks.

This process has demonstrated the interconnectedness of the energy market as part of a single, global market system. That interconnectedness is being highlighted even more by the liberalization spreading through many markets. Markets in both oil and gas are becoming more open and competition is becoming more intense. This is stripping out duplication and inefficiencies and creating a straighter and simpler supply chain.

Confidence and security of supply is important, and the effects of liberalization are mainly positive, so it is important to recognize the value of diversity. We should not be paranoid about the diversity of supply as this diversity actually supports the growth in demand.

Technology: Continuity and Change

Technology has been mentioned earlier as one of the keys to unlocking future reserves. It is, of course, a critical element in shaping the future. It is a little tricky to say whether it represents a force for continuity or change. In a sense it is both. It is a force that continuously increases efficiencies and continuously enhances the ability to find and extract more oil and gas.

Technology is at the core of BP's business and is essential to its performance. The true power of technology is unleashed when effective and appropriate solutions are rapidly applied. This includes the application

[28]

of technology from other industries to BP—one example being the transfer of techniques of visualization from the digital communications world. The beauty of technological innovation is that once it has been mastered, it can be transferred from one project to another. BP's support for the Petroleum Institute in Abu Dhabi is based on this principle.

In this region, technology will provide the opportunities to increase oil recoveries significantly. As the industry moves to more complex reservoirs requiring enhanced recovery techniques, diverse challenges will be encountered, which will demand diverse solutions.

There are a number of technologies that are proving important for this region. These include the *e-Field* concept. This is an evolving set of technologies to enable massive volumes of data to be captured, transmitted, analyzed and visualized in real time, transforming the management of reservoirs.

Another development with potential is that of *intelligent wells*—those that make use of fiber optic sensing systems and down-hole flow control to improve well management capabilities.

Also relevant here are the *advanced reservoir characterization* techniques which improve understanding of reservoir complexities.

Looking at the demand side of the equation, one can also expect the unexpected in terms of technological breakthroughs in such areas as hydrogen fuels, which could change the world order very significantly—probably not overnight, but almost certainly over time.

BP: Continuity and Change

In the foregoing section, I have sketched from my perspective, the major forces at work in the energy world—forces both for continuity and change.

These forces have all played a part in BP's recent development. As you know, the geographical disposition of BP's production has changed significantly—with areas of focus shifting from the United Kingdom and the onshore United States to places such as Russia, the Caspian, Trinidad and the deepwater Gulf of Mexico.

BP is very much part of the shift towards gas. Gas has increased markedly as a proportion of BP's total hydrocarbon production.

BP is building a significant LNG business, and it has been a partner with Abu Dhabi in LNG for nearly 30 years. A dynamic new dimension has been added to LNG in Trinidad, which is increasingly supplying both the US and European markets. Australian LNG (from the NW Shelf) is growing and supplying East Asian markets. Indonesian LNG from Tangguh will quite soon supplement these volumes.

A global operation such as that of BP has a number of dimensions—environmental, commercial and ethical. BP constantly re-examines the way it does business. When it comes to relationships, a particularly powerful idea is that of "mutual advantage"—only doing business with partners, suppliers, customers or governments when it is clear that both parties can benefit on a sustainable, ongoing basis.

Therefore, when people ask what BP might do in Iraq, the answer is very simple. It will watch as the situation unfolds, which may well take some time. Ultimately BP's approach in any country of the world is that it will participate if actually invited to do so by a legitimate and stable government, under terms that are commercially acceptable to both parties. Furthermore, as already indicated, BP is looking for sustainable and mutually advantageous relationships.

Looking at the region in a wider sense, BP's heritage lies here. The company exists because it was first engaged here in the search for oil and its development. Of course, relationships have evolved. However, no energy company can afford to ignore the world's largest repository of hydrocarbon resources, and BP has no intention of doing so. We have a long-term commitment to the region, as long as we can find the appropriate mechanisms for mutual advantage.

Abu Dhabi and BP: Reflected Changes

BP works on the principle of enduring relationships and mutual benefit, and in Abu Dhabi the relationship is profound, sustainable and has evolved over many decades.

From BP's experience it is clear that Abu Dhabi understands the difference between continuity and change very well. Abu Dhabi has always taken a long view of events – and prized simple but fundamental qualities in business – such as prudence and sound management.

Since BP arrived in Abu Dhabi in the 1930s and helped to drill for water, through oil projects and the ADGAS venture, this relationship has stood the test of time, even as other related trends underwent change.

Technology is very relevant and continues to enhance Abu Dhabi's capability to find and extract more hydrocarbons out of the ground and do more with what is produced!

Gas is also very relevant, particularly LNG, as I mentioned. Having been a longstanding partner, Abu Dhabi is also now becoming part of the increasingly dynamic and responsive global LNG market. For example, during the recent nuclear power generation crisis in Japan, BP helped ADGAS to meet customer demands at short notice—working together under pressure and building on the strong relationships that had been established over many years.

Indeed, a lot can be learnt from the relationship that Abu Dhabi has developed with the international oil companies. This relationship will continue to evolve, with mutual benefit.

Conclusion

The main message of this chapter is that there is a need to distinguish short-term change from fundamental shifts in the tectonic plates. One must wait and watch before making judgments. Often it is the case that the more things change, the more they stay the same. Yet there is no room for complacency.

Whatever happens in terms of the global geopolitical framework, there are things that can be done to build an even more powerful and dynamic global energy framework. Part of this is about developing openness and strong relationships that can respond quickly to events—which can protect against shocks.

We are all part of a global energy ecosystem in which every element in the chain needs to function well for the benefit of all. This is helped by several of the factors already mentioned: liberalized markets, best technology practice, co-operation and mutual understanding. This ecosystem is interdependent and interconnected. Consumers depend on suppliers, suppliers on consumers. The diversity of supply is needed to maintain security as the future will not be built on dependency. Balance is a vital factor, as is the ability to correct imbalances.

The system is evolving all the time and the challenge for all concerned is to work with the evolutionary currents and not to overreact to the inevitable storms.

While observing this eco-system unfold over the next few years, BP looks forward to working with its partners in the Gulf region wherever there are opportunities to do so.

NEW REALITIES FOR GULF OIL

1

A New Era for International Oil Companies in the Gulf: Challenges and Opportunities

Walter van de Vijver

The Gulf region has played such a key role in Shell's history, almost from the very start of its business over a century ago. Its first tanker went through the Suez Canal in 1892. Shell signed the first concession here in Abu Dhabi in 1939 and has been working in Oman for more than sixty years. The company's relationship with the Kingdom of Saudi Arabia began in the 1940s, and the first oil was shipped from Dubai's offshore fields in 1969. There are many other examples that could be given regarding Shell's long and productive history in this region.

This shared history is very important, as it means that the relationships and partnerships that were built over the years remain strong. It also means that there is basis of mutual understanding on which to develop new initiatives and work together to ensure that the countries of the Gulf secure the full and long-term value of their energy reserves.

Today, Shell employs about 7,500 staff across the Middle East as a whole, and many thousands more have lived and worked here in the course of their careers. Almost a quarter of Shell's equity oil production comes from the Gulf region, and an increasing amount of its natural gas. The company's investment, in terms of capital employed, makes this one of the most significant regions in the Shell Group. Moreover, that role is growing, with considerable potential to develop new projects well into the future.

With two thirds of the world's oil reserves and half the gas reserves, the Gulf region will continue to play a vital role in meeting the growing global demand for energy. The challenge ahead for all of us will be to

[35]

ensure that all the region's resources – both its natural resources and the skills and talents of its people – are fully utilized and that the benefit and value is felt throughout the region.

Regional Challenges

There is no doubt that these are challenging times. Across the world, there is political uncertainty—with particular concerns about terrorism and the threat to security. The economic outlook is just as unclear. Growth has slowed down in many regions and while there does seem to be better news on an economic upturn in the US, clearly a key market for this region, that recovery remains tentative.

In addition to these global uncertainties there are a number of uncertainties particular to this region. The most obvious of these is the future role of Iraq. It remains unclear how quickly political stability and reliable security can be achieved. That makes it hard to predict how long it will take before Iraq resumes playing a major role in global oil production.

Apart from these uncertainties, Governments in the region have to address longer term economic and social challenges. It has been forecasted that the region's population could grow from 280 million to 400 million by 2020, a formidable rate of increase. That will mean growing demands on Government budgets to provide jobs, education, health care and other public services. These pressures could add to the problem of budget deficits, which can be seen in some parts of the Arab world.

Investment Climate

Many countries here in the Gulf have already recognized the need to take action to deal with these pressures. There have been some very welcome steps towards creating a more open business environment, along with an increasingly attractive investment climate.

These include progress in free trade area negotiations between the Gulf Co-operation Council and the EU and the US; the approach to business in the new constitution in Qatar; and the Council's aspiration to create a common currency and free trade area. Moreover, at the IMF meeting in

Dubai, there was much well-deserved praise for the increasingly open and forward looking business climate here in the UAE.

The privatization program in Saudi Arabia and the progress made in the negotiation for the Kingdom to join the WTO are very welcome developments. The use of the *Shura* council to debate proposed government legislation also underlines increasing openness across a range of business and political structures.

That approach is helping to build investor confidence. For instance, the performance of the Saudi stock market was one of the best in the world during the first half of 2003.

All these efforts will help to attract international investment, which can relieve some of the pressure on Government budgets, provide additional revenue and jobs and other opportunities. Of course, this must be accompanied by recognition on the part of international oil companies regarding the importance of continually adapting and refining their approach, as the business environment undergoes changes and the region develops further.

There is, however, a real need to maintain momentum, particularly with respect to energy investment. International oil companies such as Shell look at investment opportunities across the world, and clearly those opportunities are most attractive in countries where there is a stable investment climate and where performance is rewarded with appropriate returns.

Pressures on OPEC

Those opportunities will obviously be influenced by events determining the external climate—most fundamentally the oil price. With regard to this issue, there have been considerable pressures on OPEC during 2003. Perhaps the untold story has been the smooth way in which OPEC managed an unprecedented series of disruptions to production.

It may be recalled that, at the beginning of that year, there was major disruption to oil supply in Venezuela, followed by unrest in Nigeria and then, of course, the conflict in Iraq. Dealing with those successive disruptions – which led to a loss of about 2.5 million barrels per day – was an extremely tough challenge. The fact that this was managed without any supply shortages or prolonged price spikes is a great tribute to the sophistication and maturity of the oil market in general and OPEC in particular.

Such challenges will not go away. With the world security outlook remaining uncertain, the resilience of the system may well be tested again. Of course, oil prices will remain volatile because, as is widely known, the market is acutely sensitive to wider political and economic events.

There may well be further challenges to OPEC and producers in the region in the medium term. While there has been some surprise that the oil price has remained high in the aftermath of the Iraq conflict, there are a number of factors that could provide significant downward pressures on the price in the medium term.

One of those factors is the continuing growth in non-OPEC production. Non-OPEC countries already supply two thirds of the world's oil. Half of the fourteen countries in the world which produce more than two million barrels a day are not in the OPEC grouping and their role is growing. These non-OPEC suppliers have increased production by 15 percent over the last decade and are expected to add a further 1.1 million barrels per day during 2003.

Nearly three quarters of that growth is likely to come from the Former Soviet Union. This underlines the fact that Russia is going to play an increasingly significant role in global oil supply. It is already the world's second biggest oil producer and oil exporter and will continue to be a clear competitor to Middle East producers. No doubt this was one factor driving the progress made in the bilateral oil discussions between Saudi Arabia and the Russian Federation.

The Role of Iraq

In addition, there will be competition from Iraq. When that competition will emerge is not clear, but the extent of Iraq's resources means that it will certainly, in time, play a major role. At this juncture, a distinction needs to be made between the timetable for resuming exports from existing Iraqi facilities and that for developing increased production capacity. Despite setbacks to the industry, it seems likely that existing exports will recover fairly soon.

However, the speed at which Iraq can increase production significantly is more uncertain. The respected energy commentator, Daniel Yergin, has suggested that adding another two million barrels a day of production capacity on top of pre-Kuwait invasion levels could take seven to ten years and cost more than $30 billion.

This means that Iraq will not only be a competitor for market share but also for capital investment from international oil companies, further underlining the need for resource holders to create that attractive investment climate mentioned earlier.

In fact, the next decade may well see an intense period of competition for capital as the Gulf states seek to accelerate their oil and gas development plans. It must be stressed that this situation will pose challenges to all concerned—international oil companies as much as resource holders will need to face up to growing competition.

Russia's rise, along with the growth of national oil companies with international aspirations will put more competitive pressures on other oil businesses. However, that competitive pressure is a very powerful incentive to improve the efficiency of operations, to keep a relentless focus on technological improvements and to look for opportunities to combine skills and expertise.

The continued success of the oil business will depend on the ability to provide attractive opportunities for cooperation with governments and national oil companies. Of course, this is not a new challenge for Shell, which has a long record of partnership with national oil companies. There are many clear examples in this region where that combination has been worked powerfully to the mutual benefit of both parties.

International Oil Companies

Partnership is the key as success cannot be achieved in isolation. The reason why Shell's work in this region has been so successful is because the company has actively worked to involve and develop local talent. Whether as employees, contractors or external critics—their efforts have strengthened the business and allowed Shell to make the best use of resources for mutual benefit. It is by reinforcing and strengthening those combinations that the challenges ahead can be met successfully. At this point, it is appropriate to pinpoint some particular areas where international oil companies can make an ongoing contribution to the region.

The first is their ability to make the significant capital investment which energy projects need. As outlined earlier, governments are facing growing claims on their revenues and if the burden can be shared there will be considerable benefits for both parties. However, in order to secure that investment, there must be some assurance of future income and, in particular, a supportive contractual framework. There are a number of models that can achieve these ends.

One option is the greater use of production sharing agreements (PSA), which have proved very effective in achieving an appropriate balance of incentives between Governments and oil companies. These agreements ensure a fair distribution of the value of a resource while providing the long term assurance required for securing the necessary capital investment for energy projects. Whatever the contractual model that is pursued, the key will be to ensure that they provide incentives for performance and align the incentives for all parties to the agreement.

Another key area where international oil companies can play a role is in applying cutting-edge technology. This is becoming increasingly important as a number of fields in the region reach maturity. It is in these mature areas – for example, Oman – where technology can really make the difference, prolonging the lives of those fields and increasing the amount of oil that is recovered. Shell has been meeting the demands of maturing areas in a number of regions. The company has increasingly considered how to leverage its technological strength to ensure that the maximum value is extracted.

In Oman, this approach is being applied to Shell's operations, in which the deployment of leading edge technology is helping Petroleum Development Oman (PDO) to arrest the decline in production. The lessons being learnt in Oman about enhanced oil recovery techniques and other technologies will be a vital tool in other mature areas in this region. These lessons will help to prolong the lives of Shell's existing fields and to discover new resources, and by developing the company's expertise in managing the reservoirs more effectively, will improve the long term viability of all its projects.

Prospects for the Gas Industry

That long term future will include an increased focus on the gas resources of the region. There is a natural tendency to focus on oil production in the Middle East but gas needs to be recognized as another extremely important part of the region's production. Gas demand is growing across the world. It is a cost competitive fuel, relatively abundant and offers environmental advantages, especially over coal, in power generation. What this implies is that the Middle East producers should not see gas as a threat but as a very attractive commercial opportunity. The gas reserves in the Middle East are extensive, comprising thirty six per cent of world's total. It is clear that gas projects in the region can complement and supplement oil and bring added value.

Earlier this year, Shell reached an agreement to explore for gas in a joint venture with Saudi Aramco and TOTAL in the Rub Al-Khali. This is the first time since the creation of Saudi Aramco that foreign international oil companies have gained access to gas acreage in Saudi Arabia, and presents a very exciting opportunity for all the partners in the project.

Flexibility is one of the key advantages that gas can offer as a fuel. In particular, the ability to produce liquefied natural gas, or LNG, which can then be transported by tanker to any market around the world, offers great potential value. Shell has an extensive LNG portfolio, leads globally in equity LNG sales and has particular expertise in developing and marketing LNG with two major projects currently being developed in Nigeria and Sakhalin. The company is also developing the Hazira re-gasification LNG terminal in India which will have a capacity of five million tons per annum and will open next year, providing access to a new market.

Alongside LNG, Shell has developed a new fuel from gas by using gas-to-liquids technology. This process converts gas into an ultra clean liquid fuel as an alternative to diesel that can be used in road vehicles without the need for any modifications. This fuel therefore provides significant environmental advantages and is believed to have a huge potential market across the world, especially in urban areas which suffer from air pollution problems. A key part of Shell's gas-to-liquids business is the project being developed in Qatar.

[41]

Support for Local Communities

With Shell's long ties to the region and its special relationship in the local communities, the company hopes to make a contribution to the region in its widest sense. It is working to develop all local resources including its human resources. In the seventeen Middle East countries where Shell works, as much as 88 per cent of its staff are locally hired. Their expertise is invaluable and the company is constantly seeking ways to develop and extend those skills here in the Gulf.

Equally, Shell can also provide those staff with new skills and opportunities around the world. Increasingly, they are taking the opportunities that an international company like Shell can offer them, to develop their expertise elsewhere in world and then return to the region with enhanced skills. The company's jobs are open to all and Shell staff members face no barriers in developing their careers anywhere in the world, regardless of which region they started work in.

Shell has long recognized that it has a duty to contribute to the local communities and one way is by supporting a number of initiatives to develop education and skills within the region. One example of this work can be seen in the Petroleum Institute, which opened here in Abu Dhabi in 2001. It is a centre of excellence for teaching skills related to the oil and gas industry and provides training to more than four hundred students.

In Oman, we support a 100 per cent Shell social investment program. We also make a contribution through PDO, which provides more than 4.5 million Omani riyals to support university education for Omanis. That meant that last year PDO sponsored sixty two postgraduates and two hundred and thirty six undergraduates who will provide a pool of highly skilled and talented people who will be very attractive to any employer.

It is a matter of pride that international oil producers have been able to play their part in developing the region's human resources alongside the region's oil and gas wealth. Shell looks forward to continuing to provide more such opportunities to local people.

[42]

Conclusion

In conclusion, I would restate Shell's clear view that both in gas and oil, this region is going to play a key role in meeting the world's energy needs right through to the end game of oil, and Shell intends to play its part right to the very end. This means that, despite the challenges outlined, there is a very bright future for the region. It has rich resources, firm foundations for growth and an increasingly attractive climate for investment.

Shell has taken the time to build successful partnerships in the Middle East over the past century. As a result, its relationships in the region are based on mutual respect, and a knowledge that by working together maximum value can be created. Both sides share a common goal—this region's progress and prosperity. Shell's success as a business depends to a very significant extent on its performance in this region. That means that there is a powerful joint interest at work—the more this region prospers, the greater the return on Shell's investment. Working together can boost the success of this region.

Finally, I would emphasize one fundamental point about Shell's approach. The company does not think that oil companies ought to get involved in politics—although the gap between oil and politics can sometimes be very small! The company's aim, in every country in which it works, is to strive to help Governments deliver change for the better, and play its part in meeting the challenges mentioned earlier. All this is undertaken within a framework of clear values and principles and a commitment to long-term engagement—an approach which I believe can help the Shell Group continue to make an effective contribution to the future stability and prosperity of the region.

2

Gulf Oil Investment Outlook: Trends and Issues

Fatih Birol

The investment requirements of the oil sector in the Middle East and Gulf region are analyzed in this chapter. After assessing the amount of investment that will be needed through 2030, attention will be focused on the obstacles to be overcome in order to mobilize this capital in a timely manner. The concluding part of the chapter will assess the global implications stemming from lower-than-projected levels of investments occurring in the region. The analysis is based on the *World Energy Investment Outlook* (WEIO) released in November 2003 by the International Energy Agency (IEA). The IEA is currently updating and expanding its analysis of oil/gas sector investment issues in the Middle East and Gulf region. Their findings will form an important part of the 2005 edition in the *World Energy Outlook* series due to be released in November. This report will analyze the rate of development of the Middle East and North Africa's energy sector and draw implications for the availability of exports to world markets.

Global Investment Outlook

To meet projected demand growth of 1.7% per year over the next three decades, $16.5 trillion, or almost $550 billion a year, will need to be invested in global energy supply infrastructure. This is equal to around 1% of projected global GDP and 4.5% of total investment on average. Capital needs will grow steadily through the projection period. The average annual rate of investment is projected to rise from $455 billion in the decade 2001–2010 to $632 billion in 2021-2030. This compares with estimated energy investment of $413 billion in 2000. Actual capital flows will fluctuate around these levels according to project and business cycles.

For the whole energy sector, 51% of investment in production will be needed simply to replace existing and future capacity. The rest will be needed to meet the increase in demand. The share of investment to replace existing production capacity is highest for oil upstream (78%), followed by gas upstream (70%) and coal mining (65%). In the electricity sector, investment to replace existing power plants will be 30%. Table 2.1 details developments in key aspects of the global supply infrastructure for each fuel.

Table 2.1
Global Energy Supply and Infrastructure

Fuel	Infrastructure Development	Units	Year 2000	Year 2030	Annual Average Rate of Growth (%)
Oil	Production*	mbpd	75	120	1.6
	Refining capacity	mbpd	82	121	1.3
	Tanker capacity	million DWT	271	522	2.2
Gas	Production	billion cubic meters	2,513	5,280	2.5
	Transmission pipelines	thousand km	1,139	2,058	2.0
	Distribution pipelines	thousand km	5,007	8,523	1.8
	Underground storage working volume	billion cubic meters	328	685	2.5
Coal	Production	metric tons	4,595	6,954	1.4
	Port capacity**	metric tons	2,212	2,879	0.9
Electricity	Generation capacity	GW	3,498	7,157	2.4
	Transmission network	thousand km	3,550	7,231	2.4

Notes: * Oil production includes processing gains.
    ** The port capacity figures in this table do not include the capacity required for internal coal trade in China, India and Indonesia (cumulative additions for internal trade are 192 Mt of capacity).

Source: IEA analysis.

Global Oil Investment Outlook

A little over $3 trillion of investment will be needed in the oil sector through to 2030 (Figure 2.1). Investment needs will average $103 billion per year, but will increase steadily through the period as demand increases. The share of investment spending in OECD countries is high relative to their production capacity because unit costs are higher compared to other regions particularly in the upstream segment of the supply chain.

Figure 2.1
World Cumulative Oil Investment by Decade

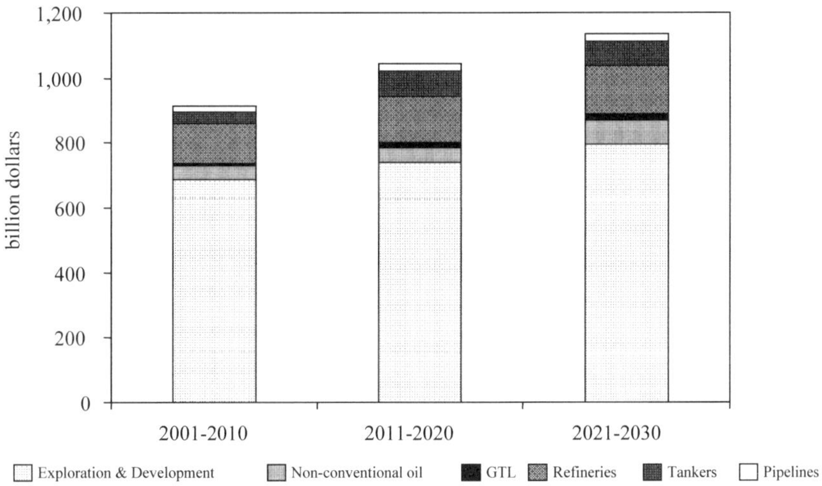

Source: IEA analysis.

The projected increase in world oil demand from 77 mbpd in 2002 to 120 mbpd in 2030 will require more than 200 mbpd of new production capacity to be brought on stream. Most of the new capacity will be needed to replace depleted wells that are currently producing or wells that will be brought into production and depleted during the next three decades. Bringing all this capacity on stream will entail upstream investment of $2.2 trillion. Inter-regional trade in crude oil and refined products is projected to increase by around 80% over the period 2001-2030. The construction of tankers and pipelines to enable this trade will cost $257 billion. Investment in refining, with new capacity concentrated in the Middle East and Asia, will be $412 billion dollars. Development of non-conventional oil projects, which are expected to contribute over 8% to total world oil supplies by 2030, will cost $205 billion, mainly in Canada and Venezuela.

As indicated in Table 2.2, OECD countries will account for the largest share of total oil investment (31%), followed by the Middle East (18%), the transition economies (16%) and Africa (13%). Nonetheless, the largest addition to production capacity will take place in the Middle East, where the unit capital cost of exploration and development per barrel is only one quarter that of the OECD countries. Although 69% of all oil-sector investment, excluding transportation, will occur in non-OECD countries, more than 40% of such investment will be in projects to supply crude and oil products to OECD countries. In the Middle East, over half of the oil investment is geared towards exports intended for OECD countries.

Table 2.2
Global Oil Cumulative Investment by Region and Activity, 2001-2030
(in billion dollars)*

Region	Exploration & Development	Non-Conventional Oil	Refining	Total
North America	466	114	43	622
Europe	199	1	22	222
Pacific	19	1	24	44
Total OECD	**684**	**116**	**89**	**888**
Total transition economies	**422**	**0**	**26**	**448**
China	69	0	50	119
South and East Asia	87	7	69	163
Middle East	408	16	99	523
Africa	311	7	42	360
Latin America	241	59	37	336
Total developing countries	**1,116**	**89**	**297**	**1,501**
Total non-OECD	**1,538**	**89**	**323**	**1,949**
Total world	**2,222**	**205**	**412**	**2,837**

Note: * Not including global transportation investment of $257 billion.

Source: IEA analysis.

Global Oil Exploration and Development Investment

Cumulative global investment in oil exploration and development from 2001 to 2030 will amount to $2.2 trillion, or around $74 billion per year. Investment will grow over the projection period, from an estimated $69 billion per year in the first decade to $79 billion per year in the third decade. In comparison, spending was somewhat lower, at $64 billion, in 2000 as a consequence of the low oil price in the previous year. Although capacity additions will be substantial, average upstream investment costs per unit of output will fall as more oil is expected to come from the Middle East, which is by far the world's lowest cost region (Figure 2.2).

Figure 2.2
Average Development Costs and Proven Reserves by Region

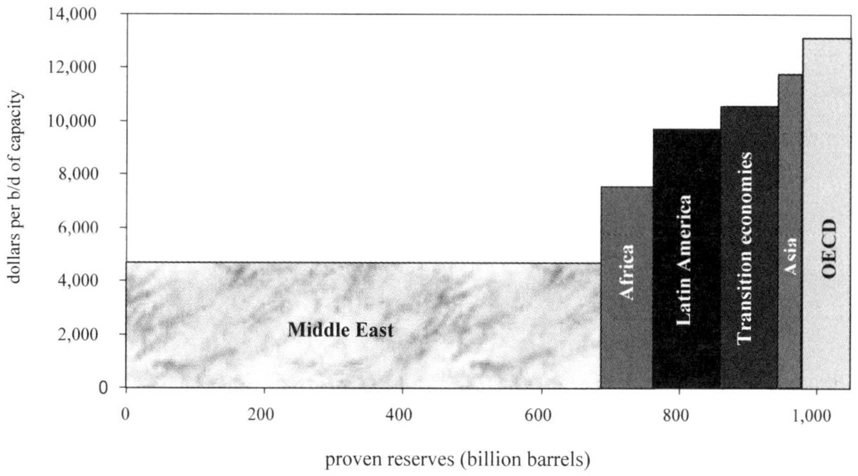

proven reserves (billion barrels)

Note: The extent of the area for each region provides an indication of the relative amounts of investment that would be notionally required to develop all existing proven reserves.

Source: IEA, *Oil & Gas Journal*, December 24, 2001.

Estimated investment requirements for each region depend on projected production, oil-well decline rates, and exploration and development costs. Developing countries are expected to account for nearly 55% of global upstream investment. Investments in OECD countries will remain large despite the small and declining share of these countries in world oil production, which is projected to fall from 30% in 2002 to only 11% in 2030. In contrast, investment in the OPEC countries of the Middle East represents only 18% of total investment, because of low unit costs in this region. This region will account for 43% of world oil supply in 2030, up from 29% at present.

In total, more than 200 mbpd of new production capacity will have to be added during the next three decades. This will be required mainly to replace progressive declines in production capacity from wells already in production or that come onstream during the projection period, as well as to meet demand growth. Replacement capacity of 175 mbpd will be more than five times larger than the 33 mbpd of capacity additions required to meet demand growth (Figure 2.3). Of this replacement capacity, 37 mbpd will be needed simply to maintain capacity related to the increase in demand over the projection period. The rest will be needed to maintain *current* capacity.

Figure 2.3
Conventional Oil Production Capacity

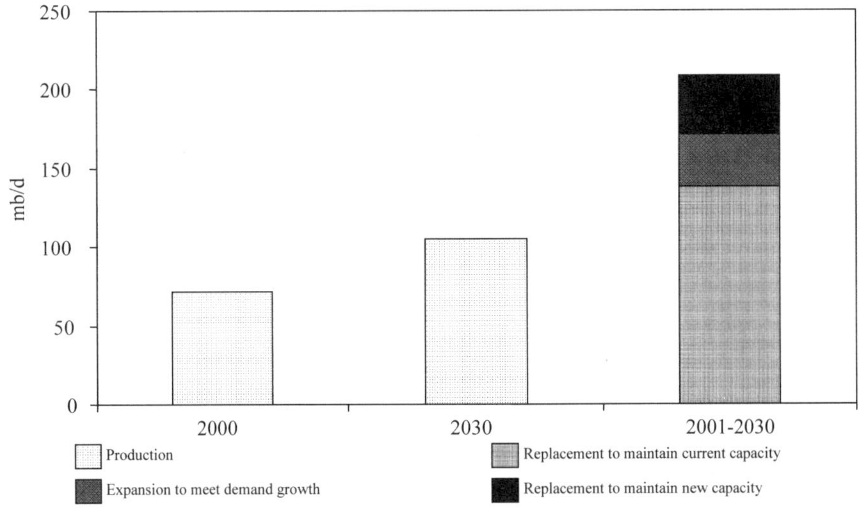

Source: IEA analysis.

Although the oil investment flows projected for the next three decades will be large and will rise progressively, the availability of capital is not expected to be an investment constraint. However that does not guarantee that all those investments will be made or that capital will flow to where it is needed. Several factors could discourage or prevent investment from occurring in particular regions or sectors. In other words, investment may be constrained by a lack of profitable business opportunities rather than any absolute shortage of capital. Table 2.3 summarizes the necessary and sufficient conditions for an oil company to invest in a particular upstream project.

Table 2.3
Investment Conditions for Upstream Oil Investment

Sufficient Conditions	Necessary Conditions
• Profitability	• Confidence in market demand
• Acceptable risk	• Resource base—quantity and quality
• Repeatability—opportunity to sustain profitable stream of investment	• Access to reserves
• Fit with corporate strategy	• Legal and institutional framework
• Fit with portfolio of current and planned assets and projects	• Rule of law

Source: IEA analysis.

Where necessary investment conditions are fulfilled, profitability and risk are the key factors that determine whether the investment goes ahead. The required rate of return, or hurdle rate, on any investment varies according to the risks associated with it. As investment shifts to regions where country risk is likely to be higher, the average hurdle rates of oil companies will increase.

The most volatile element in the investment equation is the oil price. Upstream global oil and gas investment in recent years has tended to fluctuate in line with oil prices. A price collapse, such as occurred in 1985 and 1998, typically leads to a subsequent reduction in investment spending. Conversely, higher prices tend to encourage investment spending, as seen in recent years. The rate of investment, in turn, affects prices. There is also evidence that the increasing short-term volatility of oil prices, by increasing risk and therefore hurdle rates, is constraining investment.

Gulf Oil Investment Outlook

Investment in expanding oil production capacity in the Middle East and Gulf will be vital to global energy market prospects in the medium to long term. Mobilizing that investment will depend largely on the production and

[51]

investment policies of the key producers, particularly Saudi Arabia. Although the costs of developing the region's vast reserves are lower than anywhere else in the world—restrictions on foreign involvement in many countries and the dependence on national oil companies for a large share of state revenues might constrain the amount of capital available for investment in expanding production capacity. Of course, investment prospects in Iraq are particularly uncertain.

Investment Outlook

The projected growth in Middle East oil production implies a need for around $523 billion of capital spending in exploration and development over the next three decades. Investment flows will need to rise substantially from an average of $12 billion a year in the current decade to around $23 billion a year in the last decade of the projection period. Almost half of this investment will be to supply OECD countries.

It is assumed that exploration and development costs for new supplies will be broadly constant for both low-cost onshore and higher-cost offshore fields over the projection period, but a gradual shift towards offshore drilling in some countries will raise average costs slightly in the region as a whole. Costs in the Middle East are nonetheless expected to remain the lowest in the world, and well below assumed price levels. The average capital cost of new onshore capacity in Middle East OPEC countries is around $4,600 per barrel per day compared with $10,200 worldwide and around $22,000 in the North Sea.

Downstream oil investment needs will also be substantial. Refining capacity is projected to surge from just over 6 mbpd in 2002 to 10 mbpd in 2010 and 15.6 mbpd in 2030—equivalent to one large new refinery a year. This will entail capital outlays of around $99 billion, or $3.3 billion a year. Investment in gas-to-liquids (GTL) capacity, most of which will probably be built in Qatar and Iran, will amount to $12.7 billion, more than 30% of the world total.

Investment Uncertainties

The principal uncertainties clouding future Middle East supply and consequently investment needs, is the rate of growth of global oil demand, the resulting call on OPEC supply and the supply policies that producers choose to pursue. A slightly lower rate of increase in demand than that projected in *WEO-2002* would have a particularly marked effect on investment needs in the Middle East as the main residual supplier of oil to the international market.

There are also uncertainties on the supply side. The policies of the host countries on opening up their oil industries to private and foreign investment, the fiscal regime and investment conditions, and government revenue needs may constrain capital flows to the sector.

These factors must be seen against a backdrop of continuing political instability in the region. The US-led occupation of Iraq, endless and exhausting negotiations over a peace deal between Israel and Palestine, and social and political tensions throughout the Gulf compound the political and economic unpredictability of the region.

Future trends in the natural decline rates of Middle East oilfields will have a major impact on how much investment will be needed. Much of the oil produced in the Middle East today comes from gigantic fields that have been in operation for several decades. The natural decline rates at some of these fields are thought to be rising.

Iraq

Nowhere are short-term oil production prospects more uncertain than in Iraq, following the overthrow of the Saddam Hussein regime by US-led forces in early 2003. The immediate objective of the administration is to restore production capacity as quickly as possible in order to generate the export earnings needed for reconstruction. Looting and sabotage have reduced sustainable capacity, which was estimated at 2.8 mbpd before the war. Restoring output to even that level may take many months as Iraqi oil infrastructure has suffered years of under-investment. Achieving the 1990 level of 3.5 mbpd is expected to take several years. The provisional administration announced in July 2003 that it had accepted a $1.1 billion

[53]

investment plan to return crude output to the pre-war level. Achieving this goal will depend on how quickly order can be restored to the country and the extent of the damage to oilfields caused by poor production engineering practices and maintenance during the 1990s.

In the longer term, there is considerable potential for expanding capacity. According to the *Oil and Gas Journal*, Iraq has 112 billion barrels of proven reserves. Other estimates range from 95 to 120 billion barrels. Of 73 known fields, only 15 have been developed. However, there are enormous uncertainties and questions about the future development of the Iraqi oil industry:

- How quickly can the transition to a stable government be achieved and how effective will that government prove to be?
- How extensive will the damage caused by looting and attacks on facilities and pipelines be before law and order can be restored?
- Will foreign oil companies have any role, and if so, what commercial and fiscal terms might they be offered?
- What will be the role and ownership of the Iraq National Oil Company (INOC) and the availability of oil revenues for re-investment in the industry?
- Will sufficient pipeline capacity be available for exports?
- What will be the legal status of contracts signed or negotiated with foreign firms prior to the war?
- What will Iraqi policy be *vis-à-vis* OPEC membership and acceptance of production quotas?

It is estimated that raising capacity to around 3.7 mbpd by 2010—the Reference Scenario projection—will require cumulative investment of close to $5 billion. However, government revenues from production over the period 2003-2010 would be much higher, at over $20 billion. The economic return on upstream investment will, nonetheless, decline with rising investment. The marginal cost of an additional barrel of capacity will be particularly low in the short term, but as production increases, the marginal cost of a barrel will increase substantially. Extending production beyond about 4 mbpd will require major new projects, which would call for investments in exploration, new production capacity and new export facilities.

Figure 2.4
Oil Upstream Investment Needs in Iraq
for Different Production Profiles

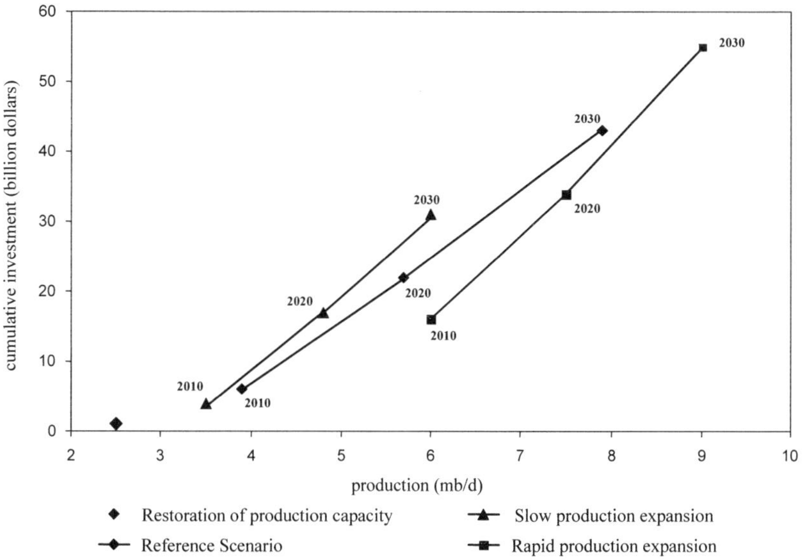

Source: IEA Analysis; Restoration of Iraqi Oil Infrastructure Final Work Plan, July 2003.

To illustrate the uncertainties clouding future Iraqi oil developments and their implications for investments, we have devised two alternative production profiles corresponding to faster and slower development (see Figure 2.4 above). In a rapid growth case in which production reaches 9 mbpd in 2030, investment needs would be around $54 billion, about $12 billion more than in the Reference Scenario, where production reaches 8 mbpd. The rapid growth case assumes that capacity of 3.5 mbpd is reached within two years and that production rises in a linear fashion through to 2010. This trend implies that Iraq's share of total OPEC production would rise significantly.

In the slow production growth case, investment is about $12 billion less than in the Reference Scenario, with production reaching 3.5 mbpd only in 2007 and 6 mbpd in 2030. In this case, once production of 3.5 mbpd has been achieved, the subsequent production increases keep Iraq's share of total OPEC production more or less constant.

Restricted Middle East Oil Investment Scenario

This scenario assesses the implications of investments in Middle East OPEC countries occurring at a lower level than projected in the *WEO-2002* Reference Scenario.

I-Background

The *WEO-2002* Reference Scenario projections of oil production, from which our investment projections are derived, are subject to several uncertainties. Expectations of the Middle East are particularly important in view of the region's central role in meeting global oil (and gas) demand in the coming decades, but there is a real risk that production capacities in the region will not be developed as quickly as expected in the Reference Scenario. The purpose of this section is to assess the consequences for global oil supply and demand, oil revenue and upstream investment of a scenario in which investment in the region is limited. The investment needed to meet the projected growth in production may not be forthcoming for several reasons, which include the following:

1. *Resource availability:* If reserves prove to be smaller than expected or difficult to recover due to operational difficulties, the need to find and develop new resources would be greater.
2. *Infrastructure:* Inadequate infrastructure could constitute another barrier.
3. *Labour availability:* Operational and financial performance could be affected by a shortage of qualified labour.
4. *National financing constraints:* In countries with national oil companies, financing new projects could become a problem where the national debt is already high and national issues such as sovereignty discourage reliance on foreign investment.
5. *Foreign investment policies:* The policies of producing countries with regard to opening up their oil industries to private and foreign investment, the legal and commercial terms on offer and the fiscal regimes will have a major impact on how much capital Middle East producers will be able to secure.

[56]

6. *Oil prices and depletion strategy:* Prices will affect the ability of producing countries to finance investments from their own resources and therefore, their need to turn to private and foreign investment. Governments could choose to delay development of production capacity in order to achieve higher profits by driving up international prices. Some may slow the development of their resources in order to preserve them for future generations.

7. *Competition for financial resources:* In countries with state-owned companies and a rapidly growing population, education, health and other sectors of the economy could command a growing share of government revenues and constrain capital flows to the oil sector.

In order to simulate the effect of restricted oil investment in OPEC Middle East countries, their share of global oil production is assumed to remain flat at 28%, rather than growing to 43% in 2030 as in the Reference Scenario. This is close to the level observed in recent years. Under this assumption, production in the region keeps growing, but at a much slower pace than indicated in the Reference Scenario.

Under the Restricted Investment Scenario, prices are assumed to be on average 20% higher than in the Reference Scenario. As a result, the average price for imports into IEA countries rises to around $35 per barrel in 2030 (in year 2000 dollars). Prices are also assumed to fluctuate around this rising trend, peaking in some years at around $40 per barrel when global production approaches short-term capacity.

II-Results

Oil Demand

In the Restricted Investment Scenario, world oil demand grows by 1.3% per year, reaching 110 mbpd in 2030 (Table 2.4). This is 8% lower than in the Reference Scenario because of higher prices, which promote more efficient energy use and switching to other fuels. The share of oil in the global energy mix is 35% in 2030, compared with 38% in the Reference Scenario.

Table 2.4

Global Oil Supply in the Reference

and Restricted Investment Scenarios

Region	Scenario	2000	2010	2020	2030
Price ($ per barrel)					
	Reference	28	21	25	29
	Restricted Investment		27	30	35
Demand (mbpd)					
OECD	Reference	47	52	56	60
	Restricted Investment		49	52	53
Non-OECD	Reference	28	37	48	60
	Restricted Investment		36	46	57
World oil balance (mbpd)					
	Reference	75	89	104	120
	Restricted Investment		85	97	110
Supply (mbpd)					
Middle East OPEC	Reference	21	26	38	51
	Restricted Investment		24	27	31
Rest of the world	Reference	54	62	66	69
	Restricted Investment		61	70	79

Source: IEA analysis.

Oil Supply

OPEC Middle East production in the Restricted Investment Scenario is 20 mbpd lower in 2030 than in the Reference Scenario but it still increases from 21 mbpd in 2001 to 31 mbpd in 2030. The shares of non-conventional oil producers and other major oil resource holders in OPEC are substantially higher, to make up for lower production in the Middle East

OPEC Revenues

Oil revenues in OPEC countries outside the Middle East grow continuously over the projection period in the Restricted Investment Scenario, thanks to higher oil prices and higher production. The situation is different in OPEC Middle East countries, where cumulative revenues are lower than in the Reference Scenario (Figure 2.5). For OPEC as a whole, higher oil prices do

[58]

not compensate for lower production. Cumulative revenues over the projection period are more than $400 billion lower than in the Reference Scenario. Even on a discounted cash-flow basis, cumulative OPEC revenues over the projection period are lower.

Figure 2.5
OPEC and OPEC Middle East Cumulative Revenues
in the Reference and Restricted Investment Scenarios (2001-2030)

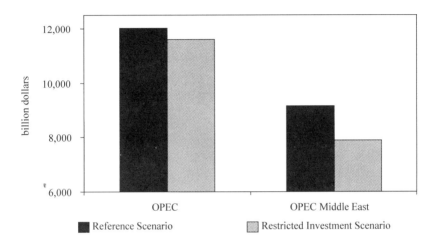

Source: IEA analysis.

Implications for Upstream Investment

In the Restricted Investment Scenario, despite lower global production, upstream oil investment requirements are 3% higher. Investment needs are higher in all regions, except OPEC Middle East, where they are $100 billion lower. The bigger investment requirements in Africa and the transition economies reflect faster production growth. However, the bulk of additional investment goes to non-conventional oil, which becomes more economically attractive. Investments in non-conventional oil are more than four times higher in the Restricted Investment Scenario than in the Reference Scenario.

Concluding Remarks

This chapter has presented the oil investment outlook globally and for the Middle East under a Reference and Restricted Investment scenario. The investment required is large and increasing in each succeeding decade. Funding this investment will represent a significant challenge, despite the low development costs in the Middle East. Whether investment occurs in a timely and efficient manner will depend critically on the production and investment policies of the major producers. The continuing consumer-producer dialogue will play an important role in bringing together both parties in order to examine the challenges that confront the oil industry.

3

Stabilizing the Oil Market during Unstable Times: Economic Dilemmas for the Gulf

Thomas E. Wallin

The international oil market took its current form and acquired its major characteristics in the late 1980s, following the price crash of 1986, and during the intervening period, price volatility has been a key element of the market. The instability of prices has become a fixture in the international oil business. The price fluctuations stem from the structure of the market itself, the large number of actors and the difficulty that OPEC or any other actor or group of actors encounter in imposing their will on the market. Moreover, given the unexpected convulsions in oil supply and demand caused by political disruptions and other external influences, instability in prices seems inevitable and inherent to the market. Futures and other derivatives markets have developed alongside the physical market in order to hedge the price risk caused by this volatility and to base speculation upon it. International oil companies have learned to manage their businesses quite well despite the instability. Whether dealing with refinery margins or long-term upstream investments, the companies have developed strategies for managing price instability. On a certain level at least, the commercial world has adjusted and accepted the commoditization of oil and the attendant price fluctuations that form an integral part of it.

Nevertheless, for oil producers and consumers, the instability of the market remains a serious problem when they confront the financial pain caused by low or high oil prices respectively. The price swings can also

[61]

have other onerous impacts on the economies of producer and consumer countries. Obviously, oil producing and oil exporting nations that lack a diversified economic base, such as many of those in the Middle East and Gulf region, are particularly vulnerable. However, for consuming countries the impacts are significant too. High oil prices have also played at least a contributory role in every US economic recession over the last 40 years. High prices for gasoline and refined products are not only economically damaging but also politically contentious in the United States and Europe. For these reasons, governments in both oil exporting countries and oil importing countries have pursued policies to deal with the dislocations caused by oil market instability.

Some key periods of oil market instability over the last 15 years will be examined from my perspective as a petroleum journalist who has closely followed developments in the industry. As an observer without any direct interest, I am inclined to view the evolution of international petroleum markets in rather unconventional terms. After tracing the general trends over the last 15 years, a few key episodes of extreme instability will be analyzed to illustrate some of the critical factors influencing oil prices. This will be followed by a review of the policies pursued by governments in their efforts to influence oil markets and assess their effectiveness. By projecting how these policies and oil markets dynamics are likely to play out, some predictions can be made about the future prospects for oil price stability. Based on this assessment of past and future trends, some ideas will be offered on other ways to deal with instability and forge a sounder commercial and corporate basis for oil markets in the future that would lead to a reintegration of the international oil business and a more stable oil market.

Before looking at the recent periods of price instability and the lessons that they provide, it is important to be clear about what is actually meant by stability and instability. Stable oil prices are universally favored. The term "price stability" sounds objective and clear but it is actually loaded with differing connotations depending on who is using it. For oil producers and for OPEC the term usually means stable and fair or equitable oil prices—implying that prices must be stable and above a certain minimum acceptable level. On the other hand, the oil consumers and importers talk of stable and reasonable or attractive oil prices—which means stable prices that are low enough to encourage economic growth and restrain inflation.

At the outset, one must recognize that the entire discussion regarding oil market stability and efforts to improve it are closely tied with the interests and perspective of producers and consumers about broader issues of oil security and economic vulnerability. The policies and actions taken by producers and consumers with regard to market stability are very much driven by and informed by these underlying assumptions, so it is important to acknowledge them. Both sides may agree that market stability is good, but if that stability is at prices that are $10 per barrel apart, such a consensus is meaningless.

Recent Trends in Market Instability

Over the last fifteen years the instability of oil prices has varied. The most extreme period of price instability was during the Gulf War (1990–1991). However, price instability has become more pronounced in the 3–4 years preceding 2003 as compared to the immediate post-Gulf War period of 1991–1996. Figure 3.1 illustrates these trends on the basis of monthly fluctuations in the OPEC basket price from January 1988 until July 2003.

Figure 3.1
Month-to-Month Oil Price Changes (1988-2003)

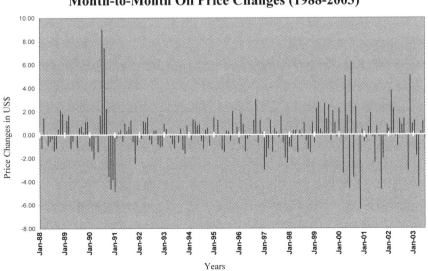

Source: *Oil Market Intelligence*, Energy Intelligence Group

In terms of overall price levels, the period of the last four years also marks a period when oil prices have been at a substantially higher average level than in the preceding period. The higher price level is due in large measure to the success of the OPEC price band mechanism and the market management coordination among OPEC producers. Prices have been about $5–$10 per barrel higher than they were during most of the 1988–1999 period, as can be observed from Figure 3.2 below. Despite the success of OPEC in achieving its higher price objectives much more effectively than before, this did not reduce price volatility but on the contrary, added to market instability. The following chart shows the trend in the OPEC basket price in relation to various OPEC price targets.

Figure 3.2
OPEC Basket Price: Monthly Average (1988-2003)

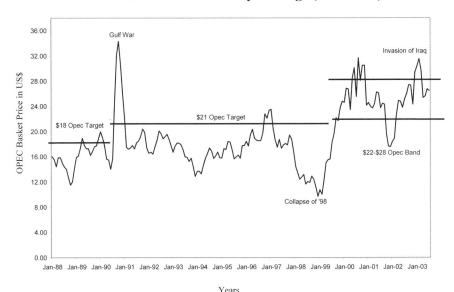

Years

Source: *Oil Market Intelligence*, Energy Intelligence Group

One of the main reasons that prices have shown greater instability in recent years is the lower level of inventories that are available to cushion the market from minor shifts in supply and demand. In the absence of surplus stocks, market pressures translate much more quickly into higher or lower prices. One way to look at this inventory pressure is by examining the forward price curve. Figure 3.3 below shows the discount or premium that forward oil prices held over time in relation to prompt prices of West Texas Intermediate crude for a period 8 weeks ahead. When forward prices are discounted the market is said to be in backwardation and stocks are low because there is no incentive for oil companies to hold extra inventory. This almost always corresponds to periods of relatively high prices like the last few years. By contrast, when forward prices are at a premium in relation to prompt prices the market is said to be in contango and stocks are abundant because there is a clear financial incentive to hold stocks and lock in the profit by selling the oil forward. Periods of contango are associated with low oil prices. Both contango and backwardation tend to be self-sustaining and require some major event to displace them. In general, low stocks and price backwardation seem to be closely linked to increased price volatility.

Figure 3.3
Backwardation and Contango (1988-2003)

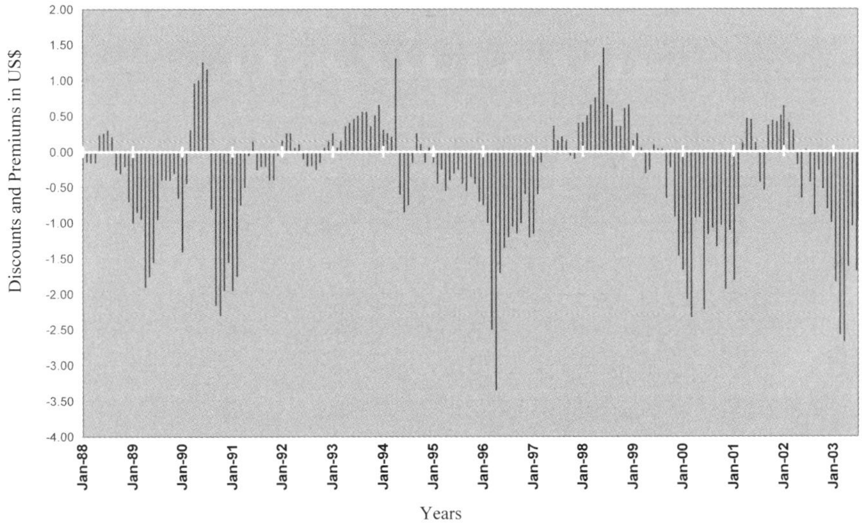

Note: Contango is for values above zero and backwardation is for values below zero.
Source: *Oil Market Intelligence*, Energy Intelligence Group

Moving from these basic observations about market instability, it is worth focusing on three particular events that were marked with extreme price instability: the Gulf War period of 1990–1991, the price collapse of 1998 and the US invasion of Iraq in 2003. On the basis of these events, some specific observations can be made about market dynamics and government policies aimed at dealing with unstable markets.

The Gulf War

The Gulf War of 1990–1991 is in many ways the classic price shock event of the modern oil market and many parallels were drawn with it during and before the US invasion of Iraq. Prices collapsed in the first half of 1990 due to high production within OPEC and then more than doubled in August and September with the Iraqi invasion of Kuwait and the loss of oil exports from both countries. Prices then collapsed again just as quickly in early 1991 with the liberation of Kuwait.

One of the key observations to be drawn from this period is that during a politically driven supply crisis like the Gulf War, the fundamentals of oil market supply, demand and inventories become secondary to market psychology. The fact that oil inventories were high and markets were in contango did little to restrain the immediate price increase, but those fundamentals did reassert themselves immediately afterwards. Government policies that seek to contain price volatility during a crisis must be focused on market psychology and perception more than actual supply and demand.

In terms of the policies of consumer country governments, the decision by the United States and the International Energy Agency (IEA) to wait until the end of the conflict to release stocks to the market, added to the post-conflict price decline rather than mitigating the initial price upswing. With hindsight, the focus of the IEA release on the supply–demand balance rather than market psychology did not help much in dealing with price volatility. The policies of Saudi Arabia and Iran to move significant volumes of crude oil outside the Gulf in the autumn were probably much more helpful in terms of restraining upward price pressure at a time when market psychology was at fever pitch, but these supplies also contributed to the severity of the post-war price collapse. The lesson for governments of both producing countries and consuming countries is that they need to focus on countering market psychology and must be careful not to contribute to volatility by the way in which they respond to the crisis. Given these constraints, the use of surplus capacity and strategic stocks by governments

[66]

to contain price instability is inherently difficult and may lead to unintended consequences.

1998 Price Collapse

In contrast to the Gulf War period and the oil price increases of the 1970s, the price collapse of 1998 is generally viewed as having been driven by a demand shock rather than a supply shock. Asia is the main force behind global oil demand growth, and the domino-like recession that hit key Asian economies in late 1997 and 1998 led to a collapse in oil demand for which OPEC producers were unprepared. Ultimately, it took several attempts by OPEC in cooperation with non-OPEC producers to tighten the market enough to reverse the price decline. The actual volatility of oil prices during the decline was not as great as it was during the subsequent rebound, mainly because stocks were in surplus.

Given the dire revenue impact of the price collapse for oil producers, this period was one of the most difficult for the Middle East and the Gulf and it is important to look at the internal problems within OPEC that led to the inability to deal with the unexpected drop in Asian demand. Already in 1997, Venezuela's aggressive production policy coupled with its abandonment of OPEC quotas was creating serious difficulties within the group that led to lower oil prices and rising inventories. In the OPEC meeting in Jakarta held in late 1997, Saudi Arabia pushed for an increase in quotas that augmented supplies just at the time when demand was weakening. Although never publicly acknowledged as a policy, this move was intended to punish Venezuela and other OPEC producers for non-compliance with their quotas, by imposing a period of lower prices upon them. It also forced some non-OPEC producers to partially shoulder the burden of restraining supplies. While partly driven by external demand factors, the price collapse prompted stricter enforcement of discipline on other exporters. Ultimately, this price collapse led to the formation of the $22–$28 OPEC price band mechanism and a period of very successful OPEC market management. The internal dynamics of OPEC and the tensions between OPEC and non-OPEC producers can seriously aggravate periods of market weakness and instability.

The US Invasion of Iraq

The oil market's response to the US invasion of Iraq was widely expected to be a replay of the Gulf War situation, but this was not the case. While oil prices were driven once again by market psychology and rose immediately before the conflict, the increase was much less in percentage terms, rising from a much higher base than during the Gulf War. The prices also dropped much less after the conflict. This much more moderate price spike occurred although oil inventories were much tighter in late 2002 and early 2003 than they were in 1990. Moreover, it occurred despite the fact that the oil market was facing serious secondary supply disruptions from political strife and labor strikes in both Venezuela and Nigeria. Although the oil supply lost due to the invasion of Iraq was less, it was anticipated that these other factors might have caused the price impact to be almost as great as during the Gulf War.

More successful government policies in dealing with oil markets were clearly part of the reason why the price impact was not as great as during the Gulf War. OPEC's success in the preceding years with its price band and the fact that Saudi Arabia controlled the lion's share of surplus capacity meant that the producer group responded not only to the Iraq War but also to the Venezuelan and Nigerian shortfalls with carefully modulated increases in production. Meanwhile, the United States and the International Energy Agency made it clear that emergency stocks would be made available if needed, but these stocks were never actually used and the potential for their release was used as a psychological tool to influence the market. While the surplus capacity in OPEC countries and the strategic stocks of the consuming countries were used more effectively than during the Gulf War, they were still not able to contain the volatility of oil markets completely. However, on balance, government policies were much more successful at restraining prices than they were during the Gulf War or the collapse of 1998.

Success of the OPEC Price Band

The OPEC price band mechanism, in effect since early 1999, has not significantly decreased oil price volatility but has probably increased it through the low inventories that resulted. In fact, the price band has brought

[68]

a period of much higher prices. This mechanism is worth considering more closely because it represents a highly successful market management period for OPEC. Although somewhat lacking in terms of strict market stability measures, the recent period has proved a success in terms of the broader objectives of oil-exporting countries in achieving stable and fair oil prices. The higher prices have boosted revenues for all oil producers. With higher prices, the higher level of market volatility has essentially gone unnoticed. In short, market instability can be manageable for OPEC and other exporters if it occurs at relatively high prices. This reality underscores the importance of viewing market stability in the context of a broader package of producers' goals related to fairness and revenue growth and stability.

OPEC's success in managing the market and defending the $22–$28 per barrel price band comes from a pro-active approach and careful coordination within the group. While quota discipline has not been perfect, it has been reasonably good compared to earlier periods. The fact that idle capacity is not excessively large and is concentrated mostly in the hands of Saudi Arabia and its allies means that there has also been less scope for internal disagreement. OPEC has also shown a much greater sensitivity to market psychology, taking decisions and timing their announcement to maximize market impact, rather like a central bank. As noted above, these market management policies worked reasonably well during the invasion of Iraq and its aftermath in helping to contain upward price pressures and also to avoid a post-war price collapse. Some commentators have been quick to point out that other mitigating factors have helped OPEC to keep prices within the band. However, given the record of the last four years the maintenance of the price band must be seen as more than luck.

While successful in the medium term, the market management policies pursued by OPEC countries in relation to the $22–$28 band also pose problems. Part of OPEC's success has been in keeping commercial inventories low, which in turn helps support prices. However, these lower levels of commercial inventories make markets more vulnerable to minor imbalances, price swings and instability. This volatility in turn requires constant fine tuning of the market and a willingness and ability to respond to even minor price swings. The term "micro-management" of the market has been used with some validity, and some critics expect that OPEC will

[69]

misjudge this delicate balancing act at some point, leading to an unexpected price downturn.

In the longer term, the $22–$28 price range is encouraging increased production from several non-OPEC sources. Within OPEC itself, it is encouraging the development of new production capacity in most member countries. As will be detailed in the section focusing on the future market outlook, OPEC is encountering a situation in which its market share is declining at a time when the capacity of member countries is increasing. While the ambitions of member countries to expand output can be delayed in the short-term, it will be extremely difficult to restrain in the longer term. Market forces are likely to make the price band unsustainable, leading to a period of extreme price instability and weakness.

While the OPEC price band represents one of the most effective policy responses of oil exporters to counter market instability and price weakness, it does not represent a longer term solution. Internal and external pressures are building up that are likely to be impossible to contain in the longer term, leading to a new stage of extreme price weakness and greater instability.

Policy of Oil Importers

Since the late 1970s, the United States and other major oil importers have been largely committed to energy policies that seek to advance free market principles, and there has been a broad consensus that this approach ensures that all market participants receive valid signals and incentives. Government regulation of energy markets, no matter how well intentioned, is seen as a source of distortions that lead to economic inefficiencies detrimental to the whole economy and to consumers in particular. The result is a policy that is essentially passive with regard to price instability except under crisis conditions.

The only policy area in which consumer governments are willing to influence price volatility is with the establishment of strategic stocks such as the US Strategic Petroleum Reserve (SPR). These large stocks of crude oil have been accumulated to deal with loss of supplies in a crisis but their release also has the potential to significantly restrain upward price pressures and thus help to stabilize a volatile market. The trigger for using such stocks has almost always been supply losses rather than specific price levels or the extent of price increases. By measuring the loss of supply rather than price signals, government officials have tended to release supplies late in a crisis after the economic damage caused by high prices has already hit oil-consuming countries. As seen above, this was clearly the case in the Gulf War. Unless policy makers consider using a release mechanism more closely tied to oil price levels, which seems unlikely for both political and operational reasons, the existing policy is unlikely to have a very significant impact on restraining oil price volatility. Perhaps the best contribution that it can make is through the threat of potential release—as was the case during the US invasion of Iraq.

Beyond the limited and largely ineffectual policy responses of oil consumers to oil price instability is a broader set of issues and concerns. Just as oil exporters seek oil price stability as part of wider concerns related to fairness and revenue enhancement in the form of higher prices, oil consumers follow policies that are predicated on the broader goals of reasonable and economically efficient prices that are lower than those that producers are hoping for. Price stability is also valued for its own sake because of the benefits it provides by assuring longer term investment. In the ultimate analysis, price volatility can be tolerated by consumers if oil is cheap.

The free market policy of the United States and other consumer countries toward oil is consistent with the economic ideology of liberal democracy but in reality it is a historically new development. For much of the history of the US oil industry, prices have been under some degree of control, either by corporations, in the form of Standard Oil until 1911, or later by a combination of state or federal government policies from the 1920s until 1980. These policies took the form of allocations by the Texas Railroad Commission and other state bodies, protectionist tariffs for domestic oil producers and federal price controls. The embrace of free market principles in oil in the later 1970s spared the US government the politically impossible job of managing the market while promoting the interests of consumers by maintaining the lowest possible prices most of the time.

In a free market, the prices of oil and other energy sources tend to be driven to low levels around the cost of production during periods of surplus, which usually last much longer than periods of scarcity or tightness. The problem for politicians is that long periods of depressed prices are eventually followed by periods of extremely high prices in a free market environment. The high capital costs and long lead times of energy production projects mean that supply comes not evenly but in spurts, and periods of low prices and under-investment lead to shortages and high prices as supplies catch up with demand growth. This cycle means that there is inherent price instability that can be extreme and politically very unpopular, with the free market energy approach advocated by the United States and other large consumers.

The governments and politicians who have reaped the benefits of low energy prices through free market policies in the 1980s and 1990s are increasingly encountering the dark side of that policy in the form of high and volatile prices. High and volatile prices for energy helped to spur the recall of Governor Gray Davis of California in 2003. US motorists had become used to cheap gasoline and price spikes have become a hot political issue. In Europe, high taxes on motor fuels have led to revolts by consumers. The energy policies of consumer countries are exposing their governments to greater political risks because consumers want assurances of low and stable prices that governments can provide some of the time but cannot deliver all the time. In short, consuming countries are encountering the volatility of free energy markets and the voters will only tolerate such policies if prices are low or kept from rising too high. At some point, these political pressures may force governments to seek an alternative policy.

Oil Security and Limits of Government Policy

From the examination of market instability over the last fifteen years and the responses of government policies in both oil exporting and oil importing countries it is clear that concerns for price stability clearly involve a broader package of issues relating to oil security. Price stability is considered desirable by both sides but it is seen from very different perspectives when it comes to overall oil security. Market stability and the broader concept of oil security do not mean the same thing to oil exporters and oil importers.

At the risk of oversimplification, oil exporters see oil security in terms of fairness, which essentially amounts to revenue stability and growth. Thus market stability is central but equitable prices are most important. The relatively higher prices represented by the OPEC price band seem to fill this objective. More broadly, exporters also need secure market outlets and prospects for future demand growth. These goals of expanded sales volumes are harder to achieve. In fact, under the OPEC price band mechanism they may be completely out of reach because of the growth of non-OPEC supply and the decline of OPEC's global market share. The policies of producing countries can at best only achieve some of their oil security objectives and only for part of the time.

By contrast, oil importers see oil security in terms of reliability and reasonableness—reliable supplies at reasonable or relatively cheap prices. Market stability is less important from this perspective than stable supplies and some protection from high prices, but obviously volatility is harmful to investment and volatility also generally accompanies price increases. By making most efficient use of available resources, the free market government policies of consumer countries should theoretically go a long way towards delivering these oil security objectives. One obvious obstacle is the fact that OPEC as a dominant group of oil exporters does not fully embrace free market objectives. Equally, if not more problematic for consumer country governments is that their citizens also do not accept the full implications of the free market—which brings with it inevitable periods of tight supplies and high prices. The free market approach cannot consistently provide the kind of oil security that voters in consumer countries want—abundant, low cost supplies. So far, no politician has been brave enough to tell them this, and none is likely to do so in the future.

The current oil market structure makes price instability unavoidable, and the market policies of producer and consumer country governments can reduce such instability only to some extent. Furthermore, government policies on both sides are only partially successful at achieving their respective broader oil security objectives, which are very different, particularly in terms of price levels. In fact, the differences in overall objectives and policies pursued by governments tend to reinforce market conditions leading to price volatility and the inability of both sides to reach their security objectives. While much progress has been made in recent years toward a productive producer and consumer dialogue, at a certain basic level, these meetings are unlikely to make significant progress when it comes to the core issues of oil market stability and energy security.

Future Price Pressures and Potential Instability

Given this overall past performance and the limitations of government policies, it is worth considering some of the market forces now in place in order to assess the future prospects for both price instability and the broader oil security objectives of both oil exporters and importers. The future outlook seems particularly challenging for the policies and objectives of oil producers and for Arabian Gulf exporters in particular, creating a critical economic dilemma for the region.

The success of the OPEC price band mechanism has created a wide incentive for all oil producers, both inside and outside OPEC to increase production. In the last few years, most of the non-OPEC rise has come from Russia and other countries of the former Soviet Union (FSU). The FSU has been boosting oil production steadily since 1998, with gains of well over 500,000 bpd every year since 2000. While these increases have accounted for the bulk of recent non-OPEC production growth, that picture is changing now, with several other non-OPEC producers showing significant gains. Energy Intelligence's *Oil Market Intelligence* did a careful survey of these additional volumes and projected a record annual increase in non-OPEC production of 1.4 mbpd in 2004. Half of that volume was estimated to come from the FSU, while the remainder would be divided somewhat equally between increases from Latin America, West Africa and North America. New deepwater production and Canadian synthetic crude production are key growth areas, with projects in place that should extend these gains into future years. At $22–$28 per barrel crude oil prices, this kind of rapid growth is likely to continue from a wide range of sources, thereby putting a squeeze on OPEC's own efforts to expand production.

In addition to non-OPEC growth, production volumes and capacity are also rising within the producer organization, OPEC. Iraq is the most obvious source of these additional supplies. While there is still great uncertainty about the pace and scope of Iraq's recovery, the country hoped to reach pre-war output levels in early 2004 and perhaps hit parity with Iran a year or two after that. Ultimately, it is targeting an output level of 6.5 mbpd by 2010—an increase of about 4.5 mbpd over a six-year period. In addition, Algeria, Nigeria, Libya and Qatar have plans in place to significantly expand production and in some cases they already have growing productive capacity in excess of their output quotas.

Over the next few years, these rising crude oil supplies from so many sources will put mounting pressure on the core OPEC producers in the Arabian Gulf. These countries will find it very hard to meet rising global oil demand and will probably need to give more market share to non-OPEC producers and even other OPEC nations including Iraq in order to defend the OPEC price band of $22–$28 per barrel. Given the close coordination and pro-active approach required for successful market management within the price band, strains may well grow within the organization and with the key non-OPEC countries such as Russia that are aggressively expanding production at the expense of Saudi Arabia and other key Gulf producers.

Unless OPEC is able to constructively engage key non-OPEC producers in restraining supplies, which is possible but far from assured, the group and Saudi Arabia in particular, will face some difficult choices. One option would be to reduce the level of the OPEC price band significantly and endure a very difficult period of uncertain duration, trying to maintain market stability at a lower price level. Another alternative would be for Saudi Arabia to increase production and allow prices to fall sharply in an enforcement action designed to force other producers inside and outside OPEC to restrain production, much as that which occurred in the price collapse of 1998.

Given the near certainty of these rising supplies, the oil market is expected to pose serious challenges to OPEC over the next few years that are likely to bring a period of market instability and low prices that will be particularly harmful to the Arabian Gulf economies. The broader oil security objectives of the oil-exporting countries will also be frustrated under these conditions. As for the large oil importers, while their free market approach should continue to be beneficial in a period of rapidly rising supplies, they too will be exposed to increased price instability, and a period of low prices would lead to underinvestment that sets the stage for future price spikes. Moreover, even in the context of a growing supply surplus, the risks of a political upheaval or conflict that disrupts oil supplies remains real and unavoidable.

In a nutshell, the future prospect for the oil markets over the next 15 years looks very much like the pattern of the last 15 years. Price volatility is likely to remain a central feature with a persistent tension between the security concerns and interests of the main oil exporters and the main oil importers. While the market will remain vulnerable to supply shocks, price collapses caused by internal OPEC pressures and market share pressures from non-OPEC producers are likely to grow. In short, under the prevailing circumstances and the current outlook for global oil supplies, the economic dilemma for the Gulf will remain the same or quite possibly become more acute in the coming years.

Time to Re-think the Market

With the prospect of little improvement in price stability or overall oil security in the future under existing trends and policies, what would it take to significantly alter and improve the picture? Is there a way beyond the apparently irreconcilable objectives of producers and consumers that would improve market stability and enhance the oil security objectives of both groups? These are difficult questions, and cannot be addressed with minor changes and modest adjustments to the existing system. What is required is a re-thinking of the structure and assumptions that have framed the oil market for the last 15 years. Such an effort can yield some alternative directions and different commercial structures that could provide the potential for change and improvement, but this means casting off old assumptions and opening up to new ways of thinking about the market.

A good way to start is to return to the basics. Looked at coldly, it is hard to escape the conclusion that the economics of the international petroleum business is highly paradoxical. Consider the following questions:

- How is it that five countries in the Middle East represent 65% of proven global oil reserves but account for only 25% of global production?
- Despite the preponderance of reserves and some of the lowest production costs in the world why are these countries among the last to see an increase in production when global oil demand increases? Why is their market share falling?
- Why do petroleum regions that are more costly and technically difficult to develop attract the major share of investment dollars of the international oil companies, while these Middle East countries see relatively little international investment? Why do they bear the cost of carrying most of the world's cushion of excess production capacity?
- Why does the region with the lowest cost of production in the world play the role of incremental, market balancing supply rather than base load supply?
- Why do the world's largest holders of oil reserves have a relatively small role in supplying the world with petroleum products?

The short, simple answers to these questions are factors such as: politics, OPEC, output quotas, resource nationalism, and distorted investment incentives. However, the historical reasons and explanations for these fundamental contradictions about the oil business are not important. What is important to recognize is that these kinds of basic contradictions must be addressed in a fundamental commercial and economic way in order to alter the structure of the global petroleum market and bring the interests and objectives of producers and consumers more closely in line.

In this chapter, an attempt will be made to develop some ideas for changing commercial and investment relationships in ways that would address these basic paradoxes and also alter the structure of the oil market. Most of these ideas are not new but have been discussed by others in the past and have even taken tangible commercial form under certain circumstances. However, it is worthwhile to re-examine these ideas from the current perspective and test their potential usefulness and benefit when applied on a large scale.

As will be seen, the basic driving force behind most of the ideas below is to seek solutions at the commercial and financial level rather than at the political level. The group with the greatest ultimate interest in the smooth functioning of oil markets and the enhancement of oil security is the oil industry itself—both the national firms and the international companies. The companies in their widest sense have a profound interest in a business that runs efficiently within a framework of clear incentives, sound investment choices and maximum efficiency. While some governments may be understandably distrustful of some companies or may question their inherent self-interest, they must also recognize that the companies have a tremendous amount at stake in a more rational and economic industry structure. By building upon the relationships between national oil companies and major integrated oil firms, a new kind of commercial and investment environment can be created that could enhance mutual interests and help to reconcile the differences between large oil exporting countries and large oil importers. In this way, the divide between producers and consumers can be bridged.

The new approach described below essentially involves the re-integration of the international oil industry on a global scale, tying the primary upstream exploration and production region more closely to the primary oil consuming regions. While the integrated global oil supply systems of the majors were broken in the 1970s in the name of national self-determination and resource nationalism, I believe it is now time to move into a new phase that would seek to regain the broader advantages of an integrated petroleum industry on the basis of partnership. What is envisioned is a win-win solution that does not involve anything as radical as the dismantling of OPEC or the privatization of state oil companies. In fact, the basic elements of the existing petroleum business and oil market would remain. The changes are envisaged in how the key commercial players interact at the level of investment and commercial dealings.

This global re-integration of the international oil industry would operate on two tracks: the international oil companies would gain access to reserves and production in the key producing countries of the Arabian Gulf and the national oil companies of the Middle East would gain substantial downstream refining and marketing positions in key markets outside the

[78]

region. Essentially, the national oil companies are upstream production companies that rely on commercial relationships with major oil companies and other integrated firms for outlets for their crude oil, while the international oil companies have a similar imbalance between their large downstream operations and their more modest, higher cost upstream operations. The result of re-integration would be a group of large global petroleum companies with more balanced upstream and downstream positions—a new group of "seven sisters" with the national oil companies playing a dominant role by virtue of their strong upstream positions. The process by which these companies would be transformed is essentially an asset swap, with national oil companies exchanging upstream assets for the downstream assets of the international oil majors. Since the upstream assets earn higher margins and are thus inherently more valuable than the downstream assets, the asset swap is likely to favor the national oil companies. At one point in the early 1990s, Saudi Aramco and TOTAL came close to negotiating such an arrangement but the deal collapsed due to political pressures on both sides.

Upstream Projects: Building on the Abu Dhabi Model

In recent years one of the main conundrums of the petroleum industry has been the difficulty faced by international oil companies in striking upstream investment deals in key Middle East oil producing countries such as Saudi Arabia, Kuwait and Iran. Essentially, these countries have been searching for ways to attract significant amounts of foreign investment in their petroleum and energy sectors but have yet to arrive at a formula suitable for both sides. Meanwhile, the international oil companies are eager to gain access to the large, low cost hydrocarbon reserves of the Middle East. They have had difficulty in expanding their upstream businesses for years. In fact, the large mergers of the late 1990s that created the super majors are predicated on the assumption that larger corporate scale was required to invest in the big projects that were expected to become available in the current time period in the Middle East and the former Soviet Union. Apart from Qatar, with its emphasis on production sharing contracts, there has been little new foreign investment by international oil companies in the Middle East in recent years.

[79]

The points of contention have mainly involved ownership of reserves and rates of return. Part of the problem regarding rates of return on investment has been the expectation by international oil companies that they should be able to earn upstream returns of 15%–20% as they do elsewhere in the world. However, the low level of geological risk in Middle East countries makes it understandable that governments in these countries would be unwilling to offer those returns. Some form of ownership of reserves is viewed as critical by international oil companies because without it their relationship is that of a service company rather than an investor, and they need to get full valuation for the investment from their shareholders. While production sharing arrangements and traditional concessions can provide most of the things that international oil companies want, the producing countries have been reluctant to offer them. Moreover, they tend to target investment in new exploration and production, which have limited scope in countries such as Saudi Arabia and Kuwait, with their surplus output capacity.

Given these constraints, one of the best approaches might be to follow the example set by Abu Dhabi over the last 25 years in its partnerships between the national oil company and foreign equity companies. Despite all the ups and downs of the oil market and the petroleum business over the last 25 years, these companies have always found Abu Dhabi a highly attractive place for investment because the partnership relationships that were established are solid win-win propositions for both sides. This has allowed for the stable and consistent development of the country's productive potential and continuing eagerness on the part of oil companies to invest despite what might be viewed as fairly limited returns. This model could be used quite successfully in other countries to provide similar benefits and a considerable increase in foreign investment in the region without compromising national control over resources or undermining petroleum policy.

Under the Abu Dhabi upstream model, the international oil companies are long-term partners rather than temporary service companies or firms that get only the secondary upstream prospects that are of limited interest to the state oil firm. The foreign oil companies hold minority equity stakes in the key producing companies and can thus claim genuine ownership of some core oil reserves. They receive a guaranteed profit margin of $1 per barrel. While this is a modest return, the fact that it is assured regardless of the price level is a significant benefit. Moreover, accelerated depreciation of investment significantly enhances upstream returns for the companies. Furthermore, investment decisions are made jointly by the international oil companies and the state oil company to assure that they are sound and serve the mutual interests of all parties. The resulting package has historically been very appealing to the international oil companies, which have tended to give the country investment priority over other alternative options. Furthermore, the investment priority given to Abu Dhabi is not out of some long-term strategic view based on the hope that the project might open other doors in the future but rather because the Abu Dhabi upstream model provides genuinely attractive current benefits to the companies. At the same time, the government retains majority control of the upstream operations and preserves national sovereignty over petroleum while benefiting from significant foreign investment. The fact that Abu Dhabi has not made any major alterations in this basic partnership approach over the last 25 years and has the best record for attracting foreign upstream investment in the Middle East over that period provides clear evidence of its success.

The Abu Dhabi model also provides an avenue for significant investment in the Middle East petroleum sector on a scale not seen in over 30 years. Such a flow of investment would tilt the global pattern of upstream financing much more heavily in favor of the Middle East, thereby redressing the imbalance that has long existed. The implementation of the Abu Dhabi model could take the form of an invitation by key Middle East nations to international oil companies to acquire minority equity positions in their national oil firms or in their key operating units. This approach would replicate the kind of ownership structures that exist in Abu Dhabi. Given the kind of interest that super majors have shown recently in investing in Russian firms such as TNK and Yukos–Sibneft, the level of interest in minority stakes in companies like Saudi Aramco or KPC would probably be huge. These minority equity investments would give the international oil companies highly valuable participation in the core reserve assets of these companies—an important investment opportunity that is significant for their long-term future. These stakes would be structured as investment partnerships proceeding along the lines of the Abu Dhabi model. Such an opportunity would create a huge reorientation in the upstream investment priorities of international oil companies, diverting significant capital away from other projects in other regions and downgrading the priority now being given to non-OPEC development projects.

Thus the Abu Dhabi upstream investment model provides both a proven workable approach toward upstream partnership between national oil companies and international oil firms. It also creates a highly scalable investment mechanism that enables a major shift in upstream investment priorities in favor of the Middle East. Of course, such a policy would have to be adopted broadly in order to have a big impact on investment incentives and priorities, and would need to be implemented carefully. Under the right conditions it could have a profound impact, while also preserving national control of petroleum for the host governments.

Downstream: Inheriting Rockefeller's Legacy

The re-opening of the Arabian Gulf to significant inflows of foreign investment in the upstream oil industry based on the Abu Dhabi model would attract large amounts of new capital and fundamentally alter international petroleum investment flows, but it would only provide true re-integration for the international oil firms. The national oil companies would still remain largely domestic upstream companies unless there is also a downstream portion of the asset swap in which these firms gain direct access and interests in significant refining and marketing assets in key consumer country markets. A broader re-integration of the downstream petroleum sector in key markets around the world by the national oil companies themselves would also yield further benefits and could also profoundly alter the way that the oil market works to help provide greater stability and broader benefits of oil security.

In making their choices about upstream partners, the national oil companies of the Middle East would be able to select companies willing to provide them with significant downstream assets in key markets as part of the upstream deals. The huge attractiveness of the upstream assets would give the national oil companies considerable leverage in these negotiations

[82]

and they could seek to be paid in part for the minority stakes in upstream activities by an exchange of key downstream assets.

National oil companies would thus be in a strong position to acquire interests in key downstream assets as part of a re-opening. However, the question that arises is why would they want such interests given their relatively poor financial performance compared to the upstream sector? Although the financial performance of the downstream sector has been weak, the value of international downstream assets to national oil companies is much broader than pure financial benefit. The main attraction of downstream re-integration for national oil companies is that it gives them more control over their oil and allows them to participate directly in adding value. National oil companies enjoy the additional benefit of becoming true global corporations with much wider reach and influence. Perhaps most importantly, integration allows national oil companies to lock in outlets for a significant volume of their production, putting them securely in a base load supply position with much less worry about direct competition from other crude oil exporters. They would also be able to carve out strong downstream positions in key growth markets such as China or India, making sure that they can benefit from future demand gains. Furthermore, the national oil companies could be in a better position to participate in and influence the evolution of the petroleum product market in the main consumer markets as they change due to environmental pressures.

National oil companies in the Middle East, with their abundance of upstream reserves, have understandably tended to think of themselves as primarily upstream companies with perhaps minor stakes in export refining or even in international downstream systems such as those of Saudi Aramco and KPC. However, this re-integration of the industry by the Middle East national oil companies would be on a much larger scale than anything attempted thus far. The big advantage of downstream integration – as Rockefeller and the major oil companies have shown in the past – is that it provides much greater control over the business at every stage and allows the producer to move from being the remote seller of a raw commodity to a direct distributor of an essential product of modern life. It is a truism to say that crude oil has no inherent value—it only has value in terms of the

[83]

refined products that can be made from it. The benefit of downstream integration is that it puts the producer in much greater control of the entire system and makes the producer a direct participant in the consumer market. In an oil market prone to instability, this can be a major advantage.

Through their large reserves and the kind of asset swap envisioned here, the national oil companies of the Middle East would have the opportunity to become true global companies, extracting value from their output in remote downstream markets and benefiting directly from the growth of those markets. Such a transformation requires a change in mind set by the national oil companies of the Middle East. They must aspire to be true global players, recognizing that they hold a significant comparative advantage and can use their massive upstream positions to become primary suppliers of petroleum to final consumers all over the world. Such a transformation means taking full advantage of the commercial and business opportunity that is implicit in their huge reserves. It is a legacy to be seized upon that could also help transform the economies of the Gulf and the roles of these countries in the world.

Benefits of Re-integration

The re-integration of the global oil business would create a new kind of Middle East national oil company that would be much more like a major oil company, but possibly on an even larger scale. It would also give the international oil companies that invested in the Middle East a stronger upstream position and better balance with their downstream capabilities. Yet, beyond the structural transformation of the companies involved in the swap of assets would be a number of other changes that should help address a wider set of issues that include the inherent instability in the oil market.

With the opening up of the Middle East to significant investment in the petroleum sector, other regions, both inside and outside of OPEC that have been primary targets for the budgets of international oil companies, would take a back seat. While a number of existing projects would continue to move ahead, attracting funds to higher cost, technically difficult ventures that require the expertise of the large oil companies would become harder and some projects would be abandoned or delayed. If OPEC were to lower its target price level a bit – a move it might countenance with the help of rising market share – these investments would become even more problematic. Overall, there could be a tectonic shift in global petroleum investment incentives and priorities that would help Middle East producers see a reduction of competition from rising non-OPEC supplies and also begin to eventually benefit from more consistent gains in market share.

With downstream integration, Middle East national oil companies could lock in permanent sales outlets in key markets, further reducing the potential impact of competition from non-OPEC producers. They could carve out positions in key growth markets as well as establish important refining and marketing capabilities in large, mature downstream markets. The Middle East producers would be almost entirely suppliers of base load barrels, increasing or decreasing refinery runs in key markets, which would provide maximum and immediate impact on the market in key areas. In short, downstream integration would provide a much more sophisticated understanding of market pressures and much more sensitive tool for influencing the market.

By strengthening the upstream positions of international oil companies, the national oil companies would enhance the standing of potential competitors. However, as the majority partner in the upstream relationships, the national oil companies could be selective in their partnerships and have considerable leverage with their partners. Additionally, in their efforts to gain entry to downstream growth markets, they could also turn to partnerships with new emerging majors such as those from Asia and Latin America. This would make for a diversified group of partners that would limit the potential benefits to any single player.

In terms of the stability of oil markets and the broader oil security objectives of the Gulf producers, reintegration would provide clear benefits by diverting investment away from non-OPEC countries and towards the Middle East. This would promote growth in market share for Middle East producers that is more commensurate with their global share of reserves. Middle East producers would also gain more secure outlets for their oil through downstream integration. Global downstream networks would also provide the basis for more efficient systems that could operate effectively with low inventories and at the same time apply more effective control of supply when seeking to manage the market. The operational efficiency benefits of large unified supply systems of the re-integrated industry would be significant for the market, reducing the need to rely on spot markets and derivatives to balance the system and thereby moderate price swings. Moreover, the large integrated supply systems might be better able to respond in a crisis by shifting supplies internally without resorting to volatile markets and taking full advantage of inventories across the entire supply chain to absorb disruptions or other unexpected problems.

Beyond all these benefits, there are some other important secondary advantages for the Gulf producers. Depending on how the upstream partnerships are structured, they should be able to promote significant economic development and diversification in Gulf countries by freeing up investment dollars that would otherwise have gone to the oil sector. Furthermore, a global, more commercially focused national oil company would also serve as an important catalyst for domestic economic expansion, opening up the potential for other investment and development projects.

On an international political level, the much greater economic integration between the Gulf countries and the main consumer markets would help to break down polarization and mutual suspicions, while fostering interdependence. Closer economic and investment links would improve relations and make the existing trade linkages much more tangible and direct. Russian oil companies are already rebranding gas stations in the US in order to make political statements. Middle East companies could take similar steps and go much further.

As the largest holders of oil reserves in the world, Arabian Gulf countries have a critical stake in the issues of global warming and the development of cleaner fuels. As direct participants in the downstream refined product markets of the main consumer countries, the Middle East national oil companies would have greater scope to participate in and shape the debate on these issues as well as play a more direct role in the eventual energy transition away from oil and toward alternative fuels. The Middle East countries would be able to take a longer term view on the energy transition, anticipate and invest in new technologies and be in a strong position to take commercial advantage of the change as direct distributors of energy products. This is the strategy that major oil companies are already pursuing and Middle East national oil companies could benefit in the longer term by following suit.

Conclusions

The re-integration of the global petroleum industry described here would represent a radical change for the Middle East producers and would transform the oil market and the investment incentives underpinning it. These are massive changes that would reduce the instability of oil markets and provide greater oil security. For Middle East oil producers, the primary benefit would be secure and growing markets for their oil. The shift in petroleum investment toward the Middle East and away from more marginal areas would eventually help to expand the market share of the Middle East. Greater integration would also provide for more market efficiency and put more sensitive tools in the hands of OPEC producers to manage oil markets. All of these changes would allow OPEC producers and Middle East members in particular to provide greater price stability and oil security. For oil consumers, the re-integration of the global oil industry would provide greater security of supply and stronger ties with key producer countries in terms of both upstream and downstream activities. The mutual interests of both oil exporting and oil importing countries in the re-integrated supply system also tends to emphasize common interests in oil security and ultimately a more cooperative producer-consumer relationship.

Although these changes seem radical, the basic components of the current oil market would continue to exist. Volatility in spot and futures markets would not disappear, nor would the risk of supply disruptions and political upheavals that threaten market stability and foster uncertainty over prices. OPEC's internal politics would remain a critical concern as would the pace of overall oil demand growth. Re-integration would simply be a force that would make some of these components of the market more manageable, particularly for Arabian Gulf producers who would be major beneficiaries, but also for consumer countries. The national oil companies would emerge from the process of re-integration as much more significant global players in the petroleum business and through their partnerships with traditional major oil companies and major oil companies in newly emerging markets, they would have a broader impact. The flow of much larger volumes of the world's oil through the integrated systems of these companies would generate operational efficiencies but would not completely insulate any of them from the impact of market forces.

For the oil consumers, this new reintegrated global petroleum industry would provide greater stability and efficiency but could also be a somewhat more intimidating place. The upstream investment attractiveness of the Middle East would tend to undermine the supply diversity that has been relied upon as a central pillar of oil security in consuming countries. In response, some consumer countries might pursue policies that actively foster the development of alternative supply sources and alternative fuels. While the free market energy policies of the major consumer countries helps to facilitate the kind of reintegration of the oil industry described here, some consumer countries might well abandon such policies if they feel threatened. With that potential in mind, the oil producers of the Arabian Gulf might seek to adopt policies that would reassure consumer countries and amplify re-integration benefits to them. With significant downstream activities and a desire to promote investment in their upstream petroleum sectors, producer countries would have a greater interest in maintaining a lower level of oil prices, which would be regarded favorably by oil consuming countries. Thus, lowering the OPEC target price over time might be a specific policy goal. Consumer countries would also feel less threatened if national oil companies from the Gulf avoid taking large downstream positions in any one market. Clearly, one of the risks to Middle East producers in moving toward re-integration of the industry is the potentially negative reaction of consumer countries, which would need careful handling.

Whether or not the Arabian Gulf producers ever take the radical step of re-integrating the global petroleum industry, just considering the possibility reveals some basic insight about the global oil market. Market stability and oil security involve much more than managing prices—sound underlying investment incentives across the industry are also needed to achieve these goals. Only by shifting more investment back to the Middle East and turning the national oil companies into true global players can the economic paradoxes that plague the oil industry be addressed. Without changes of that magnitude, it is hard to see how the world can avoid reliving the oil market instability of the last 15 years.

IRAQ IN THE
ENERGY SCENARIO

4

The Future of Iraq's Oil in the Global Energy Market: Strategic Options in the Aftermath of the War

Herman T. Franssen

In order to assess the potential impact of Iraq's reentry into the world oil market and its future role in OPEC, one needs to review Iraq's past production history, its current and future oil production capacity, the possible future role of international oil companies (IOCs) in the development of Iraq's oil reserves, the role of oil in the Iraqi economy, the advantages and disadvantages of OPEC membership as well as political and strategic developments in post-war Iraq. The outcome of such political, strategic and economic developments will lead to possible oil production scenarios, which will be tested against the current and expected future demand for OPEC oil. The question is: Will OPEC be able to absorb rising Iraqi oil exports in the years ahead?

Iraqi Oil Production Prior to the Invasion of 2003

Iraq is not a newcomer to the world of oil. Following the First World War, the victors carved out three provinces from the Ottoman Empire and founded the State of Iraq. British-controlled Iraq gave concession rights to the Iraq Petroleum Company (IPC), a company formed by major British, US and French oil companies. In 1927, the Kirkuk field was discovered and seven years later the field was brought on stream. A few other fields were found but development was slow, largely due to internal IPC conflicts and political problems.

[91]

As early as 1961, rising nationalism restricted IPC activities to producing fields, limiting it to nine out of thirty five discovered oil fields. Kirkuk and Rumaila (North and South) were the main producing Iraqi oil fields and remain so even today. In the early 1970s Iraq nationalized the assets of the IOCs and transferred them to INOC, the Iraq National Oil Company. For a few years, Iraq benefited from a combination of post-1973 high oil prices and rising oil production (1.9 mbpd in 1973 to a peak of 3.5 mbpd in 1979). While most production still came from Kirkuk and Rumaila, INOC began to develop several new fields and by 1990, some 38 new fields holding 78 billion barrels had been added to the reserve base, which is estimated to be in excess of 110 billion barrels.

Oil production averaged about 2.4 mbpd in the 1980s during and following the Iran-Iraq war. The war resulted in huge losses in human lives, military equipment and infrastructure. Little oil and gas exploration occurred during this period. The following decade proved even more disastrous for the Iraqi oil industry. For the first six years after the Gulf War oil production was limited to 0.5-0.6 mbpd for internal consumption only, as sanctions were imposed on Iraqi exports after the Gulf War. After 1995, when the UN Oil-for-Food Program was initiated, oil production once again rose to about 2.6 mbpd in 2000 but dropped thereafter. The Ministry of Oil claims that pre-war capacity was 3 mbpd even though production averaged only 2.2 mbpd in 2002. However, production did reach 2.7 mbpd in February 2003. The average for the decade of the 1990s was 1.6 mbpd. Wars and sanctions have left an outdated infrastructure in need of costly rehabilitation and Iraqi petroleum engineers have indicated significant downhole damage to several reservoirs.

In the 1990s, Iraq had plans to increase oil production to some 6 mbpd over a ten-year period with the help of IOCs from Europe, Russia and Asia. Although over twenty IOCs had advanced discussions with INOC over terms of engagement in Iraq's upstream industry, UN sanctions prevented all but a few of the oil companies from signing agreements on the development of Iraqi oil fields in the 1990s.

Iraq's State Oil Drilling Company (ISODC) emerged from the Gulf War with less than two dozen working drilling rigs. Moreover, no new rigs could be purchased due to sanctions. The ingenuity of Iraq's petroleum sector engineers allowed ISOC to repair damaged rigs and by early 2003 the number of working rigs was raised to 36, bringing it close to the level that prevailed before the Iraq-Iran War. Drilling activity more than doubled between 1999 and 2002 but despite the increase in drilling, production steadily declined over the same period. Service contracts had been signed with foreign drilling companies under the Oil-for-Food Program but such activities had hardly begun when the invasion of Iraq occurred in March 2003.

Restoring Iraq's Pre-War Production Capacity

Prior to the war, it was generally assumed that if Saddam Hussein failed to ignite oil wells anywhere near the scale of the Kuwaiti disaster in 1991, Iraq would quickly return to the pre-war average production level of close to 2.4 mbpd. While the Iraqi army did not use a scorched earth policy towards the end of the coalition campaign, widespread damage was done to the surface infrastructure in the field, not so much by the war itself but by extensive looting during and immediately after the war.

Muhammad Ali Zainy, an oil advisor with the American team between May and August 2003, described the damage inflicted in the oil sector as follows:

> The kind of damage inflicted on the oil industry was wide ranging, from the littlest item to the incredibly heavy equipment. Direct damage, looting, sabotage or a combination of these were inflicted on degassing stations, oil pumping stations, gas compressor stations, production facilities, industrial water supply and water injection facilities, storage tanks, vehicles, cranes, drilling rigs, field laboratories, office equipment, electric generators, stores, workshops, chemicals, tools, spare parts, control and safety equipment, civil, mechanical and electrical works, gasoline and LPG filling stations, field offices and camps.

Moreover, the pipeline from Kirkuk to Ceyhan in Turkey was blown up several times, interrupting exports from the northern fields.[1] The damage was not limited to the Northern and Southern Oil Companies but included also the Northern and Southern Gas companies, the Northern, Southern and Central Refineries Companies, the Oil Products Distribution Company, the

State Company for Oil Projects (SCOP), the Iraqi Drilling Company and the Oil Exploration Company.

Oil production collapsed during the invasion and remained below 0.5 mbpd until late July 2003. In early August, production reached 1.3 mbpd but fell again to about 0.7 mbpd by the third week of August due to acts of sabotage. The situation improved in September and by the middle of October 2003 production was just above 1.6 mbpd.

The Iraqi Ministry of Oil, the US Army Corps of Engineers and Kellogg, Brown & Root (KBR) identified a list of 220 projects for restoration. The Restoration Plan was to be implemented in three phases:

- *Phase 1:* To be completed by end of September 2003, aimed to restore production to 1.5 mbpd
- *Phase 2:* To be completed by the end of 2003, aimed to bring production capacity up to 2 mbpd
- *Phase 3:* To be completed by the end of the first quarter of 2004, aimed to restore production capacity to 2.8 mbpd. The total cost was estimated at $1.1 billion.

The first phase was completed successfully but exports are lagging behind planned levels due to sabotage of the northern pipeline (for details and updates see post-script section at the end of this chapter).

The State Oil Marketing Company (SOMO) projected a growth in Iraqi oil exports from about 0.9 mbpd in October 2003 gradually increasing to 2.3 mbpd in December of 2004 (averaging about 2 mbpd for 2004). Assuming consumption at about 0.35 mbpd in 2003 and 0.4 mbpd in 2004, the Ministry of Oil expected total production to rise from 1.25 mbpd in October 2003 to 2.7 mbpd in December 2004, and averaging 2.4 in 2004.[2]

Assuming that steady security can be provided for oil field workers, that sabotage will be reduced and that oil equipment arrives on time to replace looted and damaged parts, the production and export targets may be achieved. However, many Iraqis and non-Iraqis with in-depth knowledge of the Iraqi oil sector who fully comprehend the current level of oil field security are less optimistic about these targets than the Ministry of Oil.

If all goes well, by late 2005, the production capacity of currently producing fields may be restored to 3.5 mbpd by INOC with the assistance of international oil services companies. Recent cost estimates to achieve this target are in the vicinity of $3 billion. At the Middle East Petroleum and Gas Conference (MPGC) held in Dubai in September 2003, INOC President Thamer Abbas Ghadban indicated as follows:

- the upstream sector of the oil industry would not be privatized
- INOC would restore production capacity to 3.5 mbpd with outside technical assistance
- IOCs may be needed in Iraq if the country decides it wants to increase capacity to 5 or 6 mbpd.

Most experts would agree with Dr. Ghadban that to achieve production capacity considerably in excess of the pre-war 3.5 mbpd level within the next decade, participation by IOCs would be essential. The international oil industry has the capital, technology and managerial skills to raise Iraqi oil production capacity to 5–6 mbpd within a decade. However, even under the most optimistic scenario, it will take many years before this level can be achieved.

Prerequisites for Major Capacity Expansion with IOC Assistance

IOCs possess the capital as well as the technical and managerial know-how to nearly double Iraq's production capacity if that is what a future Iraqi government wants to do.

The issue of the possible reentry of IOCs into Iraq is politically very sensitive and if undertaken prematurely and without a clear legal and fiscal regime regulating foreign investments in the petroleum sector, the result could be chaotic. Before they are ready to commit the vast sums required to expand Iraqi production capacity, the IOCs would like to see solid preparation leading to an acceptable petroleum law in Iraq. A new petroleum law and other laws governing foreign investment, taxation and foreign exchange repatriation, are essential ingredients for the successful reentry of IOCs into Iraq. Such legislation will have to be approved by a legitimate Iraqi government. Only a legitimate, duly elected Iraqi government can define the long-term relationships between the host country and IOCs. It is expected that an elected government will be in place in 2005 as part of the unfolding constitutional process.

[95]

Since it normally takes a few years to develop a legal regime for the petroleum industry in a host country, the interim government in Iraq can help to put into place all necessary ingredients, perhaps with the help of the World Bank and internationally known consultants. The question that arises next is: Why is legitimacy so important for IOCs?

- It is an essential pre-requisite to create an acceptable degree of political, economic and fiscal stability for investors
- It avoids the risk of being precluded from dealing with a legitimate government through hasty deals with an interim government or foreign power
- IOCs do not want to compromise dealings with other Arab countries.

Prior to signing petroleum agreements with IOCs, Iraq will need a body of laws and an approved constitution that clearly defines the power of the government. Based on the constitution, the newly elected government would then pass or reconfirm a set of laws governing foreign investments in general and the petroleum sector in particular.

Once a legitimate government is in place, a new Constitution adopted and legislation covering foreign investments and the petroleum sector has been passed, negotiations with IOCs can be concluded on the terms of engagement—ranging from service contracts to buybacks or buyback-plus, joint ventures, production sharing agreements (PSAs) or hybrid agreements. There are many options and combinations of these to choose from. The Iraqi government may decide to implement several different regimes for different fields and exploration blocks. The new government will also have to rule on the legitimacy of contracts signed with the Saddam Hussein regime.

However, in the meantime, INOC can undertake various activities in anticipation of the adoption of a future petroleum law. The Ministry of Oil and INOC can prepare data in digital form (from what is left after the looting) and prepare a status report on the Iraqi oil industry. The interim government can prepare a draft petroleum law (as well as other necessary laws and regulations) for submission to an elected parliament.

The interim government can also legally engage the services of oil service companies as well as oil companies to assist INOC in restoring oil production to the pre-war level.

The Politics of Iraqi Oil

It is generally accepted that Iraq's oil reserves are second only to those of Saudi Arabia and also that there are other significant oil and natural gas prospects in the country. Experts also agree that except for Kirkuk and Rumaila (North and South), Iraqi oil fields are among the least developed in the world and therefore Iraq has the potential to become another Saudi Arabia in terms of future oil production. Indeed, Iraq has the resources to become one of the top three key actors in the world of oil but these vital resource statistics have not changed in decades. The key issue remains—when is this potential likely to become reality?

From the experiences of Iraq in the 1980s and 1990s, Iran after the Islamic Revolution and Russia following the collapse of the Soviet Union, it is evident that after these wars and revolutions, oil production initially fell and it took years for production to return to pre-war levels. In Iran, production collapsed in 1980 following the 1979 revolution and never returned anywhere near the pre-revolution level. In fact, average oil production in Iran during two decades after the revolution, was only about half of the pre-revolution production. In Iraq, production fell sharply during the Iran-Iraq War and again after the Gulf War of 1990–1991. The collapse in Russian oil production in the late 1980s and early 1990s coincided with the collapse of the Soviet Empire. Production increased again from 2000 following oil sector privatization and the emergence of Vladimir Putin's government. In each case, however, there was a period of declining oil production triggered by a war, revolution or collapse of an empire. Is Iraq going to suffer a similar same fate or will the outcome prove different this time?

Some optimists in Iraq believed that after a period of very slow oil production recovery following the US invasion, security and stability would be restored and oil production would reach pre-war capacity sometime in 2004. Dr. Ghadban of INOC, speaking at MPGC 2003 in Dubai estimated

[97]

that pre-war production capacity would be reached by the end of 2003 and 3 mbpd by the end of the first quarter of 2004. Optimists also assume that early reentry of IOCs into Iraq's upstream oil industry is all but certain and Iraq may reach its pre-war goal of 6 mbpd by 2010 or 2012.

Pessimists, on the other hand, believe that security will not be restored any time soon, that violence will continue and restoration of pre-war capacity and steady production of 2.4 mbpd will take longer than a year and in a worst-case scenario, the Balkanization of Iraqi society may keep production low and volatile for years to come. Without a legitimate and stable Iraqi government, IOCs will delay any plans for reentry into Iraq and the desired pre-war goal of 6 mbpd will remain a dream until years after the internal political situation has stabilized. Under this scenario, Iraq's oil production may still be below 4 mbpd by 2015.

Both scenarios are possible. The early optimism following the spectacular US military success in April and the collapse of Saddam Hussein's regime, has been replaced by growing concern about the failure of the US to bring security and order to Iraq. An early return to full and unfettered Iraqi sovereignty is not likely and there is growing fear that the internal political situation could turn into the kind of chaos that Lebanon encountered in the 1980s. US failure to restore security and carry out an orderly transfer of full and unconditional power to an elected Iraqi government could bring about the Balkanization of Iraq and could raise more regional tension. If human costs (expressed in terms of the lives of US and other coalition forces) and budgetary requirements (both military and civilian) continue to mount, how long will the US public support the occupation of Iraq?

On the other hand, in case major progress is made in restoring security and basic services to Iraqi society in the months ahead; if there are signs of economic improvement; if there is early internationalization of the effort to maintain internal stability; if Iraqi political forces succeed in reaching a quick consensus on the political structure of the country; and if there is a timely transfer of full power to Iraqi nationals, the political outcome may still be positive. Moreover, if the democratic model were to work in Iraq, it will probably have far-reaching repercussions in the entire region.

[98]

Table 4.1

Implications of Iraq Oil Production Scenarios on the Iraq Budget

Optimistic Iraqi Oil Production Scenario (Average for the Year)					
	2004	*2005*	*2006*	*2007*	*2008*
Iraqi oil production (mbpd)	2.5	2.8	3.2	3.5	4.0
Iraqi net oil exports (mbpd)	2.1	2.4	2.8	3.0	3.5
Assumed oil price (US$/per barrel)	22	20	20	20	20
Oil income (in $ billion)	16.8	17.5	20.4	21.9	25.6
Pessimistic Iraqi Oil Production Scenario					
Iraqi oil exports (mbpd)	1.6	2.1	2.2	2.3	2.4
Oil income (in $ billion)	12.8	15.3	16.1	16.8	17.5

Source: H. Franssen.

These are two possible scenarios for Iraqi gross oil income based on specific oil export and oil price assumptions. Other credible scenarios, showing the impact of lower or higher production and lower or higher prices are possible. Based on these specific oil price and production assumptions, Iraqi gross oil income could range between $79 and $102 billion over a five-year period (2004–2008). Higher oil exports and/or higher oil prices will increase dollar income from oil; a lower level of oil exports and/or lower oil prices will cut dollar income.

Iraqi government expenditures may average $15 billion per year for recurrent expenditures (rising in the later years) and perhaps as much as $50 to $75 billion to restore basic electrical services, sanitation, water, transportation (including roads), health care facilities, educational facilities and oil sector restoration to pre-war capacity. In total, civil expenses could range between $125 and $150 billion over a five-year period.

Future US military expenses, now running at about $3 billion a month, will depend on the size of the US forces and the duration of their deployment in Iraq. If no major foreign commitments are made, it is assumed that the US will have to maintain military forces at the current level for 2-3 years, gradually reducing their numbers if and when stability returns and Iraqi forces are able to gradually take over US military commitments. Assuming that US forces will remain at 150,000 through the end of 2005, being reduced to 75,000 in 2006 and 2007 and further reduced

[99]

to 50,000 by 2008, military costs over a five-year period would exceed $150 billion.

Estimated civilian and military costs could total as much as $300 billion between 2004 and 2008 (not including Gulf War reparations and interest on Iraqi foreign debt), versus gross oil income ranging from close to $80 to $100 billion. It should be emphasized that this is not a forecast but an initial attempt to illustrate possible oil income under different assumptions of production, exports and price and also possible recurrent and capital expenditures in Iraq for the next five years (2004–2008). Including expenses already incurred in 2003 and possible cost overruns, the US government may well end up paying nearly $500 billion for Iraqi reconstruction.

If the ultimate outcome includes the emergence of a workable democratically elected federal government; improved socio-economic conditions for the Iraqi people; enhanced regional security; considerable progress on the Roadmap to Peace in Palestine; and progress towards the participation of citizens in regional governments, it would be a worthwhile price.

If, however, the US fails in its effort to bring security and stability to Iraq; does not improve the economic conditions of the Iraqi people; is unable to develop Iraq's oil sector; and makes no major progress on the Roadmap to Peace, regional security will be adversely affected and autocratic governments will feel strengthened in their efforts to preserve the status quo. If that happens, the money would have been badly spent on a failed foreign adventure with all its adverse political and strategic consequences being felt for years to come.

Iraq's Potential Impact on Near and Medium Term Oil Market Developments

Oil Market Developments in 2003

Global economic growth in 2003 has again been at least one percentage point below the long term past trend of 3% annually. Economic growth has been weak in the US (about 2.3%) and weaker in the European Union and Japan (0.9%). While the overall economic performance in the Asia–Pacific region has not been high, both India and China showed strong growth rates (5.7% and 7.4% respectively).

Overall oil demand growth may turn out to have been around 1.3%, low by historic standards but more than double the demand growth in the previous year and triple the demand growth in 2001. Demand growth was very strong in the first quarter of 2003 due to a cold winter and fuel-switching from natural gas to oil in the US as well as the replacement of shut-in nuclear capacity in Japan. Taking out all the special demand factors, global oil demand growth was close to 1%, equal to about half of global economic growth.

Non-OPEC incremental oil production has once again been robust at about 1.2 mbpd in 2003, with almost 70% coming from the FSU and close to 20% from Mexico and Canada (heavy crude).

Commercial stocks were historically low throughout most of 2003 and were expected to culminate at the bottom of a 5-year low by year end. There is some uncertainty about the reason for the continued low commercial stocks. Some of it is due to structural change in the downstream industry; streamlining following mergers and acquisitions (M&As); financial constraints faced by many independent refiners; and the fact that the oil market remained in backwardation throughout 2003, making it commercially unattractive to build stocks over and above minimum operating requirements. The low level of OECD commercial stocks may have been due more to decisions made by refiners than the result of OPEC undersupplying the global oil market.

Table 4.2
Global Oil Demand and Supply in 2003
(in million barrels per day)

	2002					2003				
	Q1	Q2	Q3	Q4	2002	Q1	Q2	Q3	Q4	2003
Demand	76.9	75.6	77.1	78.6	77.1	78.7	76.5	78.8	79.4	78.1
Non-OPEC	50.8	51.3	50.9	51.8	51.1	52.1	51.8	52.5	53.1	52.2
Stocks	-1.1	0.1	-0.8	-0.7	-0.7	0.4	1.4	1.4	0	0.8
OPEC Production	25.1	24.6	25.5	26.2	25.4	27.0	26.6	26.9	26.5	26.8

Source: H. Franssen.

[101]

For OPEC-10,[3] the year 2003 proved to be an excellent year both in terms of production and price as OPEC production rose by about 1.5 mbpd. Declining Iraqi production and the impact of political developments in Venezuela further increased the market share of OPEC-9.[4]

It may be noted that in Table 4.2, non-OPEC production figures include non-OPEC and OPEC NGLs as well as processing gain. The numbers for the third and fourth quarters of 2003 are estimates. On average oil prices in 2003 were about $5 per barrel higher than in 2002. At more than $250 billion, OPEC in 2003 earned the highest income since the early 1980s.

Growth Estimates for 2004

Although the global economy remained weak, most public and private economic estimates for 2004 were cautiously optimistic. Most estimates for global economic growth in 2004 fell between 3 and 3.5 percent, which is 1 and 1.5 percentage point higher than in 2003. Continued very low interest rates combined with massive Government deficit spending, was expected to raise US economic growth to close to 3.5 percent in 2004. European growth was projected at 1.9% and Japanese growth projected at 0.9% for 2004. Asian economies were also expected to undergo higher economic growth, particularly China and India.

Oil Demand

Based on the assumption of a return to a normal winter in North America, a restoration of shut-in nuclear power plants in Japan and 3% global economic growth, Petroleum Economics Ltd. (PEL) estimated a global increase in oil consumption of about 1.1 mbpd average for 2004. A comparison with five other major oil market assessments for the same year showed a rather narrow range of oil demand growth from 1 to 1.2 mbpd. This is a rather narrow range, given the uncertainties surrounding global economic growth, the possibility of fuel-switching to oil in case of high natural gas prices during the US winter and uncertainties related to the Japanese nuclear power sector.

[102]

Non-OPEC Oil Production

After several years of robust growth in non-OPEC incremental oil production, 2004 was expected to shape up as another year of high growth in non-OPEC oil supplies, perhaps the highest in recent years. PEL estimated a growth of non-OPEC production of 1 mbpd and another 130,000 bpd of growth in OPEC condensates. In comparison with five other studies, PEL is at the low end of the range. Other studies showed a growth in non-OPEC production of up to 1.5 mbpd and up to 0.4 mbpd of OPEC condensates in 2004. The difference between the various studies is so high (up to 0.7 mbpd), that the actual outcome could have a serious impact on OPEC's ability to manage global supplies.

Stock Changes

Stock changes are the difference between apparent oil demand and supply. To maintain oil prices within the desired range of $22–$28 per barrel, OPEC would want to manage its production in such a way as to keep global commercial stocks sufficiently tight and keep the futures market in backwardation. In light of the uncertainties on future oil consumption; the large differences in non-OPEC oil production and OPEC condensates; and uncertainties surrounding OPEC and in particular Iraqi production, OPEC's task will be very difficult.

As in 2003, oil analysts will continue to discuss whether commercial stocks are tight in view of historical analyses or adequate and in line with industry requirements as viewed by refiners today. The International Energy Agency maintains that the market is not well balanced and that commercial stocks are low and are keeping prices artificially high. OPEC maintains that the market is adequately supplied, that refiners can buy the crude they want at the market price and that oil prices within the desired OPEC range are fair and sustainable. The debate on the adequacy of commercial stocks is old and reflects different perceptions on what the level of minimum operating commercial oil stock ought to be. There is no doubt about the fact that a low level of commercial oil stocks can lead to upward price pressure in case of supply disruptions (such as occurred in Venezuela in early 2003 and in Iraq for much of 2003).

[103]

OPEC Production in 2004

Assuming that OPEC aimed at keeping oil prices within the desired price range of $22–$28 per barrel, PEL estimated that OPEC output would need to fall by an average of just over 1 mbpd in 2004 from the estimated average 2003 production level of about 27 mbpd (Table 4.3). To keep OECD commercial stocks sufficiently tight and thus achieve its price objectives, PEL calculated that OPEC production should fall from close to 27 mbpd to about 25.5 mbpd average in the first half of 2004, rising to 26 mbpd during the second half of 2004.

Table 4.3

Estimated OPEC Production for August and September, 2003

	Estimated Production		Quotas	
	August (mbpd)	September (mbpd)	June quota (kbpd)	Nov. quota (kbpd)
Saudi Arabia (including Neutral Zone)	8.63	8.55	8,256	7,963
Iran	3.71	3.78	3,729	3,597
UAE	2.34	2.23	2,038	1,966
Kuwait	2.10	2.12	2,216	2,138
Qatar	0.73	0.75	658	635
Nigeria	2.23	2.20	2,092	2,018
Libya	1.42	1.43	1,360	1,312
Algeria	1.13	1.15	811	782
Venezuela	2.25	2.62	2,923	2,819
Indonesia	1.00	1.00	1,317	1,270
OPEC-10	**25.54**	**25.83**	**25,400**	**24,500**
Iraq	1.1	1.45		
Total OPEC	**26.64**	**27.28**		

Source: Petroleum Economics Ltd, London (PEL).

Of the six studies examined (including the PEL assessment), four had put the average annual call on OPEC at 25.5 mbpd or lower and two studies had estimated close to 26 mbpd. Since Iraq will not be subject to production cuts for the foreseeable future, OPEC-10 will have to bear

[104]

the full brunt of future quota adjustments. How successfully this situation can be managed would depend primarily on the speed and extent of Iraq's production increase as well as on OPEC's ability to implement quota reductions in the light of capacity growth in some OPEC countries and the desire by some members to raise their individual quotas (it may be noted that some member countries have persistently exceeded their OPEC production quotas).

Iraq's oil production growth will remain very difficult to predict. Sabotage, looting and limited security for workers in the field, have kept crude oil and natural gas production considerably below pre-war estimates. Iraqi production growth has been erratic and oil exports slow to recover. Slow production growth has limited the associated gas production needed to produce electricity, which in turn is needed to build up refining capacity. Average Iraqi oil production in August 2003 was estimated at about 1 mbpd. Dr. Ghadban, the INOC President, while addressing the MPGC conference in Dubai in September 2003 provided optimistic estimates, stating that Iraq would reach 3 mbpd of oil production by the end of the first quarter of 2004. Most Iraqi oil industry experts were considerably less optimistic.

Even though oil production reached 1.5 mbpd during the first week of September 2003, conservative estimates for Iraqi oil production were between 1.5 and 2.0 mbpd average for the first half of 2004. Most Iraqi experts believe that Iraqi oil production and exports will remain considerably below pre-war capacity due to the lack of security, slow replacement of looted surface facilities in the South and the expected continuation of acts of sabotage on the northern pipeline in the future.

It was estimated that Iraqi oil production would increase gradually to 2 mbpd in the first quarter and to 2.2, 2.4 and 2.6 mbpd respectively in the subsequent quarters of 2004 (Table 4.4). Under this scenario, OPEC-10 would have had to cut production to a level between 23 and 23.5 mbpd for the first half of 2004 (6–9% cut) from the current level of just below 26 mbpd. Such cuts were considered feasible but possibly complicated by claims of some OPEC members to raise their individual quotas and also by an estimated OPEC capacity growth of about 0.5 mbpd in 2004.

[105]

Table 4.4
PEL Summary of World Oil Demand and Supply 2003-2004
(in million barrels per day)*

	2003					2004				
	Q1	Q2	Q3	Q4	Year	Q1	Q2	Q3	Q4	Year
Demand	78.7	76.5	77.8	79.4	78.1	79.3	77.4	79.1	80.9	79.2
Non-OPEC	52.1	51.4	52.5	53.1	52.2	53.1	52.7	53.3	54.1	53.3
Stocks	0.4	1.4	1.4	0	0.8	-0.8	0.7	0.7	0.3	0
OPEC (crude)	27.0	26.6	26.9	26.5	26.8	25.5	25.5	26.5	26.5	26.0
of which Iraq	2.1	0.3	1.1	1.5	1.3	2.0	2.2	2.4	2.6	2.3
OPEC-10	24.9	26.3	25.8	25.0	25.5	23.5	23.3	24.1	23.9	23.7

Note: * Iraq numbers for 2004 were the author's assumptions.

Source: Petroleum Economics Ltd, London (PEL).

Price Pressures

The perception among most oil analysts was that oil prices would soften in 2004 from the 2003 level, which many believe is unsustainable in view of modest oil demand growth and continued robust non-OPEC incremental supplies, particularly from Russia and other FSU countries. OPEC NGL production is rising and crude oil capacity growing at close to 1 mbpd. The insistence by some members on getting a bigger share in the future reallocation of quotas at a time when demand is weakening for OPEC oil may result in downward price pressures. Iraq's oil production, which stood at 2.5 mbpd in February of 2003, collapsed in April and has so far been rather slow to recover. While average Iraqi oil production was below 0.5 mbpd in the second quarter, it may double in the third quarter and rise further in the final quarter. While few oil analysts believe Iraqi oil production and exports will return quickly to pre-war levels, even a modest increase over the average Iraqi oil production level of 2 mbpd in 2004, would require further cuts by OPEC-10.

The US Energy Information Administration (EIA) assumed in its short term market forecast that oil prices would average $3 per barrel lower in 2004 than in 2003. The OPEC decision in September 2003 to cut production by another 0.9 mbpd from November 2003 helped to moderate Wall Street's average oil prices at least through the end of the first quarter of 2004. Oil prices were expected to remain at the same levels through the first quarter of 2004 and depending on future OPEC cuts, to decline gradually to the low twenties but still averaging around $24 a barrel for Brent crude for the year.

During 2003, geopolitical developments kept oil prices robust on the high end of the OPEC price objective of $22–$28 per barrel. In the five years from 2004 to 2008, OPEC will face increasing difficulties in managing the global oil market due to modest levels of anticipated global oil demand growth; robust non-OPEC incremental production; continued growth in OPEC natural gas liquids (NGLs) and crude oil capacity; and demand for quota adjustments. At the current price level, industry and Wall Street analysts expect demand for OPEC crude oil through 2008 to average just over 26 mbpd, which is lower than OPEC's current production. It may prove increasingly difficult to deal with rising OPEC capacity and the return of Iraq to pre-war capacity or higher.

Table 4.5
Demand for OPEC Oil through 2010*
(in million barrels per day)

	2003	2004	2005	2006	2007	2008	2010
Global Consumption	78.1	79.2	80.5	81.9	83.2	84.7	87.5
Non-OPEC	52.3	53.3	54.9	55.7	56.4	57.2	58.2
OPEC crude	26.8	26.0	25.6	26.2	26.8	27.5	29.3
Stocks	1.0	0	0	0	0	0	0

Note: * Iraq numbers for 2004 were the author's assumptions.

Source: Petroleum Economics Ltd, London (PEL) and H. Franssen.

Some medium term projections for the industry are even more optimistic on future non-OPEC production and show demand for OPEC oil at below 27 mbpd through 2008.

The difference between various global oil demand projections for the medium term is much smaller (ranging between 1.1 and 1.4 mbpd annually for the next five years from 2004 to 2008) than the assessments of incremental non-OPEC and OPEC NGL production. For the year 2004 alone, the six studies projected incremental non-OPEC crude oil production at 1.1–1.5 mbpd and OPEC NGLs at between 0.1 and 0.4 mbpd (one study which is not included showed OPEC NGLs set to rise by 0.5 mbpd in 2004). For the five year period, projections show non-OPEC crude oil and OPEC NGLs to grow at an average annual rate of between 1 and 1.3 mbpd.

Can OPEC Manage Global Oil Supplies?

Most industry estimates show little demand growth for OPEC oil at least for the next five years from 2004 to 2008 based on current estimates of rising non-OPEC production. In the 1990s, non-OPEC oil production rose by about 2.5 mbpd, with rising production in the North Sea (2.5 mbpd), East Asia (1 mbpd), Latin America (2.5 mbpd) and Africa (1.4 mbpd) offset by declining production in North America (0.5 mbpd) and the Former Soviet Union or FSU (almost 4 mbpd).

In the first decade of the 21st century, the biggest surprise is the amazing turnaround in FSU production. From a fall of 4 mbpd in the 1990s, FSU production has already increased by more than 2 mbpd between 2000 and 2003 and is projected to increase by another 4 mbpd by 2010. In addition, North American production is projected to increase perhaps more than 1 mbpd (compared to a fall of 0.5 mbpd in the 1990s) largely due to Canadian heavy crude developments. Further increments are expected from Latin America (2 mbpd) and Africa (4.5 mbpd). On balance, non-OPEC production this decade is projected to rise perhaps by as much as 1 mbpd annually. About 60 percent of the growth in incremental non-OPEC production is projected for the FSU (Russia and Kazakhstan in particular). Uncertainties remain about the timing and actual growth in FSU production as well as the ability to add timely pipeline capacity to provide external outlets for the oil. Domestic oil demand is expected to continue to grow only slowly in both Russia and the Caspian region.

In the 1990s OPEC depended on cooperation from Norway and Mexico as well as smaller oil producers such as Oman, to make small production cuts during periods when OPEC faced difficult supply management problems. Russia and the Caspian region never actively cooperated with OPEC by reducing even projected output. Since production in Norway is projected to remain fairly stable over the next five years, Oman's production is declining and Mexico's production is expected to grow by no more than 0.15 mbpd over the next few years, there is little that OPEC can expect from these traditional allies. Instead OPEC will have to deal with Russia and the Caspian region, which are expected to produce the bulk of incremental non-OPEC production. Based on past experience with those countries, OPEC should not expect active cooperation in arresting a downward price adjustment unless the oil prices fall significantly below $18–$20 a barrel for Brent crude.

While OPEC will need to adjust to rising FSU production, the organization also faces rising production capacity in member countries, particularly in Algeria and Nigeria. Recent behavior by those oil producers and official statements from those countries suggest that they are not likely to make significant cuts from their current production levels. On the other hand, Indonesia has become a net oil importer and Venezuela (which has the largest natural production decline rate in OPEC) is rapidly losing capacity due to action taken in 2003.

Due to political uncertainties, it is impossible to project Iraq's future output. Instead, the impact on OPEC of two Iraqi production scenarios may be assessed—one an optimistic scenario and the other a pessimistic one. The optimistic scenario assumes that Iraq will succeed in gradually restoring pre-war production and export capacity by 2005 and gradually expand production with the assistance of IOCs to about 4.5 mbpd by 2010. The pessimistic scenario assumes the absence of political stability in the country, the continuation of violence, very slow recovery of downhole capacity in the South and the continued sabotage of pipelines. Under this scenario, production and average annual export growth remains at or below 3 mbpd until the end of the decade.

Table 4.6
Scenario 1: Impact on OPEC of Steadily Rising Iraqi Oil Production
(in million barrels per day)

	2003	2004	2005	2006	2007	2008	2010
Demand for OPEC oil	26.8	26.0	25.6	26.2	26.8	27.7	29.3
Iraq	1.3	2.5	3.0	3.2	3.5	4.0	4.5
OPEC-10	25.5	23.5	22.6	23.0	23.3	23.7	24.8
OPEC-10 capacity	28.5	28.3	29.8	31.0	31.3	31.6	33.6
Spare capacity	3.0	4.8	7.2	8.0	8.0	7.9	8.8

Source: Petroleum Economics Ltd, London (PEL) and H. Franssen.

Table 4.7
Scenario 2: Impact on OPEC of Slow Rise in Iraqi Oil Production
(in million barrels per day)

	2003	2004	2005	2006	2007	2008	2010
Demand for OPEC oil	26.8	26.0	25.6	26.2	26.8	27.7	29.3
Iraq production	1.3	2.5	2.5	2.6	2.7	2.8	2.9
OPEC-10	25.5	23.5	23.1	23.6	24.1	24.9	26.4
OPEC capacity	28.5	28.3	29.8	30.0	30.3	30.6	31.6
Spare capacity	3.0	4.8	6.7	6.4	6.2	5.7	5.2

Source: Petroleum Economics Ltd, London (PEL) and H. Franssen.

How Will OPEC manage?

Based on industry assessments of medium term global oil demand growth rising at 1.3–1.4 mbpd annually and some 5 mbpd of non-OPEC incremental supply (including OPEC NGLs, which are not counted against quotas), the demand for OPEC crude oil under prevailing OPEC policy, will remain fairly stagnant throughout the next five years from 2004 to 2008. Industry assessments suggest that some 75 percent of incremental global oil demand will be satisfied from non-OPEC incremental production through 2008.

Superimposing a recovery in Iraqi oil production, even very modest growth to only 2.8 mbpd in 2008 (below the point at which Iraq might become subjected to OPEC quotas), would keep the demand for oil from

[110]

OPEC-10 below the 2003 level until at least 2008. Assuming an optimistic production scenario for Iraq, with the production level rising to 4 mbpd by 2008, demand for OPEC oil would remain well below the 2003 production level through 2008.

With rising production capacity in Algeria and Nigeria and planned capacity growth in a number of other OPEC countries, including Kuwait (northern fields), Abu Dhabi and Libya, supply management will become more complicated in the next five years from 2004 to 2008. In 2003 OPEC benefited from unexpected demand growth associated with cold weather in the US; fuel-switching away from natural to oil products in the US; shut-in nuclear capacity in Japan; production outage in Venezuela in early 2003 and supply disruption in Iraq from April onward. These events helped to keep commercial stocks in the OECD low and maintain upward price pressure for much of 2003. When prices began to fall in late summer, OPEC wisely decided to cut quotas from November 2003 to avoid a potentially significant rise in commercial stocks. Assuming that OPEC would continue to observe the new quotas directionally, it was expected that oil prices would almost certainly remain robust through much of the first quarter of 2004.

Beyond early 2004, oil fundamentals appeared to be weakening and, if non-OPEC production growth, supplemented by OPEC NLG production growth, continued to rise as projected by a majority of oil analysts, supply management would then become increasingly difficult, even if Iraq's oil production recovered only modestly over the next five years from 2004 to 2008. Pressures within OPEC under this scenario will become more apparent as Algeria, Nigeria and perhaps other members seek higher quotas in a market of declining demand for OPEC oil. If Iraq succeeds in expanding production gradually to 4 mbpd between the years 2004–2008, OPEC supply management will become even more difficult and the GCC states within OPEC almost certainly will lose part of their market share.

It is possible that Russia and other non-OPEC producers may have a change of heart and work with OPEC to slow down their production growth. However, past experience does not suggest that such cooperation will add enough to make a difference for OPEC. It is also possible that oil demand will grow substantially above the projected annual growth of 1.3–1.4 mbpd after 2004, although analysis of global demand growth since the 1990s suggests that this is not likely. Geopolitical developments may reduce production in one or more OPEC and non-OPEC oil exporting countries. However, it may not be prudent to formulate policy based on possible geopolitical developments.

A slow recovery of Iraqi oil production will pose a problem for OPEC-10 while a fast recovery will create greater difficulties. From this analysis it is clear that the biggest problem facing OPEC over the next five years (2004–2008) is non-OPEC incremental production, particularly export growth from Russia and the Caspian region. Recovery of Iraqi production at almost any level will complicate an already difficult supply management situation. The possibility remains that Saudi Arabia, with support from the GCC member states within OPEC, may feel compelled to defend its market share in case all efforts to secure non-OPEC (particularly Russian) support for joint production cuts fail. The inability to maintain OPEC quota discipline and cooperation from some large non-OPEC oil exporting countries could lead to a repetition of the oil market situation that followed developments in December 1985 or December 1998.

The Global Oil Market Scenario: A Post-Script

Since the ECSSR conference was held in late 2003, the global oil market has changed quite significantly and by early 2005, Iraqi oil production has only recovered slowly to about two-thirds of its pre-war capacity in 2003.

In the first place, oil analysts from the International Energy Agency and private consulting firms increased the historical oil demand data based on better information from developing economies. This move by itself has lifted global oil demand (on paper) by several hundred thousand barrels a day.

Secondly, an unexpected surge in global oil demand, spearheaded by Chinese oil product consumption growth in all energy sectors of the economy, lifted global oil consumption in 2004 by some 2.6 million barrels a day. This surge was almost twice as much oil demand growth as expected. It shattered the earlier belief held by many oil economists that demand would not increase much above 1–1.5 percent annually—an expectation that was proved wrong.

Also in 2004, non-OPEC oil production growth from outside the former Soviet Union, was disappointingly low for the fourth year in a row, implying that non-OPEC oil production outside of the Former Soviet Union (FSU), was perhaps close to peaking. Production in the FSU continued to show a sharp increase in 2004 as it did in the previous three years.

The sharp rise in global oil consumption, coupled with increasingly tough environmental restrictions on oil products particularly in Europe and the US, stretched the ability of refiners to produce all of the products on demand with the existing refining configuration. Refiners were demanding more light, low sulfur oil, while the marginal barrel in oil exporting countries was becoming heavier and higher in sulfur. The net result was a shortage of light, sweet oil, causing escalating prices of sweet light oil and rising price differentials between sweet and sour crude oil. By 2004, OPEC no longer had spare production capacity of the kind of crude oil required by the market, leading to an escalation in oil prices. The situation in the oil market, both upstream and downstream also triggered speculative interests, adding to the upward price pressures.

Finally, Iraq, which had been expected by many observers to gradually increase oil production, has not been able to export more than about 1.8 mbpd, much below its pre-war export capacity.

The net result of all these changes in oil demand, refining capacity and crude oil supply, has been a major and unexpected tightening of the global oil market, which may last at least a few years. Most observers now believe that Iraq's oil production capacity is not likely to grow much over the next few years. On the other hand, other OPEC countries will add to production capacity, leading to somewhat softer oil prices perhaps after 2005 or 2006.

Iraq had earlier been expected to play a major role in the oil market during the second half of this decade (from 2005 to 2010) but is now expected to lag behind earlier optimistic supply estimates. Once stability and security are restored within the country, and a Constitution as well as

[113]

other petroleum-related legislation has been passed by the parliament, Iraq will be in a position (if it so desires) to turn to the outside world for assistance to raise its production capacity. However, such moves may not produce actual results until the early part of the next decade—possibly after 2010.

5

Post-War Iraq and OPEC: Present Status and Future Prospects

Dorothea H. El Mallakh

The year 1991 proved pivotal, both for Iraq and the Organization of Petroleum Exporting Countries (OPEC). The outcome of the Gulf War of 1990–1991 was to bring Iraqi petroleum exports under a sanctions regime. This measure kept Iraqi output contained and its impact on the international market restrained, while leaving demand to be filled from a reconstructed Kuwaiti oil sector and growing amounts of non-OPEC production. Quite apart from the issue of Iraqi supply, another trend was already under way, one that continues to roil the markets today and makes OPEC's perceived role of "manager" more difficult—the availability of Russian oil to global customers.

The War in Iraq in 2003 has presented OPEC with another set of challenges. The first challenge is to make room for Iraq within the current production quota system. However, this could take some time depending on the rapidity with which Iraqi output is normalized and then expanded. The second challenge is more conceptual or institutional, based on the extent to which Iraq and other members of the Organization become involved in the bidding for foreign direct investment in their oil sectors, including the upstream.

The Russian "Threat" to OPEC

Russia's supply into the global market, strictly speaking, is not a "new" source unlike much of West African deep-water development or the successor states of the former Soviet Union (affectionately dubbed the "Stans"). With the exception of some far eastern development, Russian oil is being pumped largely from fields that existed prior to that nation's economic liberalization or "opening." It may be helpful to put Russian/ Soviet supply into perspective.

In 1980, a year marked by the Iranian Revolution and by supply disruptions, the largest oil producer was the Soviet Union (11.71 million barrels per day or mbpd), followed by Saudi Arabia (9.90 mbpd), and the United States (8.60) mbpd; Iraqi output was 2.51 mbpd.[1] A decade earlier (1970), before the first "oil shock," the United States topped the list of crude producers with 9.64 mbpd (the pinnacle of US output), followed by the USSR with 6.99 mbpd, and Saudi Arabia at 3.8 mbpd; Iraqi crude production was 1.55 mbpd.[2] Soviet production would peak at 12.05 mbpd in 1987 and 1988, followed by a consistent decline until the breakup of the USSR in 1991–1992. Iraqi output followed a generally upward trend from 1960 to peak at 3.48 mbpd in 1979, just before the outbreak of the Iran-Iraq conflict and at a time of increased world supply needs because of the Iranian Revolution. Saudi output would reach its apex in 1980 at 9.90 mbpd.

Until 1992, however, Soviet oil was not traded to any major extent on world markets, but that situation would change. The Soviet bloc political system, which had bound Eastern Europe economically to the USSR through energy supply, disintegrated along with the collapse of the Soviet Union. The successor states, including Russia, now were open to outside investment and western technology. The inflow of capital would rejuvenate existing fields and assist in the new development of resources, particularly those known but unexploited. Apart from foreign capital, the privatization of the Soviet-style economies tapped into and redirected internal investment, leading to the closely watched Lukoil and Yukos as well as smaller, private oil firms currently being merged or bought out. The share of world crude oil output now dependent upon private management decisions had increased substantially. The primary stakeholder in a private firm by definition differs from the stakeholder of a national oil company, with attendant implications for world energy trade.

Given the meteoric rise of Yukos and its skyrocketing production, the Russian government's recent moves to rein in and regain control over the nation's hydrocarbon resources would appear to be more than a short-term goal. The jailing of Mikhail Khodorkovsky, the head of Yukos, seems to have been the first step in reasserting state influence. The government's pursuit of charges of delinquent and/or undercharged tax bills may be the means intended to slow the private-sector growth in hydrocarbons that had reinforced the growing dominance of market-based decisions.

Should Russian oil and gas developments continue to see a resurgence of public-sector control, this could bode well for increased coordination with OPEC on issues impacting prices and, if needed, responses in output levels. Even if semi-official coordination were not to occur between Russia and the major oil-exporter bloc, the chances of a "production war" should have lessened appreciably.

Is there an Iraqi Threat to OPEC?

As one of the oldest Middle Eastern oil producers, part of the lore repeated by oilmen for years has been the vast underestimation of Iraqi reserves. It would appear this can now be evaluated and tested. For instance, in 1965, the year-end issue of *Oil & Gas Journal* gave its statistics on production and reserves. Iraqi reserves were put at 25 billion barrels, well below those of Kuwait (68.7 billion barrels), Iran (40 billion barrels), and Saudi Arabia (60 billion barrels).[3] At that time, Kuwait held over 19 percent of the world's total oil reserves and was producing just over 7 percent of global output. In the same categories, Saudi Arabia accounted for close to 19 percent of reserves and barely 7 percent of production, with the Soviet Union at 16 percent and 9 percent, respectively.[4]

By 1970, reserve figures throughout the Middle East had risen, with Saudi Arabia taking over first place with 141.3 billion barrels, followed by Kuwait (79.9 billion barrels), Iran (70 billion barrels), and Iraq (32 billion barrels).[5] Just a decade later, Saudi reserves would reach 168 billion barrels, followed by Kuwait (67.9 billion barrels), Iran (57.5 billion barrels), and Iraq (30 billion barrels). However, in the 1980s, Saudi Arabia announced a major revision of its reserves, in part because OPEC was moving to install some form of production programming; a reserves base could be used to argue for a larger quota. This was answered by other producers/exporters. In 1990, the reserves ranking put Saudi Arabia in first place with 255.5 billion barrels, Iraq jumping into second place with 100 billion barrels, then Kuwait (97.1 billion barrels), Iran (92.9 billion barrels), and Abu Dhabi (92.2 billion barrels).[6] It is expected that a top priority of the Iraqi oil sector in the aftermath of the 2003 war would be to institute an assessment of reserves and reservoirs.

Iraq's historical ties to OPEC are profound and substantial, being one of the original participants involved in the establishment of the organization. The Iraqi oil sector is among the oldest in the Gulf. With arable land, a certain level of industrialization and manufacturing, natural resources, and a trained workforce, Iraq has the necessary ingredients for a diversified economy, which can reduce its dependence on a single commodity such as oil. Reconstruction and development demands combine to give Iraq an enormous absorptive capacity for revenue and capital. Thus, with large reserves and heavy revenue requirements, Iraq shares the interest of those in OPEC wishing to maximize revenue flows but keeping the price competitive with other energy sources, thereby ensuring vigorous, long-term demand for petroleum.

Moreover, with the removal of political friction that earlier pitted Iraq against fellow OPEC states – Iran, Kuwait, and Saudi Arabia – the shared interest in production and pricing should further enhance the core role of the Gulf members, as seen in Table 5.1. Therefore, it is not surprising that Iraq's Oil Minister announced at the September 24, 2003 OPEC meeting that his country expects to remain within this grouping. In the medium to longer term and with expected additions to non-OPEC volumes, staying within the Organization would allow Iraq to participate actively in setting output levels to impact the supply balance and prices.

In the short term, it is to Iraq's clear advantage to go along with OPEC's pricing strategy. The goal of achieving the 2003 pre-war 2.2 mbpd of crude output – let alone reaching its 1980 peak of 3.5 mbpd – is now being suggested as "doable" by around 2005.[7] Iraq's production capacity and that of the other Gulf "heavyweights" are offered in Table 5.2. Iraqi revenue forecasts for 2004 and 2005, based on exports of 1.5 mbpd and 2 mbpd, respectively, were for $12 billion in 2004 and $19 billion in 2005.[8] Volatile oil prices could complicate the economic recovery of Iraq because of uncertainty over budgetary resources.

Table 5.1
OPEC Reserves, Output and Reserves-to-Production Ratio

	Reserves-to-Production Production Ratio (years)	Jan. 1, 2001 Reserves (billion barrels)	2000 Production (million barrels per day)
Iraq	120	112.50	2.567
Saudi Arabia	87	261.70	8.264
Kuwait	126	96.50	2.099
UAE	120	97.80	2.233
Venezuela	70	76.86	3.028
Iran	67	89.70	3.682
Libya	57	29.50	1.414
Qatar	52	13.16	0.688
Algeria	31	9.20	0.809
Nigeria	30	22.50	2.034
Indonesia	11	4.98	1.267
OPEC	**79**	**814.40**	**28.085**
Rest of world	15	214.06	38.837

Source: *International Petroleum Yearbook 2002* (Tulsa, OK: PennWell, 2002), 185.

Table 5.2
Production Capacity of Selected Gulf OPEC Members, 1974-2001
(in million barrels per day)

First Quarter of	1974	1990	1994	2001
Iraq	2.5	3.66	2.5	3.1
Saudi Arabia	9.7	9.08	8.5	10.0-10.5
Kuwait	3.8	2.55	2.0	2.2
UAE	2.3	2.50	2.3	2.6
OPEC share in world total (%)	76.5	73.8	78.0	78.6-78.9

Source: *International Petroleum Yearbook 2002* (Tulsa, OK: PennWell, 2002), 185.

Mid-Term Changes in OPEC's Structure

It may be useful to think forward on OPEC's structure and membership. One possibility would be another configuration evolving in the medium term. After reaching a maximum membership of 13 countries, OPEC currently counts 11 member states. Those exiting the organization were smaller-scale producers, one African (Gabon) and the other Latin American (Ecuador). The regional distribution today includes one member from Asia-Pacific, another from Latin America, a third from sub-Saharan Africa, two from North Africa, and the remaining six concentrated in the Arabian Gulf. In November 2003, Iran's revised estimate of recoverable oil and condensate reserves to 130.81 billion barrels was reported.[9] Such a reserves base would increase the reserves-to-production ratio noted in Table 5.1 and further compound the dominance of Gulf resources globally and within OPEC itself.

Thus, one scenario in the next decade or so could involve smaller-volume oil producers/exporters such as Indonesia, Algeria, and Nigeria leaving OPEC. (It must be recalled that these three countries have extensive natural gas resources.) Thus, it is possible to envision an OPEC concentrated overwhelmingly in the Gulf. Russia would be the only single large exporter outside such a Gulf-centered body. Despite its reserves base, Venezuelan power in and support for OPEC are based largely on its political mindset. Prior to the presidency of Hugo Chavez, Venezuelan adherence to the Organization's quota system was frequently lukewarm at best. Moreover, if some type of Western hemispheric energy supply arrangement is finally implemented – a proposal advanced over many years particularly by the United States – then the Venezuelan interest in remaining within OPEC could dwindle significantly.

There is a further issue that may sharpen within the OPEC membership—states with a strong natural gas base but less significant liquids reserves. Algeria, Indonesia, and Nigeria, as noted earlier, offer concrete examples. Eventually, even Qatar may view its future as lying primarily with natural gas production and export. Does this situation create a dichotomy of interests?

Within the fossil fuels category, coal has been the chief competitor to oil in power generation. Increasingly, however, natural gas is becoming the optimal choice for incremental electricity-generating capacity. Should the competition sharpen between oil and natural gas in the primary energy mix, can OPEC serve the needs of the producers/exporters of both these fuels? Until now, because of the costs involved in natural gas export, either via cross-border pipelines or as liquefied natural gas (LNG) moved by tankers, the vast proportion of natural gas has been consumed domestically or traded to nearby countries with a transportation grid in place. However, huge and expanding gas markets such as the United States and Europe may decouple natural gas from crude oil in pricing and international trade. For example, Qatar and its international joint-venture partners are banking on rising global demand that can only be met by long-haul LNG.

Is Privatization a Threat to OPEC?

Iraq's relationship to or within OPEC will also depend on its freedom to set its oil and economic policy. As mandated by the US Congress during the Cold War, the President submits an annual report to the legislative branch on the nation's security strategy. In September 2002, President Bush presented his report on *The National Security Strategy of the United States of America*. In the introduction to the report, it is declared that the US example of freedom, democracy, and free enterprise constitutes "a single, sustainable model for international success…that is right and true for every person, in every society."[10] Whether one describes this assumption as a philosophy, doctrine or ideology, it underlies much of the current US governmental approach to international relations. Ambassador Paul Bremer, civilian head of the Coalition Provisional Authority in Iraq, indicated in July 2003 that privatization of public enterprises and the opening for foreign investment, including the oil industry, would be allowed before a sovereign Iraqi government assumed power.[11]

There was substantial response to the pronouncement, along with a similar statement hinting that Iraq might withdraw from OPEC. Such pronouncements have become muted largely to avoid fueling the widely held perception – rightly or wrongly – that one of the major motivations for the Iraq war was US access to and influence over that nation's oil and gas resources.[12] The suspicion remains, and not just in Arab or Islamic quarters.

[121]

One assessment of the political doctrine widely believed to be driving US policy – possibly before September 11 but certainly strengthened and reinforced thereafter – is that the United States has a right to "to recraft the structure of geopolitics to make the world more benign, from its perspective." This "recrafting" involves the concepts of preemption, regime change, and the "political engineering of new democratic institutions, whose advent is allegedly accompanied by greater stability and peace."[13] Moreover, among advocates of current US administration policy, there is a fervent belief that petroleum resources should be owned and exploited by the private sector, not by governments, because private entities intrinsically are more efficient, will maximize production, and will lead to lower prices.

Nonetheless, it is noteworthy that diversification of oil supply remains a pressing issue for the US administration, regardless of the flow of Iraqi crude into the market. *The National Security Strategy of the United States of America* for 2002 cited earlier asserted:

> We will strengthen our own energy security…by working with our allies, trading partners, and energy producers to expand the sources and types of global energy supplies, especially in the Western Hemisphere, Africa, Central Asia, and the Caspian region.[14]

The oil-rich region conspicuously absent from this listing is the Middle East, home to the largest reserves world-wide. Also missing from the list is Russia, although the other successor states of the former Soviet Union are included. And aside from the regional aspect, given the dominance of the Gulf producers within OPEC, one might deduce that non-OPEC supply increases will be encouraged.

However, there may be a more subtle aspect to the growth of this world view. The 1990s were a remarkable decade of sweeping political change and expansive economic well-being in the United States. The Cold War ended, the Soviet Union signaled defeat of its centrally planned and state-controlled economic system, and political liberalization was in lock-step with economic liberalization. Russia led the way with the sell-off of state enterprises and the rise of the "self-made" oligarchs. Simultaneously, the "peace dividend" for the United States helped to fuel what some characterize as the "go-go," "new" economy exemplified by dot-coms awash in venture capital. Deregulation became *de rigueur.* In the United States, the rather staid semi-public utilities, known as an investment haven for widows and orphans because of stable dividends, came under pressure because stock prices mirrored an undervaluation compared to companies the share prices of which could double in months. In state after state, utility deregulation came into effect, with each plan somewhat different from the other. However, a number of occurrences tended to return government oversight and responsibility to political respectability—the California electricity crisis in 2001; the collapse of companies with non-existent assets on the ledgers; the attacks of September 11 that made national security a matter of foremost public concern; and the massive power blackout in summer 2003 through much of north-central and northeast United States and Canada.

If the international community is offered and takes a larger direct role in the reconstruction of Iraq, it is likely that the US insistence on privatization and opening of all sectors to foreign direct investment will fall to a lower priority. What this means for the Iraqi oil industry and for Iraqi oil policy/relations with fellow exporters and consuming nations is difficult to divine. One suspects it will be a long-term work-in-progress that must reflect not only domestic sensitivities, requirements, and customs but also those of the region as well.[15]

OIL MARKET RESTRUCTURING

The Changing Dynamics of OPEC and Non-OPEC Relations: Present Status and Future Prospects

Paul Stevens

This chapter examines relations between non-OPEC and OPEC members and their implications for the international oil market and international oil prices. It sketches the historical background briefly and goes on to explore how this situation may change in the future. In particular, three key issues will be examined: the future call expected to be made on OPEC-10,[1] the future of OPEC-10 capacity and the issue of which countries will constitute OPEC in the future. Although Iraq is an OPEC member, its future role in oil production and indeed its status within OPEC is extremely uncertain.

The Basis of the Relationship

The history of OPEC and non-OPEC relations is basically one of competition and rivalry. Figures 6.1 and 6.2 illustrate this relationship since the year 1965. The main point conveyed by Figure 6.1 is that OPEC has been the residual supplier to the market. The purpose of this role has been to defend the economic rent inherent in oil prices.[2]

In the context of strong oil demand prior to 1973, OPEC increased its market share. During this period, the non-OPEC sector was irrelevant. The post World War II "OECD economic miracle" and the fact that oil demand had an income elasticity of 1, meant that global oil demand was growing at 8 to 10 percent per year. Although some of this growth went to the non-OPEC sector and the Former Soviet Union (FSU), the lion's share was captured by OPEC members. OPEC's market share increased from 45 percent in 1965 to a peak of over 50 percent in 1973 (see Figure 6.2). The period 1973–1981 witnessed a reduction in OPEC's market share as oil demand faltered following the first oil shock of 1973. However, since the fall in volume was more than offset by the quadrupling of oil price, relations with the non-OPEC sector was not yet an issue.

The real problems over OPEC and non-OPEC relations emerged after the second oil shock of 1979–1981. The dramatic reduction in oil demand fell entirely upon the OPEC producers, reducing their market share to around 30 percent in the mid-1980s (see Figure 6.2). The explanation was simple. World oil demand fell due to the two oil shocks coupled with a serious global economic recession in the first half of the 1980s. Simultaneously, the non-OPEC sector recorded strong growth as the oil companies, awash with money following the oil shocks, sought to replace the equity crude access they had lost as a result of the nationalizations of the 1970s in a world where oil forecasts anticipated ever rising prices (see Figure 6.1).

Figure 6.1
The Basis for the Relationship
OPEC versus Non-OPEC Production (bpd)

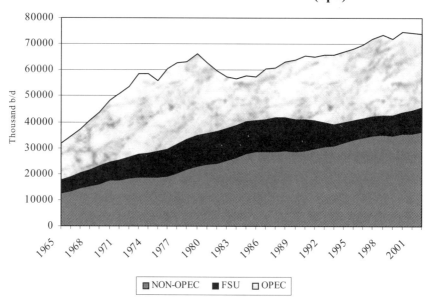

Source: *BP Statistical Review of World Energy,* 2003

Figure 6.2
The Basis for the Relationship
OPEC versus Non-OPEC Production (%)

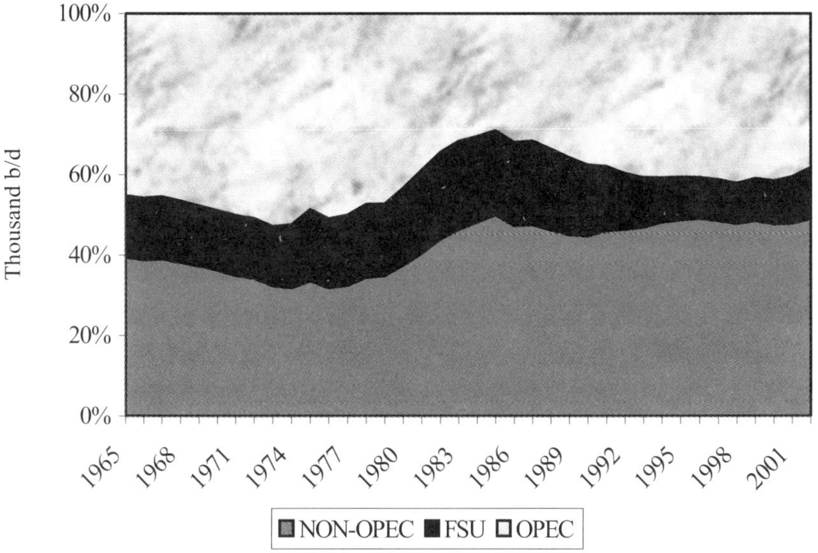

Source: *BP Statistical Review of World Energy,* 2003

It was in this period that OPEC and non-OPEC relations started to become a real issue as OPEC was forced to cut back to make way for non-OPEC production. The non-OPEC sector's willingness and ability to free ride upon OPEC generated considerable animosity. After the 1986 price collapse, oil demand began to recover as did OPEC's market share. However, between the years 1991 to 2000, the call on OPEC production has remained flat as non-OPEC production has continued to strengthen (see Figure 6.3). This trend has occurred despite a dramatic collapse in production from the FSU although collapsing consumption also meant that FSU exports remained relatively buoyant.

During the post-1986 period, there have been occasional periods of non-OPEC support for OPEC's defense of prices. However, this has generally been grudging, half-hearted and frequently not implemented at all. Invariably, this quasi-support came during periods of price crisis, most obviously following the price collapse of 1998. A few producers such as Mexico and Oman did provide genuine support although it is not

[129]

clear how much production restraint was driven by field problems rather than a genuine sacrifice of production. However, other countries, Russia and Norway among them, proved very unreliable either by promising cuts that were not implemented, or promising cuts that were due to happen anyway.

Figure 6.3

Call on OPEC: Market Share of OPEC vs Non-OPEC (including FSU)

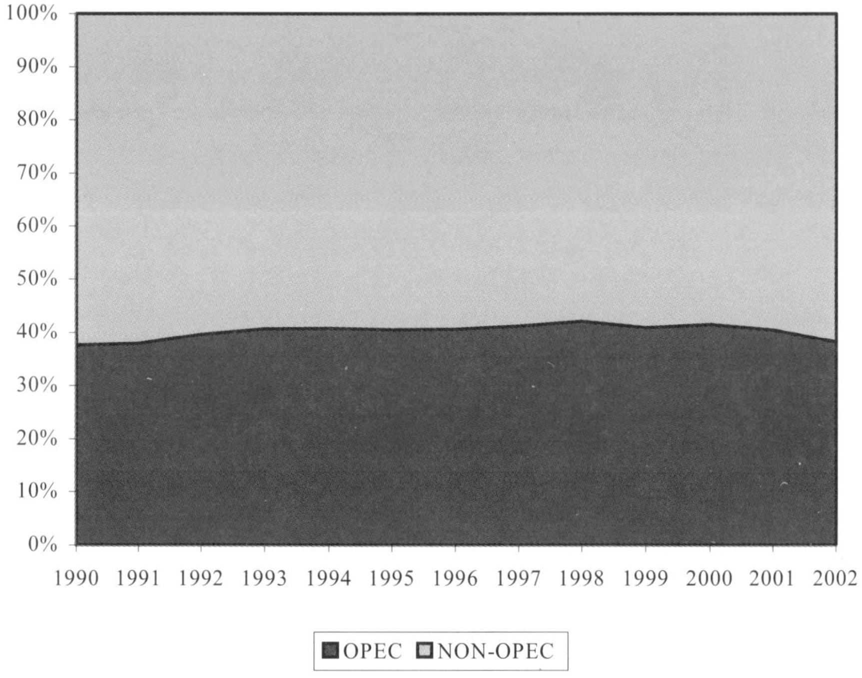

Source: *BP Statistical Review of World Energy*, 2003.

There is an important lesson to be drawn for the future, which remains a constant theme of this chapter. It appears that the better the relations between OPEC and non-OPEC, the less likely that such good relations will be sustained. This is simply because good relations imply relatively high oil prices, which sow the seeds for greater non-OPEC supply and this in turn, undermines OPEC's market share. This fundamental truth underpins the nature of the relationship and this point will be discussed further.

[130]

The Future Call on OPEC

Two key drivers that will shape the future call on OPEC production are future oil demand and future non-OPEC supply.

The Future of Oil Demand

The conventional view of future oil demand is characterized by the IEA forecast shown in Figure 6.4. Much of the strong demand growth expected in the future will be in the developing countries as their per capita income rises. Such forecasts are very common among oil analysts. However, the oil industry has always been a graveyard of consensus views and there are a number of arguments why the dramatic increases expected in oil demand forecast may not be as strong as many believe.

Figure 6.4
Forecast of World Oil Demand

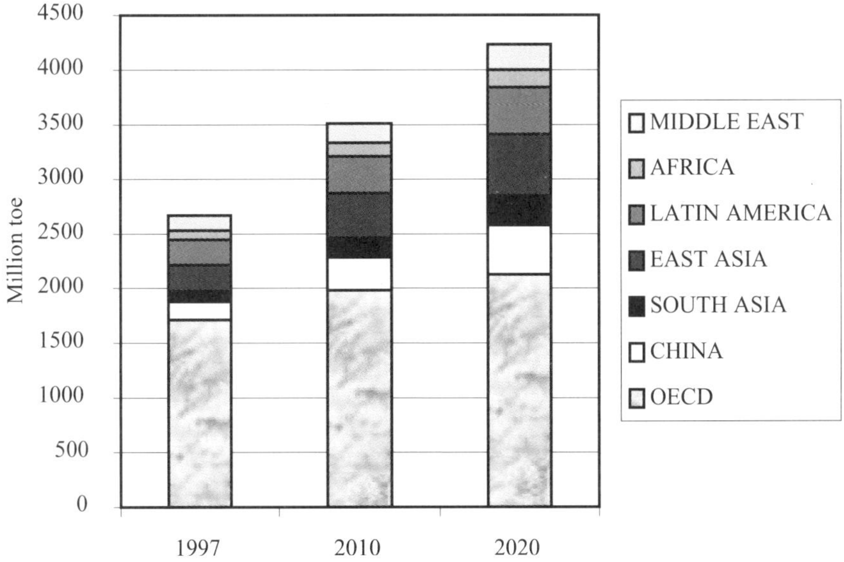

Source: *IEA World Energy Outlook* 2000.

There are clear environmental pressures to reduce energy usage. There may well be doubts over whether the Kyoto Protocol will play much of a role in reducing energy consumption. However, there are other aspects of environmental pressure which may negatively affect oil demand growth. In particular, there are strong pressures to manage the growing pollution problems arising from urban traffic congestion. As Figure 6.5 shows, while the oil shocks of the 1970s did much to damage the role of fuel oil in the static sector, it did little to dent oil's dominance in the transport sector. This explains the strong and steady growth in gasoline demand and in middle distillates—mainly diesel for road transport and kerosene for air travel. The explanation behind such growth is simple. In the static sector, raising steam under boilers can be done using many alternative fuels. However, in the transport sector, until recently, there was little by way of substitution possibilities. This situation is now changing as hybrid cars emerge and fuel cell technology receives growing attention.

Figure 6.5
Oil Consumption Patterns:
OECD Oil Consumption by Fuel (1965-2001)

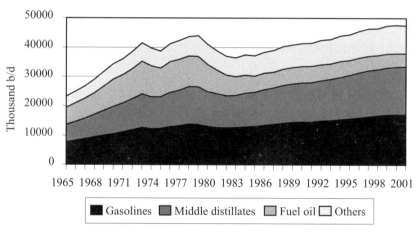

Source: *BP Statistical Review of World Energy*, 2003.

Concerns over supply security, which have been creeping back onto the agenda in recent years, have received a strong boost from the current shambles in Iraq and the generally deteriorating situation in the Middle East. Such concerns are likely to prove far more powerful drivers of energy policy than environmental concerns.

[132]

Recent developments in LNG trade and in the development of Gas-to-Liquids (GTL) technology present alternative sources of energy, which will present serious challenges to views of ever-growing oil demand. There are huge potential gas reserves which could provide serious competition to oil. In particular, they could challenge oil's role in the transport sector either through green diesel from GTL technology or by the spread of compressed natural gas (CNG).

Most of these reasons for lower than expected demand are generally known and have been well rehearsed and much discussed. However, there is one additional factor that has received little or no attention. Consumers in most developing countries did not feel the impact of the oil shocks of the 1970s as their governments protected them from higher international prices by the provision of subsidies. Figure 6.6 provides the evidence. This shows the weighted average final price to the consumer of oil products in index form for 12 developing countries. As can be seen, only three countries – Korea, Brazil and Argentina – raised their domestic oil product prices in line with the first oil shock of 1973–1974. Argentina later reverted to join the countries which protected their consumers. Again only Korea and Brazil tracked international prices after the second oil shock of 1979-1981. As the 1980s proceeded, the other countries represented in Figure 6.6 came under pressure to remove subsidies and move to border prices. This pressure resulted from the internal cost of trying to maintain subsidies and the external pressure from the IMF and World Bank as part of the fallout from the debt crisis.

A key consequence was that (as Figure 6.7 shows) those developing countries which failed to experience the oil shocks of the 1970s have very much higher commercial energy intensities than those countries that did go through the experience—the OECD countries plus Korea, Brazil and to a lesser extent, Argentina. The next stage is to consider what factors might drive these countries to improve their energy intensities as any such improvement would seriously undermine the oil demand projections contained in Figure 6.4.

Figure 6.6
Real Domestic Oil Prices in Selected Developing Countries (1970=100)

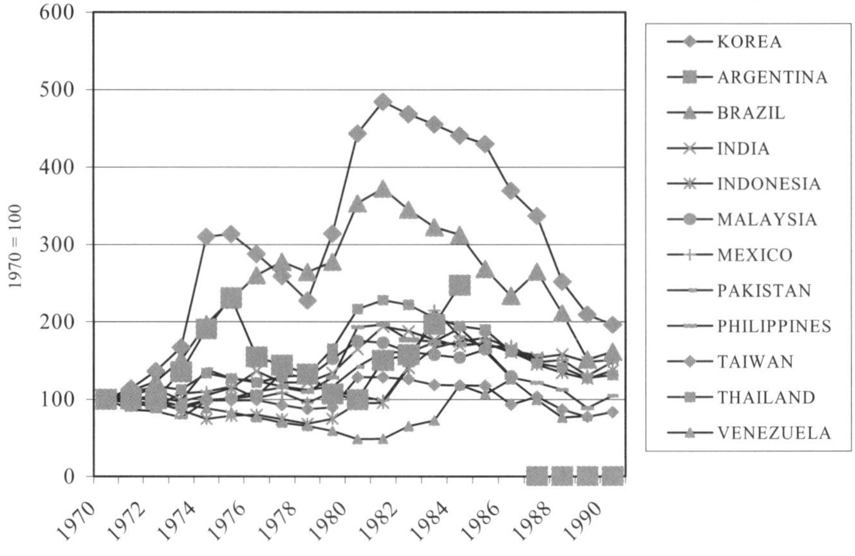

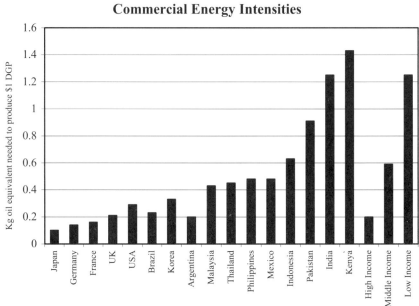

Source: Computed from Lawrence Berkeley Laboratories data 1989.

Figure 6.7
Commercial Energy Intensities

Source: World Bank Data.

For many years, as may be seen in Figure 6.8, the OECD countries have been increasing their sales taxes on oil products. Although many OPEC members view this as a conspiracy to discriminate against oil producers, there is an equally valid explanation to do with raising tax revenue. An ideal product for sales taxes is one with three characteristics—widespread use to increase the size of the tax base; inelastic demand to allow the imposition of very high tax rates; and finally low tax collection costs. Oil products score very highly on all three characteristics. The use of oil pervades all sectors of the economy. The short term price elasticities of oil demand are very low.[3] Finally, collecting the tax is cheap and simple, because it is obviously difficult to hide a refinery to avoid paying taxes. These reasons for taxing oil products are now driving fiscal policy in developing countries. Increasingly, as governments tax oil products, the domestic price of such products is rising, regardless of what happens to the international price of crude oil. There is plenty of casual empiricism to support this view. Figure 6.9 provides one illustration for Mexico and shows an inexorable rise in the prices of both gasoline and diesel, regardless of what has happened to international crude prices.

Figure 6.8
Consumer Government Sales Taxes

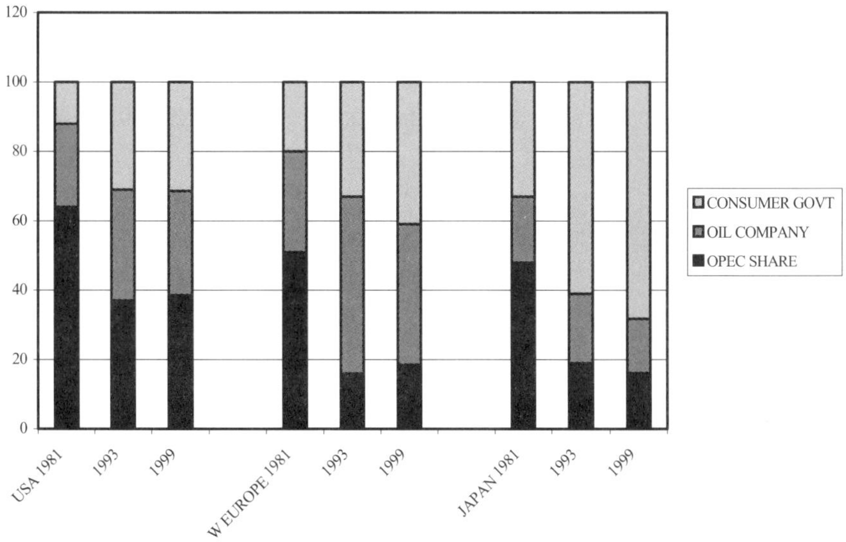

Source: OPEC data.

Figure 6.9
Mexican Fuel Prices (1990-2000)

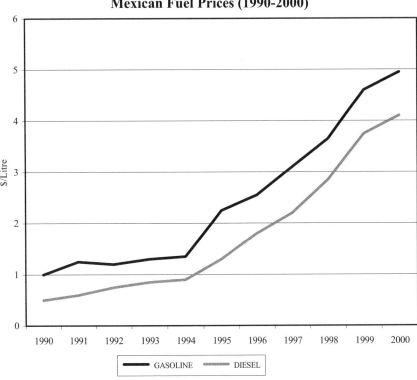

Source: F.U. Barnes, "The Dynamic Response of the Mexican Energy Sector to Regulatory Policies and Budgetary Restrictions," Ph.D Thesis, Imperial College, University of London, 2001.

The result could be a dramatic reduction in oil intensities over the coming 20 years. Figure 6.10 illustrates the impact on the IEA oil demand forecast if a sales tax regime similar to that of the United States were to be imposed in the developing world assuming a long run elasticity of -0.6. By any standards, this last assumption is conservative. Thus the IEA projections are considerably flattened as a result of the growing use of sales taxes. Of course such analysis may be over-simplified. The whole point of the oil shocks were that they were "a shock" and as such demanded a serious behavioral response. Arguably, a gradual increase in final price would, through the process of "money illusion," have less of an impact on consumer behavior.

Figure 6.10
Impact of a US Type Sales Tax Regime on the IEA Forecasts

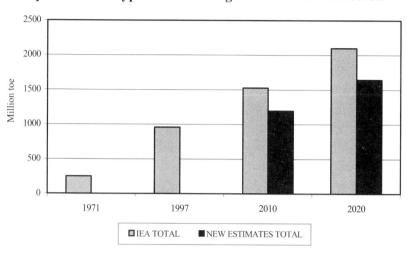

Notes: 2010 Price increases from $16.50 to $22.40; 2020 Price increases from $22.50 to 30.60 ($1990); Long run price elasticity–0.60.
Source: Author

The Future of Non-OPEC Supply

There is no obvious conventional wisdom regarding the future of non-OPEC supply. Rather there are two distinct camps. One group of recently vocal "depletionists" argues that non-OPEC (and indeed OPEC) supply is running out of steam and will peak in the very near future. Opposed to this are those who believe that human ingenuity will overcome the tendency towards the depletion of oil resources.

The argument arises because of the use of "gapology" by the depletionists. This emerged in the 1960s and probably reached its pinnacle of influence in the Club of Rome's report entitled "Limits to Growth" published in 1972.

The methodology can be described simply. First, the history of consumption (in this case of oil) is plotted and the past trend established. This trend is then extrapolated into the future. On the same diagram, a fixed stock (in this case oil reserves) is added as a horizontal line since it is assumed to be "fixed." The resulting geometry means that the two lines, one of which is parallel to the horizontal axis and the other not, will eventually cross. At this point a gap is "discovered." In trying to understand this approach, three key weaknesses in the argument become apparent:

- the assumption of ever growing demand
- the assumption of a fixed stock
- the neglect of any market dynamics and feedback loops in the system.

There is general consensus that for the next 10 to 15 years global oil demand will continue to grow. The only argument is over the speed of that growth. However, beyond that time horizon, it is perfectly plausible to argue why oil demand growth will slow down and demand will decline. The drivers of this reversal of fortune for the oil industry have already been discussed and the implicit assumption of ever rising oil demand can be questioned.

The second flaw in the logic which emerges from gapology is the assumption of a fixed stock of oil in the world. This is simply not true except in a very meaningless, pedantic, geological manner. For example, the definition of "proven reserves" is explicitly based upon assumptions regarding current technology and economics. The higher the investment made in finding oil-in-place, developing fields and increasing recovery factors, the greater are the proven reserves. Thus technology is always increasing the so-called "fixed" stock of oil.

However, the story is more complex. The United States Geological Survey put "conventional" oil reserves at 1,103 billion barrels with an estimate of undiscovered 471 billion barrels.[4] This compares to a cumulative production of 699 billion barrels since 1859. However, another source suggests additional "unconventional" oil reserves are 16,100 billion barrels! [5] Other sources have suggested similarly large figures. Of course these figures for "unconventional" oil raise many interesting questions ranging from the economic viability of development to the environmental consequences. However, in reality, if economics demands it, then "unconventional" oil will come on stream. It is considered as part of the "fixed" stock.

This is not the end of the story on "reserves." Before considering such exotica as tars sands and oil shale, it may be noted that higher oil prices can work wonders for field recovery factors. Also, developments in gas-to-liquids technology and economics could throw global natural gas reserves into the oil reserve pot. Obviously, if the "fixed" stock of oil is not fixed, then the emerging gap becomes a receding horizon. The argument of the depletionists begins to look distinctly shaky.

In gapology's argument regarding the imminent demise of oil, the final flaw lies in the neglect of market forces. The key concept is when the oil "runs out." This is indicated by the Reseves/Production ratio (R/P ratio), which is the global oil reserves divided by the annual oil production. Using data from the *BP Statistical Review of World Energy* 2002, the global R/P ratio was over 39 years. However, if the arithmetic is taken to enough decimal places, it emerges that the oil will run out at 21.50 GMT on October 20, 2040! Clearly, this is a ridiculous calculation. However, the reason it is ridiculous illustrates the serious and fatal flaw in the depletionists' argument. Let us assume that my earlier analysis is wrong and oil demand continues to rise forever and the limit of the resource base is reached. In such a case, impending depletion will create the seeds of its own demise by the feedback loops it generates. Shortage would signal higher prices. This would produce an inevitable market reaction provoking human ingenuity—Prometheus unbound once again! Higher prices would inhibit demand, not by consumers lowering usage of their oil-fueled appliances but by changes in the stock level of such appliances. Oil-burning appliances would either become more efficient or be substituted by appliances based on other fuels. Higher prices would stimulate supply, not least by making the huge "unconventional" resources accessible. Similarly, other energy sources that compete with oil would be encouraged to boost their supply. Thus the intersection on the diagram when the "gap" is supposedly reached will never occur in reality.

Two examples would illustrate this point. In the early 1980s, with a few honorable exceptions, forecasts showed the oil price rising strongly forever. Had these forecasts been correct, today's oil price should have been some $90–$200 per barrel. The current level is around $50 per barrel. Yet it should have been patently obvious to anyone with a smattering of economics that continually rising oil prices were unsustainable. The market reaction described above would inevitably undermine the higher price. In fact, this is what happened, culminating in the 1986 oil price collapse.

Earlier in history, the United States wood fuel crisis provides a second example. In the 1860s the United States began to "run out" of wood when it accounted for some 80 percent of primary energy consumption. Although this may seem implausible, wood as fuel is a "high volume–low value" item and faces economic limitations on how far it can be transported. The contemporary literature and media on the impending crisis echoes the current warnings of the depletionists: "Energy crisis looming!" "End of life as we know it!" Ultimately, all that happened was that the price of wood as a fuel rose relative to the price of coal. Consumers switched to coal. Technologists invented new and more efficient ways to mine, transport and burn coal. This widened the price difference between the two fuels at the burner tip in favor of coal. By 1900, coal accounted for 80 percent of the United States' primary energy consumption, courtesy of the market, and the "wood fuel crisis" never really emerged.

Thus the feedback loops from any impending shortage will unleash human ingenuity yet again. Of course, sudden oil price rises can and do produce undesirable macro-economic shocks. However, such sudden price shocks would arise from geopolitics, not from depletion. On October 20, 2040, at one minute past 21.50 GMT, the world will not suddenly find that all the oil has been depleted. The worst depletion could do is to cause oil prices to rise gradually, which would give time for markets to make the necessary adjustments.

The reality is that oil is similar to other depletable resources. Thus it faces a constant battle between depletion and human ingenuity. What happens to production costs and eventually prices will signal which side is winning. All the empirical work on long-term commodity price trends shows unequivocally that human ingenuity has been winning. Those who wish to make a plausible case for the oil "running out" must explain why oil is different from other commodities. In particular, they must give convincing reasons why human ingenuity in the field of oil would take a holiday or suffer a sudden attack of dementia.

Another support for non-OPEC supply strength in the next five to ten years is security of supply. This has already been discussed under demand but it also has a supply dimension. If security of supply is a concern then one obvious policy solution is to encourage domestic supply. Non-OPEC producer governments have many different means to do this. The legal and institutional framework for encouraging oil field investment is central to the ultimate recovery rate. Thus governments have great flexibility to adjust fiscal terms if recovery maximization is the prime policy objective for whatever reason.

A good example would be the United Kingdom's North Sea oilfields. In recent years, successive British governments have made it clear that the prime objective vis-à-vis North Sea crude oil production is to maximize recovery. It is clear that production is now in terminal decline but the rate of decline can be slowed if the fiscal terms are made sufficiently attractive. There are other measures that can encourage development. For example, in the 1990s the UK government forced the industry to draw up a "voluntary" code of practice regarding access to the existing pipeline infrastructure. This was explicitly designed to improve the economics of marginal fields.

Non-OPEC supply is also likely to receive support from new technological developments. Since 1986, the international oil industry has witnessed a dramatic technological revolution in oil production techniques, notably offshore. This was driven by the price collapse, which forced the major oil companies to cut their cost base, coupled with the emergence of a whole series of new technologies ranging from 3-D and 4-D seismic analysis, horizontal drilling to sub-sea completions and many more. In addition to these technologies, the oil majors themselves developed new techniques for managing large complex projects. Obviously this revolution began in areas where the oil majors had their greatest interests such as the North Sea, the Gulf of Mexico and more recently offshore West Africa. However, there are large areas of the world that still have to catch up with these changes. A good example is provided by Russia where in many important fields the recovery rate is only 5 to 20 percent.[6] Thus as innovation spreads, it is likely to provide a considerable boost to non-OPEC supplies. Combined with fiscal incentives as described above, this will create a powerful impetus for continued non-OPEC supply growth.

Finally, oil price will be a key driver of non-OPEC production. Oil price impacts production in two ways. First, it affects the profitability of projects although the more progressive the fiscal system, the less the impact on the companies. Thus, with highly progressive tax systems in a low price world, the oil majors would continue to operate the fields since their gains would be only marginally affected. It is the governments who suffer the main impact. Second, it affects the cash flow of the companies and therefore their willingness to spend. The 1998 oil price collapses caused a major reduction in expenditure by the oil majors, which was reflected in non-OPEC supply. According to the *BP Statistical Review of World Energy*, non-OPEC supply (excluding the FSU) rose on average by 580,000 bpd annually between the years 1991 to 1998. Following reductions in capital and operating expenditures by the companies, non-OPEC production fell by 141,000 bpd in 1999.

Thus the problem as previously expressed is simple. If good OPEC/non-OPEC relations signal high prices, this will boost non-OPEC supply, leading eventually to even greater erosion of OPEC's market share. Furthermore, all the current signs suggest that Saudi Arabia views $25 per barrel as an "acceptable" price and is willing to defend that price. However, a general view is that such a price level is too high since it will simply boost non-OPEC supply. This opinion is also shared by some within the Saudi oil techno-structure.

Prospects for Iraqi Exports

For analytical purposes, at this stage it makes more sense to regard Iraq as being outside the OPEC quota system. The validity of this assumption will be discussed later.

There is great uncertainty regarding Iraqi exports. Three factors hamper Iraq's return to pre-war export levels. First, the damage inflicted upon the infrastructure. In particular, unreliable power supplies are a major cause of lower production. Second, looting has seriously undermined the system. In this context, the destruction of much of the paper work in both the Northern Oil Company (NOC) and the Southern Oil Company (SOC) has slowed recovery in a society where initiative and doing without "the book" has not been encouraged for a long time. Finally, the most serious factor is the lack of security. The danger involved is not only the blowing up of infrastructure but very sophisticated sabotage in control rooms almost certainly being done by disaffected Iraq National Oil Company (INOC) employees (sacked as part of the de-Baathification policy) and their sympathizers. A communiqué from the Baath Party published in the Beirut daily *An Nahar* on November 2, 2003 called on all Iraqis to target export facilities in order to deny Iraqi oil to the Americans.

The Northern Export line through Turkey has not been operated since the end of hostilities. The allies appear incapable of defending the length of the line. Thus in the North although some 500,000 bpd is produced, at least half is being re-injected into the fields while the other half is feeding the two Northern Refineries. As for the South, estimates of exports are controversial. A best guess suggests that in September 2003 some 1 million barrels per day (mbpd) was exported via the Arabian Gulf. These export levels appear to have stabilized subsequently following improvements to the power supply in the South.

However, further expansion is likely to be difficult. The Coalition Provisional Authority (CPA) apparently had forecasted in its budget, exports in 2004 of only 1.6 mbpd despite earlier claims of 2 mbpd. More optimistic forecasts came from the State Oil Marketing Organization (SOMO), which estimated 1.148 mbpd exports for October and 2.3 mbpd by December. However, the numbers are extremely sensitive politically and should be treated with caution. One of the uncertainties is just how much money is being allocated to rehabilitate the oil sector. This is a key factor, particularly because the US service companies appear to be operating on a very much higher cost basis than appears reasonable. In the CPA budget for 2004 there was no allocation for capital spending in the oil sector. While the Bush Administration asked Congress for a $2.1 billion allocation for the Iraqi oil sector in the 2004 budget, almost half of this was intended for the import of oil products. In the CPA budgets drawn up for 2005 and 2006 there is only $1 billion allocated for capital expenditure in the oil sector.

The security situation is the key factor for Iraq to return to the level of 2-3 mbpd exports. The CPA has the legal authority to develop and produce existing fields and thus return to pre-war levels. INOC together with service companies probably have the technical capabilities to do this although the effect of de-Baathification on INOC remains uncertain. However, the security situation means that it is taking weeks to get the necessary military escorts together for the engineering crews to work on the infrastructure.

[143]

The heeding of the Baath Party call to target oil exports would clearly not allow pre-war export levels to be reached during 2004.

Unless the security situation improves, a return to pre-war export levels is unlikely before 2005 or even 2006. Such an improvement in security is unlikely without a major change in US political and military strategy. In the "Malayan Emergency" of the 1950s and at the height of the "Troubles" in Northern Ireland, the British worked on a rule of thumb of 20 soldiers per 1000 population to contain the situation. Assuming an Iraqi population of 25 million, this requires half a million troops. There is currently less than one third of that number on the ground.

Taking into account both demand and non-OPEC supply, the implications are clear. Over the next five years at least, the call on OPEC-10 at best will be flat[7] and if Iraq does spring a surprise by returning more quickly and more strongly than the foregoing analysis suggests, it could actually decline. How OPEC-10 might react depends very much upon what happens to their capacity.

The Future of OPEC-10 Capacity

The history of the international oil industry can be written in terms of how the excess capacity to produce crude (which represents the normal situation) has been managed. Figure 6.11 provides estimates of the amount of excess capacity among OPEC members between 1950 and 2003. As is evident from the figure, for most of the time, the condition has been one of excess capacity. When this excess capacity disappeared, for whatever reason, a price spike has generally followed. When the excess capacity became too great, as in the mid-1980s, a price collapse has ensued.

Four factors explain the existence of such excess, which, after all represents investment that will not generate income as long as it remains idle capacity. The existence of rent in the oil price has meant that the price has always exceeded the full built-up cost of producing a barrel. Thus the owner of the oil-in-place always has an incentive to develop. The industry has often been subject to unforeseen capacity losses requiring the development of alternatives, which become surplus to requirements once the original capacity loss is restored. Moreover, the industry has always been driven by

[144]

strong consensus. The fallacy of having such a composition is that the industry tends to witness either feast or famine as all the players are working simultaneously to achieve the same purpose. Finally, after 1985, Saudi Arabia's oil policy was deliberately designed to promote oil price stability so as to encourage a revival of oil in the global primary energy mix. A key part of this strategy was the willingness to hold enough excess capacity to be able to counter the price effects stemming from any sudden loss of supply. This strategy proved to be extremely successful in 1990 following the Iraqi invasion of Kuwait, and also in 2003 following the US invasion of Iraq.

Figure 6.11
OPEC Spare Capacity to Produce Crude Oil
(Actual to November 2002 and Estimated 2003)

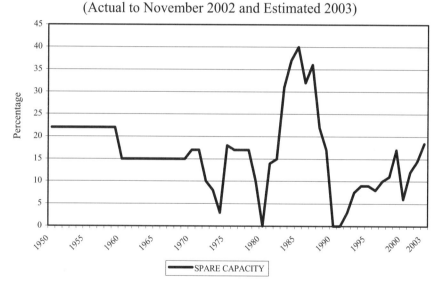

Sources: 1950-67 author's estimates; 1968-91 CIA; 1992-2003 author's estimates.

As long as the call on OPEC is flat, the system manages even if there is little excess capacity. A good example was the first nine months of 2003. The position of OPEC-10 in defending the relatively high oil prices was almost entirely fortuitous. The first half of 2003 saw a tight market. Demand was strong following a cold first quarter, high US gas prices and also high Japanese demand for fuel oil following nuclear outages. At the same time, geopolitics and internal dissension reduced supply by 2 mbpd from Iraq, Venezuela and Nigeria. Non-OPEC supply was also flat. This meant that OPEC-10 have been able to produce flat out and still have high prices. Until September, Brent crude averaged $28 per barrel. A large part of this is also because a number of OPEC members—Indonesia, Iran and Venezuela have been struggling to meet their OPEC quota which left the field free for others to produce over their quotas without disturbing the market.

Thus OPEC-10's reaction to a flat call depends upon what happens to its capacity. All the signs are that a number of OPEC members are in the process of increasing their capacity. In all cases this process is being driven by the governments, which are encouraging the entry of the international oil companies (IOCs).

Within the time frame it is perfectly possible to imagine a post-Chavez Venezuela returning to its economic liberalization policy of "Apetura" to recover capacity. PDVSA has announced that it will invest $43 billion over the next five years to increase capacity to 4.5 mbpd.[8] While this is rightly greeted with some skepticism, nonetheless, it is a declaration of intent.

Algeria is expected to see over $50 billion to be invested in the oil and gas sector over the next ten years. Recent and current projects are expected to add 650,000 bpd to current capacity in the near future. Libya is encouraging several major projects. Overall, an extra 350,000 bpd extra capacity is expected by 2005. In Nigeria there are a number of major projects and oil capacity is expected to rise by at least 1 mbpd by 2007.

The threat of Iraq opening up could also force Kuwait and Iran to break their deadlocks in relation to their own opening to the IOCs, leading to additional capacity. Similarly, Abu Dhabi and Qatar, feeling threatened by expansion elsewhere may also improve their fiscal terms to attract more upstream investment. Kuwait plans to increase capacity from 2.5 mbpd to 3 mbpd by 2005 and 3.5 mbpd by 2015. Abu Dhabi is seeking to increase its sustainable crude capacity by 400,000 bpd between the years 2002–2006. In Qatar, equity investment by the IOCs is steadily adding to capacity, albeit in gradual and small tranches.

All this suggests that the flat call on OPEC-10 will coincide with growing excess capacity. Indeed one source estimated that by the end of 2004, surplus capacity in OPEC-10 could exceed 5 mbpd.

This will create two serious problems for OPEC. The first is the obvious and long-standing problem of members ignoring their obligations and pushing more oil into the market than it can absorb, thereby creating a downward pressure on prices. The second problem is that countries that can produce above their quotas will demand additional quotas from those that cannot use all of their existing quotas for whatever reason. Such demands will seriously undermine OPEC's cohesion unless some suitable remedy can be found. One possible solution might be a leasing system for quotas,[9] whereby those with spare quotas could "lend" it to those straining to produce more than their quota at some mutually agreed price. The virtue of this system is that it would be on a bilateral basis thereby avoiding the inevitable acrimony associated with multilateral negotiations.

In the absence of such a solution, the prospects are for an increasing lack of cohesion within OPEC, including Iraq, which will inevitably spill over into deteriorating relations with the non-OPEC group. As OPEC-10 come under pressure to defend prices they will look to the non-OPEC group for support. History suggests such support is unlikely to be effective.

However, there is one possible way to remedy the situation, which relates to the detente between Russia and Saudi Arabia. At the start of September 2003 there was an historic 3-day visit by Crown Prince Abdullah to Moscow for talks with various sections of the Russian Government including President Vladimir Putin. The meeting had been preceded by a number of earlier meetings involving officials, including several by Saudi Oil Minister Ali Al Naimi. At the end of the visit several agreements were announced:

- An agreement to "coordinate their anti-terrorism efforts."
- A 5-year agreement on oil issues aimed at continuing a "dialogue" on oil policy to encourage "stable and predictable oil prices within an acceptable band." It was also intended to simplify procedures for the creation of joint ventures in oil and gas projects and to encourage the exchange of "information" on oil market issues.
- An agreement between the respective Chambers of Commerce to facilitate trade and investment.
- A series of agreements between scientific associations.

The trip and its aftermath rightly created a great deal of interest, not least because of the possible implications for the oil market.

There has been a long history of antagonism between the two countries. From the Soviet/Russian perspective, Saudi Arabia was viewed as a client state of the United States in the Middle East—an area much contested during the Cold War. Also, Saudi Arabia was active in supporting opposition to Russian involvement in Afghanistan and more recently in Chechnya. This support involved Saudi nationals actually fighting with the opposition together with allegedly wide-ranging financial support from private sources, especially from the Al Haramain Foundation (AHF). From the Saudi perspective, communism was an anathema both on religious and ideological grounds. Moreover, the Soviet Union had been a major supporter, both financially and militarily, of some of Saudi Arabia's less friendly neighbors ranging from Iraq to Syria and Yemen.

However, recent events have generated serious interest on both sides not only in improving relations, but more importantly, in generating active cooperation. Russia's interests encompass several issues:

- *Crisis in Chechnya:* One of the most pressing issues is the ongoing crisis that Russia faces in Chechnya. After the events of 9/11, Putin's support of the US "war on terrorism" effectively gave Russia a free hand to suppress the Chechen rebels. However, the fact they were still receiving substantial support from Saudi Arabia in terms of men and finance was causing problems. The prospect of isolating the rebels from Saudi support, especially financial backing, was very attractive. Although the alleged financing was from private rather than any official sources in the Kingdom, the Saudi government was well placed to at least reduce the flow of funds. This expectation was reinforced by the continuing crackdown on Al Qaida elements within the Kingdom.
- *Bilateral investments*: There has been growing interest in Russia in bilateral investments. Russian energy companies have been expressing greater interest in access to Saudi Arabia. Gazprom in particular has been discussing gas investment options including LNG export from Saudi Arabia. Such talk was explicitly encouraged by Ali Al Naimi during a visit to Moscow in March 2003. In the same month, Saudi

Aramco conferred official contractor status on Stroytransgaz allowing it to participate in Saudi oil and gas projects. At the same time, Moscow's economic strategy is to encourage greater foreign direct investment (FDI) into Russia, and Saudi Arabia represents a very large potential source of such private investment.

- *Russian elections:* The Russian parliamentary elections were scheduled to begin in December 2003 and it is possible that Putin thought that good public relations with the Saudis could attract votes from Russian Muslims. Saudi Arabia explicitly announced its support for Putin's efforts to increase Russia's cooperation with the Organization of the Islamic Conference (OIC).

- *Oil markets:* Russia is certainly concerned over the state of the oil markets. The health of the oil sector has been a key driver in its recovery following the 1998 economic collapse, which was driven in large part by the dramatic fall in international oil prices. Today the economy is in much better shape to face lower oil prices if only because production costs have fallen. In the early 1990s Russian production costs were in the range of $12-14 per barrel. Today, the costs on average are claimed to be $3.30 per barrel. It has been estimated that the Russian oil majors would break even at $10 per barrel (Yukos claimed $6.50) allowing for transportation costs. Also the IMF has estimated that at $18 per barrel, the Russian current account would still carry a $15 billion surplus and the economy would keep expanding. However, there is a clear Russian interest in maintaining oil prices above the lower end of the OPEC range ($22-28 per barrel).

Saudi relations with the United States, its traditional supporter have seriously deteriorated since 9/11. It is very difficult to determine just how serious this deterioration is from the US side since Washington is speaking with many different and conflicting voices. However, this is having two effects in Saudi Arabia. First, there is great and growing resentment at the US attitude given Saudi Arabia's steadfast role in stabilizing the oil markets since 1986 and its support for US military actions against Iraq. In July 2003, a Bill to place Saudi Arabia on the official list of state supporters of terrorism attracted 191 votes in the US House of Representatives, only just

[149]

short of a majority. This caused a major shock in Riyadh. Second, there is a concerted effort to try and seek support from elsewhere, if only as an insurance policy. Thus Saudi Arabia has been working to improve relations with the European Union. In August 2003, following over ten years of negotiations, a trade agreement was finally signed. The fact that the Saudis conceded important concessions – lifting protection to local industry and stopping the sale of gas feedstock at subsidized prices – suggests they were in a hurry to conclude a deal especially because the accusation of price subsidies on gas is extremely controversial. The moves towards détente with Russia may be seen in this context. Thus Saudi Arabia's interest in building good relations with Russia stems from several issues:

- *Source of military hardware*: Russia presents an alternative source of military hardware for Saudi Arabia and it appears that during Crown Prince Abdullah's visit, military cooperation issues were discussed.

- *Support within the United Nations:* Saudi Arabia is looking for Russian support in the United Nations to end the US-led occupation of Iraq and to force a settlement in the Israeli-Palestinian conflict.

- *Investment alternatives:* Russia does present a serious alternative home for Saudi private investment, albeit one that seems rather high risk, given the legal and other institutional weaknesses.

- *Cooperation on oil policy:* However, Saudi Arabia's key concern has been the profile of Russian oil production and avenues for Russian cooperation with OPEC. In recent years, Russia has been a major source of non-OPEC production growth, which threatens OPEC's ability to defend its price band.

In 2002 Russian production reached 7.7 million barrels per day (mbpd), a 26 percent increase on 2001. This compares with the 1998 production of 6.2 mbpd. The projections for 2003 and 2004 were 8.2 and 8.8 mbpd respectively. It is widely touted that Russia will be producing 10 mbpd by 2010. Saudi Arabia has become increasingly aware of these numbers, which have caused great concern within the oil techno-structure. As indicated above, OPEC-10 faces the prospects (at best) of a flat demand for its crude over the next couple of years and it is probably very clear to Saudi Arabia that they will need support from the non-OPEC group in general and Russia in particular. In the past, Russia has occasionally paid lip service to cooperation with OPEC, but in reality this has generally been less than effective. Either the cutbacks were scheduled anyway for maintenance purposes or they were ignored and replaced by product exports. It is possible that Saudi Arabia sees the need for serious and effective future cooperation on oil policy with Russia, especially with the prospect of Iraqi oil supply being revived.

Of course, it is a serious possibility that the September 2003 meeting and the subsequent agreements were simply a form of diplomatic rhetoric, leading to nothing of substance. At the very least, it might be perceived as a veiled warning from Saudi Arabia to Washington that patience in the Kingdom is wearing thin. The unexpected OPEC production cut in September could be viewed in similar terms. However, as indicated, the prospects for OPEC's defense of oil prices are looking distinctly poor over the next few years and it could be that the oil agreement signed in September 2003 marks the start of a serious and effective joint control of the international oil market by Russia and Saudi Arabia.

Which Countries will be OPEC Members?

A final piece of the puzzle is which countries may actually be in OPEC over the next five to ten years. There is a serious possibility that in the near future, members may well leave the organization as did Ecuador and Gabon. There is also speculation about which countries might join the OPEC grouping in future.

It is worth reliving OPEC history and examining the benefits derived from being in OPEC in the early days. The following elements will help to explain the benefits:

- The unilateral action of oil companies in cutting posted prices and hence the tax revenues of producer governments required a collective response from the major producer governments to prevent further erosion. That such a collective response was essential was clearly shown in the 1960s as realized prices of crude oil continued to fall even when posted prices were effectively frozen. Moreover, posted prices after 1960 were set too low, as for example, in Libya.

- In the 1960s, producers needed collective protection against the "Red Line" mentality of the oil majors in refusing to compete against each other. This was particularly relevant in the various fiscal negotiations that took place during the period, notably over the treatment of royalties.

- In the post-colonial world of the 1960s there was a strong sense of "Third World solidarity" and being an OPEC member also conferred on governments a sense of international importance, which for most OPEC members was the only source of such importance. In a similar vein, it provided domestic political status for governments.

- Finally, and perhaps more cynically, it allowed officials regular trips abroad to pleasant locations in the best traditions of bureaucratic privilege-seeking.

Looking at these arguments today, there is little logic left in being an OPEC member. The benefits cited above are no longer relevant. For better or worse, the spread of globalization has made the concept of "Third World solidarity" redundant. The oil companies now tend to compete far more than they used to in the days of the "Seven Sisters." Thus there is no longer any benefit in negotiating solidarity, since everyone competes now. Finally, domestic political constituents increasingly realize the particular costs attached to OPEC membership. These costs are threefold:

- Being an OPEC member most definitely constrains production through the quota mechanisms.

- Arguably, OPEC membership may constrain IOC investment if there are fears that their capacity might be affected by quotas. Together, these two constraints will and do inhibit revenue flows to the government.

- OPEC membership entails certain costs, ranging from membership dues to the expenses associated with attending OPEC meetings.

The foregoing discussion does not lead us to the conclusion that OPEC does not matter. The history of oil makes it clear that someone must act to constrain the excess capacity that is the industry norm. Without such constraints, the market would be characterized by a series of price wars, which was the case before the oil majors organized themselves in 1928 with the "As Is" agreement. However, being an OPEC member simply involves pain for no obvious gain other than that of the greater good. Free riding as part of the non-OPEC group makes far more sense, albeit from a very selfish perspective. It is therefore extremely unlikely that any new members would join the grouping as it would be supremely illogical for them to do so.

Which countries may or may not leave is a question that is obviously open to debate. Currently there is much debate over what Iraq's position will be. The official line from the oil ministry is that Iraq intends to stay in OPEC. However, if Iraq does stay, it is unlikely that it will feel constrained by its quota. This is simply because the revenue requirements to rebuild Iraq are huge. If production is physically possible, it is inconceivable that Iraq will accept not to produce. While Iraqi exports are still slowly returning to pre-war levels this issue will be less of a problem. The real problem will arise if and when Iraq's undoubted reserve potential begins to be developed by the IOCs. The "need for revenue" argument would still be valid and Iraq has a long history of being a real maverick within OPEC. As long as Iraq is unconstrained by quotas, it will remain an OPEC member. If other OPEC members insist on a quota for Iraq it is very probable that the country will choose to leave the Organization.

As for others, Indonesia will soon be forced to leave by virtue of the fact it is almost an oil importer. According to the *BP Statistical Review of World Energy*, Indonesia produced 1.278 mbpd and consumed 1.072 mbpd in 2002, with its exports being only 0.206 mbpd. In both Venezuela and Nigeria there have been long-standing and powerful lobbies in favor of leaving the organization. Both Algeria and Libya, which are formally requesting higher quotas, could also find that their interests are best served by being outside the organization.

[153]

Conclusions

If members do leave, the implication is that price defense falls on fewer shoulders. Since a smaller OPEC (by definition) means a larger non-OPEC group, the average pain of price defense arises exponentially. Furthermore, the longer OPEC succeeds in defending a relatively high price, as it has done in recent years, the more this problem is compounded as non-OPEC production rises in response to these higher prices. In such a world, OPEC and non-OPEC relations will deteriorate. Certainly, if it faces a serious price collapse as in 1998, the non-OPEC group might provide support in order to try and save the situation. However, a point may be reached when all efforts to avert a collapse end in failure, or to quote the popular children's nursery rhyme: "All the King's horses and all the King's men could not put Humpty together again." After all, the oil price was only revived in 1999 as a result of two fortuitous political events. First, there was the *de facto* accession of Crown Prince Abdullah in Saudi Arabia who was willing to sacrifice the Saudi oil policy stance in return for better relations with Iran. Second, there was the accession of Hugo Chavez as President of Venezuela who was trusted when he promised that his country would cease cheating. Without those autonomous and unconnected events the oil price could conceivably still be around $10 per barrel.

The problem is that there is no obvious solution in sight. The "high volume, low price" strategy aimed at putting the non-OPEC group out of business has been discredited. It failed in 1986 and again in 1998—if the latter was actually part of any strategy.[10] Geopolitics could remedy the situation by taking out producing capacity and allowing others to benefit from their growing capacity. Venezuela and Nigeria remain politically very unstable. Iran underwent potentially destabilizing parliamentary and presidential elections in 2004. Even Saudi Arabia is facing serious challenges following the May 2003 bombings in Riyadh. However, depending on the misfortune of others hardly constitutes a serious strategy.

The other possible hope is that reserve depletion will effectively end the non-OPEC group's capture of market share and that, at the end of a difficult road, the core OPEC producers will somehow gain their reward

[154]

whenever the world is forced to resume using their reserves. However, there are two questions which threaten such a strategy:

- How long will such reserve depletion take and can the core OPEC members survive meanwhile?
- When non-OPEC supply falters, what if global oil demand does too, for the reasons outlined earlier?

On balance, unless the Saudi-Russian détente does have a hidden agenda which will actually come into operation, OPEC and non-OPEC relations are in for a very rough ride in the next few years.

7

New Energy Markets in Asia: Opportunities for the Gulf

Fereidun Fesharaki and Hassaan Vahidy

Asia and the Middle East are the world's most promising energy markets—particularly in the area of oil and gas. Considering the low per capita use of oil and gas in Asia, the region's oil product consumption is poised to grow at an annual rate of over 3% and natural gas consumption is projected to grow at annualized rates exceeding 5% in the years to come. We consider these growth rates to be conservative estimates—the growth rates for oil and gas consumption in Asian countries can be significantly higher given stronger economic growth and improved political stability. Having a low level of energy resources, the region is heavily dependent on the Middle East for its supplies of oil and increasingly, natural gas. Currently the Gulf exports over 60% of its oil to the Asia–Pacific region and Asian countries import 73% of their oil from the Gulf. This supplier–consumer relationship is poised to strengthen as Asia's growing energy need and depleting oil and gas reserves will make the region increasingly reliant on the Gulf for its energy needs.

At the same time Asian energy markets have been undergoing a slow and gradual transformation. Some of the major consumer nations are starting to open up their energy markets—posing both challenges and opportunities for the players in the market. Furthermore, it is important to emphasize that every Asian country is unique in its own way—faced with a special set of conditions and often behaving in an isolated manner. There

[157]

are a number of examples for such behavior particularly in the region's oil markets, and this complicates the energy market situation.

Therefore, there is a need to understand the different drivers for the growth of energy demand and supply in individual Asian markets and to comprehend why the market players behave in a particular manner. In this chapter an attempt is made to analyze the key features of some important Asian energy markets, highlight recent developments and identify various aspects of these markets that Middle Eastern suppliers should take into account while formulating their strategies for the region.

Gulf Oil—Role in the World and Asian Energy Markets

The Middle East – with over half of the world's proven oil reserves – remains the center of gravity in the global oil market, and there is no doubt that its importance as a region is poised to grow. Based on estimates/forecast of 2004, the entire region produced approximately 20.86 million barrels per day (mbpd) of crude and condensate. Of this, approximately 5.56 mbpd was consumed domestically in refineries and direct burning for power generation and consequently, the remaining volumes of 15.29 mbpd approximately were exported. Of these exports, around 60% went to the Asia-Pacific region, followed by 19% to Europe and 15% to North America. The remaining volumes were exported to South and Central America and Africa. Saudi Arabia is by far the region's largest producer and exporter, accounting for approximately 41% of production from the Middle East. It is followed by Iran at 19%, and UAE, Iraq and Kuwait at approximately 10-11% each. Qatar and Oman each account for 4% of total production.

The collective output of Middle Eastern producers can be explained to some extent by the dynamics of oil prices and OPEC quotas. For example, as oil prices rose significantly throughout 2000, OPEC quotas were revised upwards and producers increased production. Middle Eastern producers produced close to 21 mbpd in 2000. Similarly, oil prices declined through most of 2001, and in response to this, OPEC output was cut sharply from the 2000 level. Hence the 2001 output of Middle Eastern producers was lower, as compared to 2000.

[158]

The Middle East supplies oil to virtually the entire world but its biggest customer is the Asia-Pacific region. (Figure 7.1) The Asia-Pacific accounts for over 60% of the crude exported from Middle Eastern countries. Europe and North America each receive exports in the range of 15-20%. The geographic proximity of the two regions, growing Asian deficit and the absence of alternatives for Asian countries, will lead to an even larger share of the eastern sales of Middle East oil.

Figure 7.1
Oil Exports from the Middle East
(including crude and refined products)

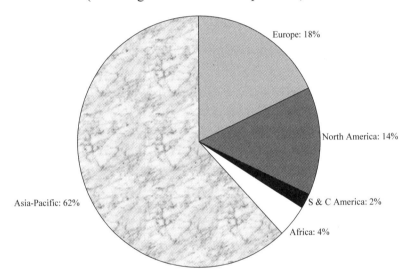

Total Exports in 2002 = 18 million barrels per day

Source: Fesharaki Associates Consulting and Technical Services (FACTS) database and analysis.

This trade pattern has more or less remained unchanged over the last several years. However in the longer run, Asian countries will constitute an even bigger share of Middle Eastern exports. The Middle East, with its massive proven reserves of oil and the lowest production cost in the world will continue to be the key player in the global oil equation. Middle Eastern crude is typically characterized as heavy and sour. Almost three fourths of the volume produced from the region has sulfur >1% and a gravity of <34 degrees API (American Petroleum Institute scale).

Most major producers in the Middle East have embarked on projects to increase production capacity—the most notable of these being Saudi Arabia, UAE (Abu Dhabi) and Kuwait. At the same time, some producers such as Iran and Oman have been struggling to maintain output and Iraq has recently resumed exports although the country's progress in restoring production to prewar levels has been slower than earlier estimates. In the longer run, we expect the region's production capacity to grow from a 2003 year-end estimate of 23.3 mbpd to 28.8 mbpd by 2010. This forecast assumes that Iraq will continue to be an OPEC member and that the organization will continue to function based on its revenue-maximizing strategy.

Gulf and Asia—Interregional Investments in the Oil Sector

Over the last several decades both Asian and Middle Eastern companies have made investments in each other's oil and gas sectors. Some investments date back to late 1950s with Japanese companies starting operations in the Gulf. This was followed by investments by Gulf producers in the Asian downstream oil sector and more recently further Asian investments in upstream interests in the Gulf. The two-way flow of these investments is likely to continue in the future.

Some key Gulf investments in Asian refineries include Saudi shares in the Petron refinery in the Philippines and the S-Oil refinery in South Korea. Similarly, the Abu Dhabi-based International Petroleum Investment Company (IPIC) holds shares in Korea's Hyundai Oil refinery and the Pak-Arab refinery and pipeline in Pakistan. In addition, the Kuwait Petroleum Company (KPC) has retail stations in Thailand under its Q8 brand.

Some other potential investments are Aramco's interest in the Southern Chinese refinery of Fujian. India's downstream sector is opening up and Aramco and KPC have expressed interest in buying the downstream company Hindustan Petroleum Corporation Limited (HPCL) which will give them access to the Indian retail market. Furthermore, KPC is also one of the bidders for a controlling share in Pakistan State Oil (PSO)—the oil marketing company.

Currently the national oil and gas companies of Japan, China, India, Malaysia and South Korea are involved in several upstream projects in the

Gulf. Some of the Asian investments in the Gulf's upstream oil are stemming from the notion that holding equity in overseas oil fields provides supply security. It may have psychological benefits but it does not provide real security. Such examples include the Chinese and Indian investments. However, some others, notably Petronas are seeking investments purely on economic terms.

Petronas opened up offices in Iran, Dubai and Bahrain to oversee the group's operations in the region. The company operates two blocks, located in southeastern offshore Bahrain, under an exploration and production sharing agreement (EPSA). Petronas has been operating in Iran since the late 1990s. It owns interests in the Sirri A and E offshore fields, an interest in the South Pars Gas Development project, Phases 2 & 3 and an interest in the Munir Block. Petronas is also involved in the exploration of two blocks in Yemen. Besides these interests, the company is also considering upstream prospects in Iraq.

India's state-owned upstream company—the Oil and Natural Gas Corporation (ONGC) is aggressively seeking out overseas investments in the upstream sector. In the Gulf, the company's overseas arm—ONGC Videsh is exploring interests in Iran and Iraq. Moreover, the two Indian state oil companies: ONGC and Indian Oil Corporation (IOC) are members of one of the three consortia approved to bid for projects in Kuwait's upstream sector.

Chinese companies have been pursuing interests in the upstream sectors of Iran and Iraq. Chinese National Petroleum Corporation (CNPC) and PetroChina are involved in exploration and development activities in Oman. Sinopec and China National Offshore Oil Corporation (CNOOC) are looking for opportunities in Iran while Sinopec is a member of a consortium that has been approved to bid in Kuwait's upstream sector. China International Trust and Investment Corporation (CITIC), the oldest state non-energy company, has teamed up with Hong Kong-based Sunwing Energy (a subsidiary of Canada's Ivanhoe Energy) to explore for opportunities. There are now six Chinese upstream companies, all government-owned, which are scouting the Middle East for acreage.

Japan has had a long-standing involvement in the region's energy sector. Japan Oil Development Company (JODCO), a subsidiary of the

Japan National Oil Company (JNOC), holds a 12% share in ADMA–OPCO (Abu Dhabi Marine Operating Company). It was established in the late 1970s and is involved in the development of Umm Shaif and Lower Zakum fields and exploration in the ADMA concession. JODCO also holds a 49% share in ZADCO (Zakum Development Company), where the company is involved in production from the Upper Zakum, Umm Al-Dalkh and Satah fields.

JNOC holds majority shares in JAPEX (Japan Petroleum Exploration Company) and INPEX (formerly Indonesia Petroleum Ltd.) both of which are involved in exploring various options for the Azadegan field in Iran.

Japan's Arabian Oil Company (AOC) has also had long standing operations in the Saudi-Kuwaiti Neutral Zone. AOC's concession agreement with Saudi Arabia expired in 2000 and the concession with Kuwait expired earlier this year. Since then, the company has entered into new agreements with Kuwait Gulf Oil Company (KGOC)—a subsidiary of Kuwait Petroleum Corporation (KPC). This involves agreements on provision of technical services and facilities by AOC, and agreement from KPC on minimum volumes of sales to AOC.

Similarly, the Korea Gas Corporation (KOGAS) has participated in several gas exploration prospects in Oman and Qatar. Besides this, Thailand's PTT Exploration and Production Public Company Ltd. (PTTEP) is also looking for investment opportunities in the region's upstream sector.

Recent Trends in Asian Oil Product Consumption

Through most of the last decade Asian oil consumption was growing in excess of 5% per year. This trend has slowed down substantially since the Asian financial crises of 1997–1998 (See Figure 7.2).

After shrinking by over a quarter of a million barrels per day in 1998, the Asian market bounced back, growing by almost 1.5 mbpd over the subsequent two years. This however was not a sustainable recovery as the region's total growth for consumption of oil products was fairly marginal over 2001 and 2002. We estimate that the growth in oil products consumption will be substantially better—at 556 thousand barrels per day (kbpd). The notable improvement comes from Japan but not because of any upturn in the country's economy. Instead, it resulted from the shutdown of the country's nuclear power capacity, which led to increased oil consumption for generating electricity (See Table 7.1).

Figure 7.2
Asia-Pacific Product Demand (1970–2015)

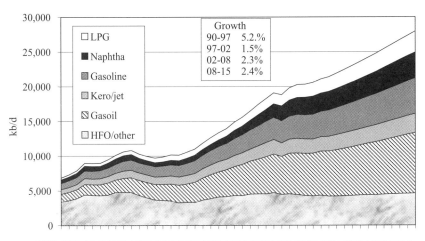

1970 1973 1976 1979 1982 1985 1988 1991 1994 1997 2000 2003 2006 2009 2012 2015

Source: Fesharaki Associates Consulting and Technical Services (FACTS) database and analysis.

Taking a closer look at developments in 2003, the first three quarters were turbulent—with the Iraqi conflict, SARS, and the nuclear crisis in Japan. As might be expected given this chain of events, Asia's petroleum product consumption was also erratic. Among the major consumers, China continued to post spectacular growth, but in India and South Korea growth was relatively subdued, as high prices seemed to be taking a toll on demand. Japan posted a temporary increase in consumption. Overall, Asia-Pacific petroleum product consumption was projected to increase by 2.7%, or 556 kbpd in 2003, a less robust growth than in the early to mid-1990s, but certainly an improvement over 2001 and 2002.

[163]

Table 7.1
Asian Oil Demand Growth, Selected Nations (kbpd)

	1998	1999	2000	2001	2002	2003*
China	87	343	320	111	168	272
India	112	154	28	3	3	15
Japan	-206	84	-40	-209	-90	87
S. Korea	-246	130	55	3	54	29
Thailand	-43	44	-5	-12	37	35
Indonesia	-57	55	73	45	26	53
Others	91	184	35	108	34	64
Total	**-262**	**994**	**466**	**49**	**232**	**555**

Note: * Projected.

Source: Fesharaki Associates Consulting and Technical Services (FACTS) database and analysis.

Our projection was that consumption would grow by 334 kbpd in 2004. This drop-off was largely due to China and Japan. China's growth was projected to slow a bit, to approximately 195 kbpd. At the same time, Japan's consumption was expected to decline by approximately 97 kbpd in 2004. This is because Japan's 2003 consumption received a one-time boost from the nuclear crisis and 2004 would therefore suffer in comparison. Over the long term, we expect regional consumption to grow by approximately 2.5% or 500-700 kbpd, on average. If Japan – a large but stagnant market – is excluded, consumption is projected to rise by over 3.0%.

Turning to the long-term growth prospects of individual products, gasoil will lead overall demand growth over the period 2002–2015, growing by approximately 200 kbpd, on average. As vehicle ownership continues to rise rapidly, gasoline consumption is projected to grow by 2.8%. Growth in the consumption of LPG and naphtha should slow down from the spectacular increases of 1990–2002 but would still average in the range of 2.6–3.7%, or just below 100 kbpd annually. Overall, growth in kerosene/jet fuel consumption is projected to be somewhat slower than other products as residential and commercial use of kerosene will stagnate. After a SARS-related slowdown in the consumption of jet fuel in 2003, demand should

[164]

continue to increase at a healthy rate (approximately 4.0%) through 2015. In contrast to other regions, consumption of fuel oil is projected to increase, albeit very slowly, spurred by Asia's rapid economic growth.

Other forms of energy have steadily taken the place of oil in sectors such as power and industry but in the transport sector petroleum products still reign supreme. Moreover, with Asia–Pacific car ownership growing at breakneck pace, transport fuels are poised for robust growth. In China, the number of cars has been growing by about 20% per year, and the potential growth is almost unlimited—there are only about 25 vehicles per 1,000 people in China, versus approximately 750 per 1,000 in North America. If present patterns persist, China's car ownership would exceed that of the US by 2030. India, the other Asian population giant, is also on a rapid growth path, with vehicle ownership increasing by approximately 7% per year for the foreseeable future.

Overall, we project that the regional consumption of transport fuels will grow by 3–4%. For some countries, such as China, growth will be in the range of 4–6%. With relatively rapid growth and quickly changing specifications, transport fuels are certainly an area to watch in the future.

Recent Trends in Middle Eastern Oil Product Consumption

With a huge hydrocarbon resource and a relatively small population, the Middle East has not been considered a major oil market in its own right, but rather an exporter, with crude oil being the main export commodity. The region often operates as a swing producer and is continually growing and evolving. In reality, demand growth rates in the Middle East – though volatile in the short term – have outpaced even that of Asia in the longer term, despite the Asian demand boom. Moreover, viewed in the broader context of the past thirty years, Middle Eastern crude distillation capacity has expanded more quickly than that of Asia, despite the attention given to the Asian refinery buildup (and the current overcapacity).

The comparison between Asian and Middle Eastern consumption growth is particularly notable in recent years. A considerable slowdown has been experienced in the growth of Asian oil products consumption. At the same time, the domestic market for oil products in the Middle East countries has continued to grow at around 5% per year. There are two primary reasons that may be noted:

- Relatively higher crude oil prices in the international market translate into higher income for the producer nations and not necessarily higher price—as oil prices in most of the Middle Eastern countries remain regulated. Therefore the combined effect of higher income and somewhat fixed domestic prices creates an environment for increased consumption.
- Over the last few years there has been considerable growth in the region's petrochemical capacity, which has spurred growth in LPG and naphtha.

Our outlook anticipates continued demand growth, with a shift away from middle distillates and fuel oil toward gasoline, naphtha and LPG. Growth in gas processing and the petrochemical sector, in fact, will create double-digit demand growth for LPG and naphtha through 2010. The near-term outlook for jet fuel demand will remain weak, as travel is constrained, but we expect recovery in the post-2005 period. The long-term trend in Middle Eastern oil product demand is illustrated in Figure 7.3.

The Middle Eastern gasoline market has been unusually dynamic, with short-term perturbations creating a need for imports even in traditional exporting and net-exporting countries such as Saudi Arabia and Kuwait. Recently, gasoline imports have moved to Kuwait, Saudi Arabia, Iraq, Oman, UAE, Yemen, and most notably, Iran. Iranian gasoline imports were generally under 25 kbpd prior to 2000, yet demand continued to grow strongly, and growth in production capability fell steadily behind growth in demand. In 2000, gasoline imports topped 30 kbpd, rising to 47 kbpd in 2001 and 79 kbpd in 2002. The 2003 imports were expected to average 85 kbpd, and imports were forecasted to exceed 150 kbpd in 2005. In fact, Iran alone this year has transformed the region into a slight net importer of gasoline. Moreover, despite a major refinery expansion program that will leave no refinery in the country untouched, gasoline imports will persist while exports of other products will grow. Fuel oil exports in particular will remain a feature of the market, and perhaps a troublesome one.

Figure 7.3
Strong Growth in Middle Eastern Demand

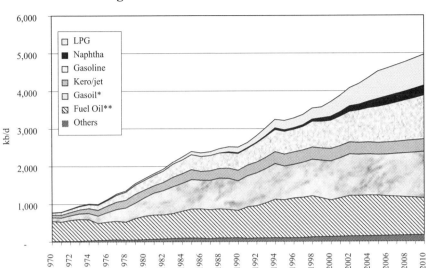

Notes: *includes bunkering
    ** includes bunkering and DU crude

Source: Fesharaki Associates Consulting and Technical Services (FACTS) database and analysis.

The Middle East as a whole may have to contend with fuel oil surpluses, as demand growth in some countries will be offset by demand declines in others. While gasoline demand is expected to grow at rates of 4–5% between 2003 and 2010, fuel oil demand in contrast will stagnate and then decline. When combined with the strong growth in demand for naphtha and LPG, it can be seen that the Middle Eastern demand is steadily being shifted toward the lighter end of the barrel and away from the heavy end. Even middle distillates, long the region's workhorse fuels, are declining in share. As Figure 7.4 illustrates, in 1980, just 18% of demand was for light products, compared with 41% apiece for middle distillates and heavy products. The share of light products has now more than doubled and accounts for 37% of demand, while middle distillates account for 34% and the remaining 29% is taken by heavy products. By 2010, we forecast that the share of heavy products will continue to slide down to 23%, while that of light products will rise to 45%, and the share of middle distillates will level off at 31%.

[167]

Figure 7.4
Middle East Demand Shifts to Lighter Barrel (1980–2010)

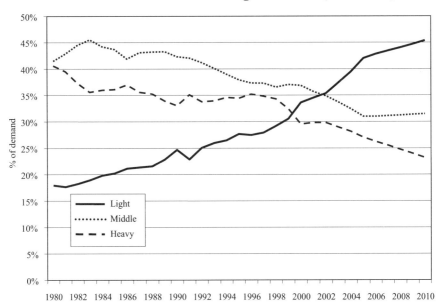

Source: Fesharaki Associates Consulting and Technical Services (FACTS) database and analysis.

Asian Crude Oil Balance: Rising Dependence on Gulf Oil

With a rather flat production profile and growing consumption, Asia relies heavily on imported oil. With production just below 8 mbpd, the region imports some 13.3 mbpd of oil to fulfill its needs. Projections indicate that over the next ten to fifteen years, oil production growth in Asia is likely to be sluggish. In the meantime, petroleum product demand in Asia will continue to grow at around 2.5% per year.

These opposite movements in regional crude oil production and petroleum demand growth results in the general rise of oil import dependence in the region, especially after 2005. In 2001, the import dependence of the Asia–Pacific region was 62 percent. It is projected to increase to 65 percent in 2005 and 70 percent by 2010, which is equivalent to a net oil import requirement of 17.7 mbpd, up from 12.9 mbpd in 2001 (See Figure 7.5).

[168]

Figure 7.5
Asia-Pacific Oil Production and Net Import Requirements (1999–2010)

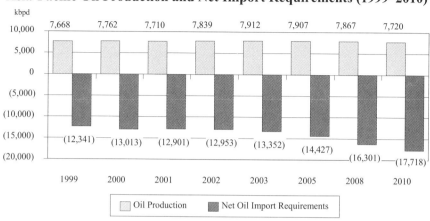

Note: Oil production = crude output plus nonrefinery LPG.

Source: Fesharaki Associates Consulting and Technical Services (FACTS) database and analysis.

These forecasts mean that oil supplied from within the region is likely to account for less than 30 percent of the region's oil consumption in the Asia–Pacific in 2010 and beyond.

Asian countries fulfill almost three-fourths of their import requirements by buying Middle Eastern crude. Approximately 15% of the imports are from within the region and 8% of the oil is imported from the Atlantic Basin (West Africa and Europe).

Crudes produced in Asia fall into two broad categories: heavy sweet and light sweet. With the exception of a few streams, all Asian crudes are sweet, with low sulfur content. Light sweet crudes are produced mainly in Australia, Indonesia, Malaysia, Thailand, India, Pakistan, Brunei, Papua New Guinea, and some other smaller countries. Indonesia, India, and Brunei also produce heavy sweet crudes, as do China, Vietnam and other countries. Asian crude production is dominated by heavy sweet crudes, the share of which is expected to increase further over the coming years.

The Asia–Pacific region's crude production (including lease condensate but excluding other natural gas liquids) had been expected to reach over 7.5 mbpd in 2002, higher than the production of 7.4 mbpd in 2001, thanks to higher oil production in China and to a lesser extent, India and Vietnam. In the meantime, production in Indonesia and Australia is declining.

[169]

Figure 7.6
Asian Imports of Crude Oil

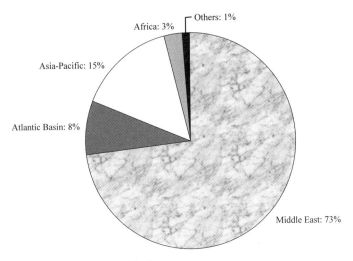

Notes: Based on 2002 data for 10 biggest Asian importers
        Total imports = 12.6 mbpd
        Atlantic Basin = West Africa + Europe

Source: Fesharaki Associates Consulting and Technical Services (FACTS) database and analysis.

China, Indonesia, Malaysia, India and Australia are the largest oil producers in Asia. These "Big Five" countries are estimated to have accounted for 89 percent of the total regional crude production in 2002. Their dominance is likely to continue in the near future.

China's crude output increased by 1.7 percent in 2001 and was estimated to rise by 3.1 percent to reach 3.4 mbpd in 2002, owing to higher offshore oil production. In the long run, China's crude production from offshore fields and the west and northwest is likely to increase while production from the aging fields in the east will decline. Overall, under our base-case scenario, the country's production is projected to increase continuously at a moderate rate.

Indonesia's crude oil production, which declined in 2001, dipped lower in 2002 and was estimated to decline further in 2003. New contracts and actual investment under the existing contracts are slow to materialize. As such, it is expected that Indonesia's crude production will decline in the long run under the base-case scenario. Although new finds are possible they may not be enough to compensate for the natural decline of existing fields.

For the second year in a row, crude and condensate production in Malaysia increased in 2002. While Tapis is reaching its peak level, additional smaller streams will be coming online, maintaining the production level at well above 700 kbpd through 2005. Unless new oil fields are discovered and developed, oil production in Malaysia is expected to decline after 2005.

India's production is stable, although growth will remain sluggish. The offshore Bombay High is the largest producing field in India, accounting for over half of the country's total oil production. Other crude streams are located in the states of Assam and Gujarat. India's entire crude production is geared for the domestic market. This production is well below the level demanded by the country's refineries, thereby necessitating large crude imports. During the coming decade, unless India adopts a more open foreign investment policy in the upstream oil and gas sector, a significant increase in oil production would be unlikely.

Australia's crude/condensate production declined notably in 2001, a trend which continued in 2002. Barring a substantial increase in upstream exploration activities, Australian production is likely to decrease in the long term under our base-case scenario.

Looking at the next five to ten years, for the Asia–Pacific as a whole, regional crude oil production is expected to be flat through 2005 and slowly decline thereafter under our base-case scenario, owing to the production decrease in Australia, Indonesia and Malaysia. Projections of the base-case scenario are based on known fields with ongoing and planned development activities. If new discoveries are taken into consideration, the regional crude oil production could be higher.

Moderate growth in China, Thailand, Vietnam, Brunei and Malaysia is counter-balanced by declines in Australia, Indonesia, India and other countries. Consequently, regional production was estimated to be 7.5 mbpd in 2003, roughly the same as in 2002. For the first time, the regional output is forecasted to rise slightly through 2008. Even by 2010, production is expected to be higher than the level prevailing in 2002. China is a major contributor to the growth, followed by Vietnam and Thailand, while Indonesia and Malaysia continue efforts to increase their production levels. Once again, the trend of regional oil production can be best described as flat and stagnated over the forecast horizon (through 2010).

The Asia–Pacific region's crude exports, which are mainly intra-regional, remain flat at 2.1 mbpd for 2001 and 2002. Little change was expected for total exports in 2003 and 2004. The region's exports are forecasted to maintain levels of above 2 mbpd through 2007 and are likely to decline thereafter. For individual countries, China, Indonesia and Australia all exported smaller volumes in 2002 as compared to 2001, while exports increased in 2002 for Vietnam, Thailand, Malaysia and some other countries. By 2010, all major producing countries are expected to export less unless there is a significant breakthrough in the upstream exploration and production (E&P) in Asia.

To determine the region's oil import dependence, we define total oil demand in Asia as refinery runs plus direct burning of crude plus net refined product imports (excluding non-refinery LPG). We define total oil production as crude/condensate output plus non-refinery LPG. The difference between these two represents the net imports for the region. During 2002, Asia's crude run was down by 66 kbpd and the direct use of crude oil was flat. There were wide variations in individual countries: China increased its crude run by 186 kbpd in 2002, India by 70 kbpd, Taiwan by 28 kbpd and Pakistan by 18 kbpd. Incidentally, China, India and Taiwan are the three countries that had the most refining capacity additions in recent years. Excluding the four countries mentioned above, crude runs were down by as much as 368 kbpd in the rest of Asia, with South Korea being down by nearly 200 kbpd, Japan by 123 kbpd, and Singapore by 40 kbpd. These developments, coupled with flat net refined product imports (excluding non-refinery LPG), led to a slight decline in overall oil demand in 2002.

The region's crude runs were projected to increase by as much as 650 kbpd in 2003, of which about 250 kbpd was expected to be from China, 130 kbpd from India, 115 kbpd from Singapore, 100 kbpd from Taiwan, and 53 kbpd from Japan. In the meantime, the direct use of crude oil was also forecasted to be higher in 2003, owing to increased burning in Japan (nuclear power shutdown) and China (power shortage), but net product imports (excluding non-refinery LPG) are likely to be flat again. These changes were considered likely to result in significantly higher oil demand for Asia in 2003.

On the supply side, total oil production was higher in 2002 because of increased crude/condensate output as well as marginally higher non-refinery LPG output. For 2003, the oil production was expected to be flat. As a result, the net oil imports for the region as a whole were slightly lower in 2002 but expected to be notably higher in 2003. Over the coming years, while oil production remains flat, oil demand in the region is likely to rise continuously, leading to higher oil import dependence, which is expected to reach 64% in 2005 and 67% in 2010.

The Middle East's crude oil exports to Asia are rising steadily. However, its share in the region's total crude oil imports has been stable lately (2000-2005). Through our forecast horizon (2010), the role of the Middle East as Asia's dominant oil supplier is irreplaceable. Nevertheless, if Russia ends up completing its crude pipelines to China (through Daqing) or the rest of Asia (through Nakhodka), it will have an impact on the volume of Middle Eastern crude exports to the Far East.

The Atlantic Basin crudes play a supplementary but unique and important role in Asia's oil supply. Nearly non-existent before 1995, Asian imports of Atlantic Basin crudes have turned into a regular flow, reaching above 1 mbpd in recent years. The need for Asian import of crudes from the Atlantic Basin stem from four main reasons:

- To improve product specifications to meet tightening environmental standards. This need applies particularly to Taiwan but also to Japan and India.
- To run any low-sulfur crudes for countries such as China and also Indonesia.
- The region's overall need for more crude intakes as crude runs are rising and regional production is flat.
- The arbitrage requirements necessary to improve refining margins when Dubai-based crude prices are too high, as reflected in the Dubai–Brent price differentials.

The Atlantic Basin crudes are attractive if the differential is low, while its market in Asia can be squeezed if the differential is high because of the disadvantage of long-distance shipping. However, since there are needs other than price arbitrage, the Atlantic Basin crude exports are likely to continue in the foreseeable future regardless of the Dubai-Brent differential.

[173]

Figure 7.7

Major Importers of Atlantic Basin Crudes in the Asia–Pacific Region

(2002 Estimate: 1,007 kbpd)

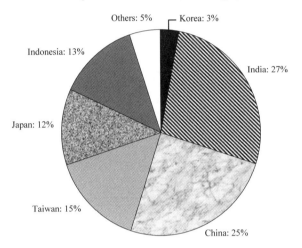

Notes: Atlantic Basin = West Africa + Europe.
         Estimate based on January-November 2002 data

Source: Fesharaki Associates Consulting and Technical Services (FACTS) database and analysis.

Apart from the Atlantic Basin crudes there are other non-Middle Eastern crudes such as those from Russia, Central Asia and Latin America. While the controversial Russian crude pipelines to Asia may continue to be delayed, the ultimate completion of one or two lines from Russia to China or the rest of Asia will raise the volume of non-Middle East oil supply to Asia significantly.

Developments in Asian and Middle Eastern Downstream Oil Sectors

In the Middle East, the Gulf countries in general are refraining from the addition of refining capacity but Iran remains a notable exception. The projected additions in refining capacity through the end of this decade are shown in Figure 7.8. In Qatar, the additions include the grass roots condensate splitter coming up at Ras Laffan. In the UAE, additional capacity is intended to ease the bottleneck situation at the condensate splitter of the Abu Dhabi National Oil Company (ADNOC). In Iraq we anticipate that by

[174]

2008 some of the existing refining capacity will be rehabilitated, allowing increased crude runs. Iran is the site of some major additions in refining capacity. The country has the potential to add some 750 kbpd of refining capacity by the end of this decade, with Abadan, Tehran and Tabriz being the planned locations for most of these additions. Moreover, there are plans to add some 250 kbpd of condensate splitting capacity at Assaluyeh—in time to receive the condensate from the South Pars field.

Figure 7.8
Middle East Crude Distillation Unit (CDU) Additions

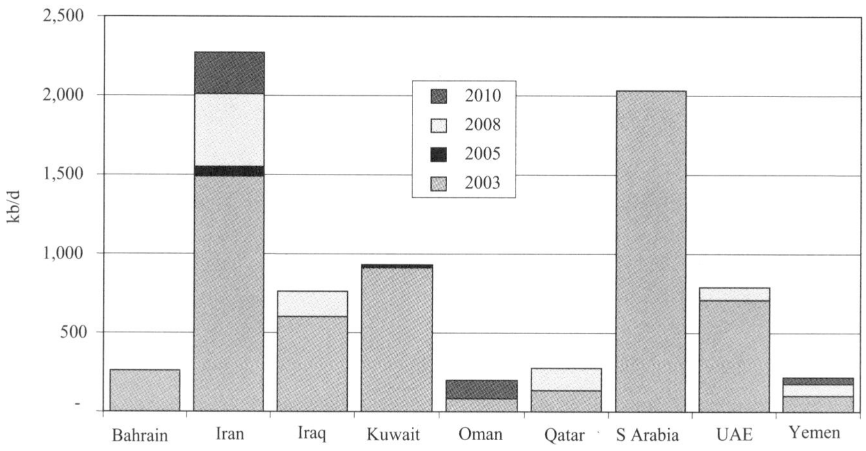

Source: Fesharaki Associates Consulting and Technical Services (FACTS) database and analysis.

To deal with impending declines in fuel oil demand both at home and in key export markets, Middle Eastern refiners are planning a number of cracking projects between now and 2010. As Figure 7.9 illustrates, every refining country in the region is planning to add cracking/coking capacity between 2003 and 2010, in order to increase the production of lighter oils. Of these, major expansions are scheduled in Iran and Saudi Arabia.

On the fuel quality side, many of the expansions and upgrades being planned are geared towards producing higher quality transport fuels to meet US and European standards, which are spreading to other markets as well. Domestic fuel quality is also being improved and goals remain for continued improvement. For example, a number of projects are planned to

[175]

hasten the phasing out of leaded gasoline and to reduce diesel sulfur levels. Kuwait is continuing to rebuild damaged units and adding even more middle distillate hydro-treating capacity at Mina Abdullah. Iran has announced a very aggressive campaign to tighten specifications, with the goal being 50 parts per million (ppm) sulfur diesel throughout the country, though achieving this stringent level will take some time—since the budget for the necessary enhancements has not yet been approved. Bahrain is adding a distillate hydro-treater plus a hydro-cracker that will cut diesel sulfur to ultra low levels. Saudi Arabia is making quality-related investments at Yanbu, Rabigh and Riyadh. With the demand shift in Asia and the overcapacity situation, Middle East refiners recognize that improving fuel quality is not only desirable for local markets but is also the key to flexibility in penetrating export markets.

Figure 7.9
Increase in Middle East Cracking/Coking Capacities (2003–2010)

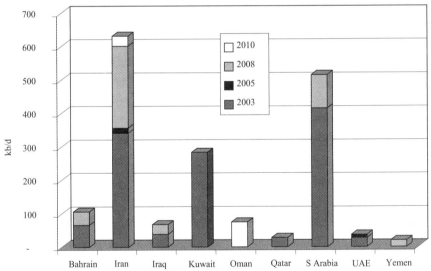

Source: Fesharaki Associates Consulting and Technical Services (FACTS) database and analysis.

Figure 7.10 summarizes some of the quality-related expansion plans in the region. Immediately apparent is the strong focus on middle distillate quality. By 2008, middle distillate hydro-desulfurization (MDHDS) capacity will approach 1.5 mbpd, compared to its current level of 0.85 mbpd. Gasoline-related projects include catalytic reforming (cat reform) isomerization and alkylation but as the figure below illustrates, these expansions are moderate in comparison. Additionally, gasoline demand is growing rapidly in the region, and most sub-markets are moving to unleaded gasolines, so the additions to gasoline production capability are geared more toward domestic markets than export markets. There is at present little emphasis on producing European and US-specification reformulated gasolines for export.

Figure 7.10
Quality-Related Refinery Expansion Plans

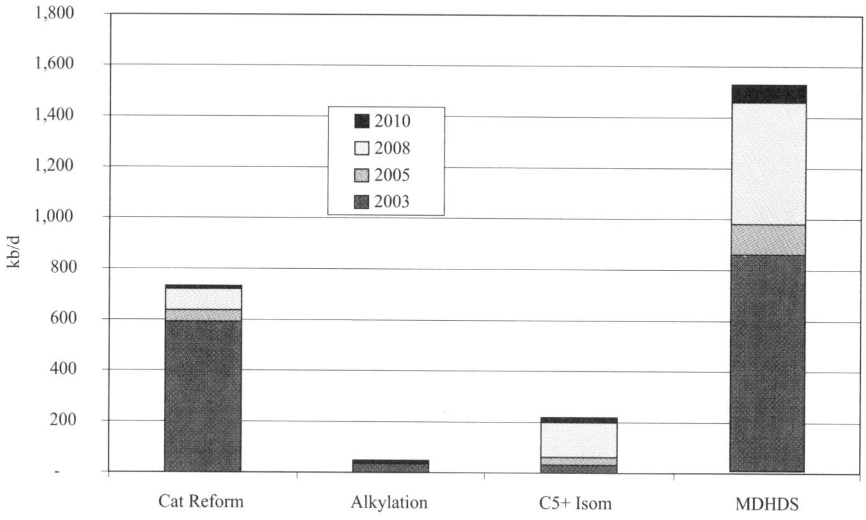

Source: Fesharaki Associates Consulting and Technical Services (FACTS) database and analysis.

On the other side of the equation, in the Asia–Pacific region, some significant additions in refining capacity are expected. The most notable will be from India, where a grassroots plant and some expansions are under way and are likely to materialize by the end of 2005—adding some 600 kbpd in refining capacity over the current level. Furthermore, expansions totaling some 600 kbpd will firm up in Chinese refineries. However, there will be closures or consolidations of approximately 300 kbpd at the same time—yielding net additions of some 300 kbpd. Simultaneously, there will

[177]

most likely be closures and mothballing of capacity from Japan, Australia, Philippines and possibly Singapore.

On the whole, Asia will continue to add some 1 mbpd of refining capacity through the end of 2005. The overall position is presented in Figure 7.11 below.

Figure 7.11
The Outlook for Asian Refining Capacity (kbpd)

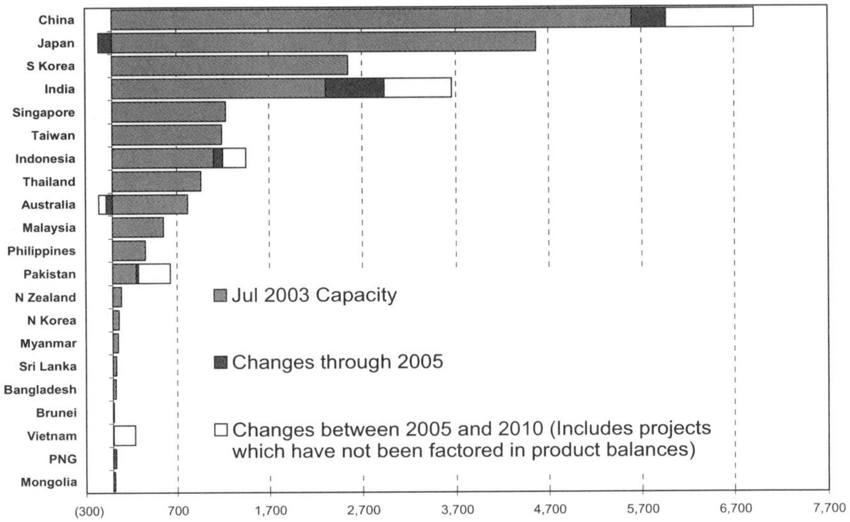

Source: Fesharaki Associates Consulting and Technical Services (FACTS) database and analysis.

Focus on Chinese and Indian Oil Markets

China and India are the two emerging markets in Asia. These are among the countries with the lowest per capita consumption levels in the world and have registered healthy economic growth in recent years. Both these markets are therefore considered to have substantial potential in terms of future oil products consumption.

China's oil product consumption grew at about 8% per year through most of the 1990s. Growth was experienced virtually across the barrel with the exception of fuel oil. In the future we foresee growth rates of the order of 3.5-4% per year. Naphtha appears to be the future fuel of choice for China's growing petrochemical sector. For this reason, our outlook for naphtha demand over the next fifteen years is bullish. The projected demand for transportation fuels, including gasoline, automobile diesel and jet fuel is also strong. In spite of the anticipated entry of natural gas into coastal cities in Guangdong, Fujian, and the Lower Yangtze region, the demand for LPG continues to grow in many other cities and areas. Fuel oil is one of the few products that have limited potential for growth, because of continuous efforts by the government to restrict the use of fuel oil for power generation. On an overall basis, the country's petroleum product demand is forecast to grow by an average of 3.4 percent per annum between 2002 and 2005 (See Figure 7.12).

Figure 7.12
China Product Demand (1970-2015)

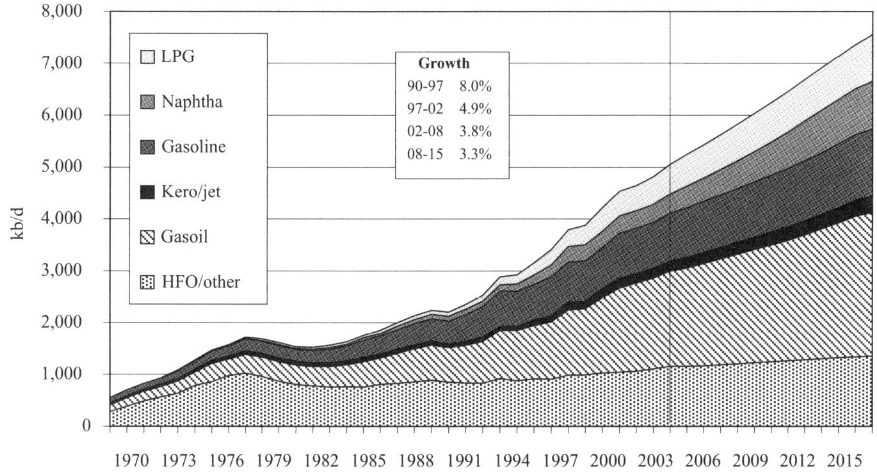

Source: Fesharaki Associates Consulting and Technical Services (FACTS) database and analysis.

With only nominal increases in the country's production, the long run outlook for the country is that it will become an even bigger net importer of oil (crude and petroleum products combined)—approximately 3.2 mbpd of imports by the end of this decade, and 4.1 mbpd by 2015 (Figure 7.13).

The 160 kbpd Fujian project (a joint venture between Sinopec, Exxon Mobil, and Saudi Aramco) is expected to be on stream by early 2006. The refinery is being designed to run 100% Saudi crude.

[179]

Figure 7.13
China Crude Production and Net Oil Import Requirements
(1990-2015)

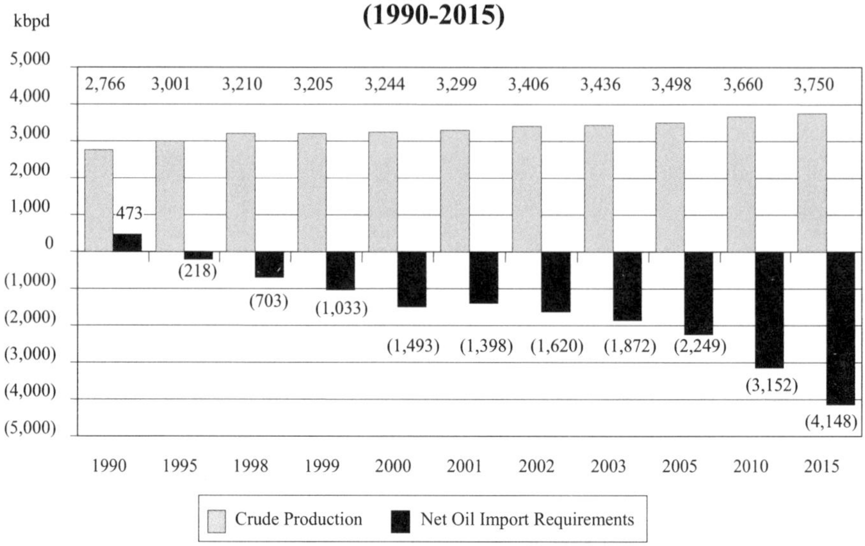

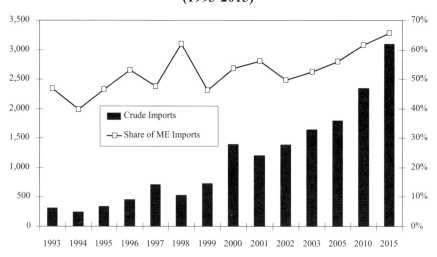

Source: Fesharaki Associates Consulting and Technical Services (FACTS) database and analysis.

Figure 7.14
China Crude Imports and Share of Middle East Imports
(1993-2015)

Source: Fesharaki Associates Consulting and Technical Services (FACTS) database and analysis.

Over the last 5 years or so, the increases in China's refining capacity have resulted in high crude runs and hence higher crude imports. Most products from the domestic refineries are absorbed in the Chinese market—gasoline being an exception. Among the individual products, there are some very notable shifts in the trade patterns. In 1995 China imported over 100 kbpd of diesel and exported under 50 kbpd of gasoline. The policy of maximizing middle distillate output over the years has resulted in elimination of diesel imports, created massive surplus of over 150 kbpd of gasoline, and a huge deficit of fuel oil with imports exceeding 350 kbpd. The overall trend of the crude and product trade balance is presented in Figure 7.15.

Figure 7.15
China's Oil Exports and Imports (1980-2002)

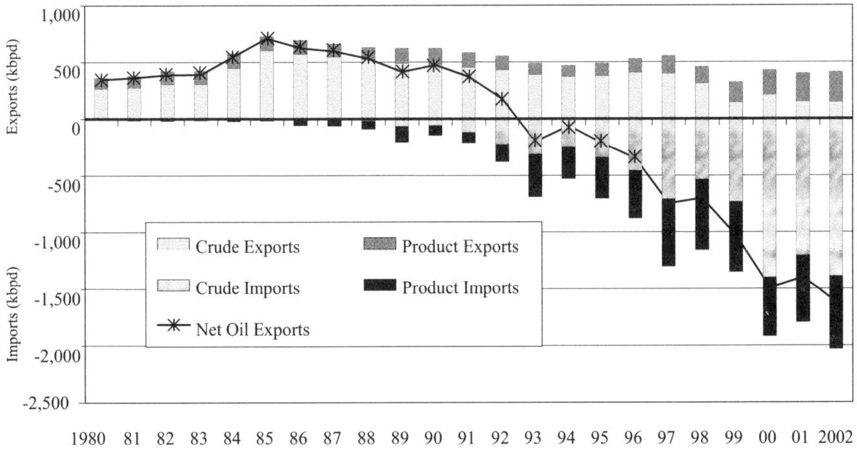

Source: Fesharaki Associates Consulting and Technical Services (FACTS) database and analysis.

India's oil consumption, during the last decade grew at close to 7% per year. The country apparently remained shielded by the effect of the Asian financial crisis. However, the country experienced a substantial slowdown in the growth of oil product consumption starting in 2001. From 2000 to 2003, Indian annual incremental growth has indeed been unimpressive. This has been quite surprising as the economy continues to expand. The slowdown in the consumption of oil products can be broadly pinned down by the following factors:

[181]

- A relatively larger share of economic growth has come from the non-manufacturing sector, which is less energy intensive.
- From April 2002, Indian consumer prices for oil products have been allowed to move with international prices thus exposing consumers to price movements in the international market.
- It is estimated that approximately 20-30 kbpd of diesel consumption has been cut back due to the substitution of diesel by compressed natural gas (CNG) in public transport vehicles in two major cities.
- Moreover, since 2000 several power plants using naphtha have moved away from using the fuel and shifted to natural gas.

We foresee a gradual recovery in oil consumption growth starting in 2005. In the long run it is estimated that the country's oil product demand will grow in the range of 3–3.5% per year. This growth will mainly be driven by road transportation fuels and liquefied petroleum gas (LPG), which is used as cooking gas in households.

Figure 7.16
Product Demand in India (1970-2015)

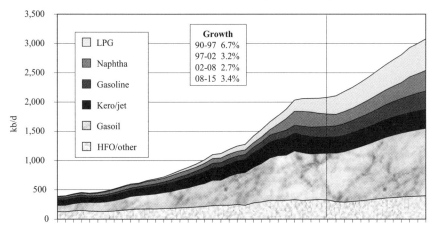

Source: Fesharaki Associates Consulting and Technical Services (FACTS) database and analysis.

One of the most dramatic developments in India and perhaps in Asia's downstream sector has been growth in the region and the country's own refining capacity. Between the years 1999 and 2001 the country's refining

[182]

capacity grew almost by 100%. This combined with the slowdown in the country's oil consumption growth had a tremendous impact on India's oil products trade and a significant impact on the regional product balance. India, once importing some 250 kbpd of diesel, turned into a major exporter of the fuel—exporting some 100 kbpd of diesel in 2003.

Figure 7.17
India's Refining Capacity and Product Balance:
Net Imports/(Net-Exports)

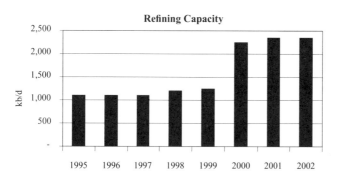

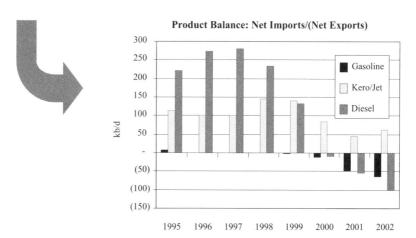

Source: Fesharaki Associates Consulting and Technical Services (FACTS) database and analysis.

Indian refiners have imported oil from all the major Gulf producers. India is also a significant consumer of Iraqi oil. Currently Indian refiners hold the largest volume of term contracts for the Basra grade in Asia.

[183]

Figure 7.18
India's Crude Imports from the Middle East

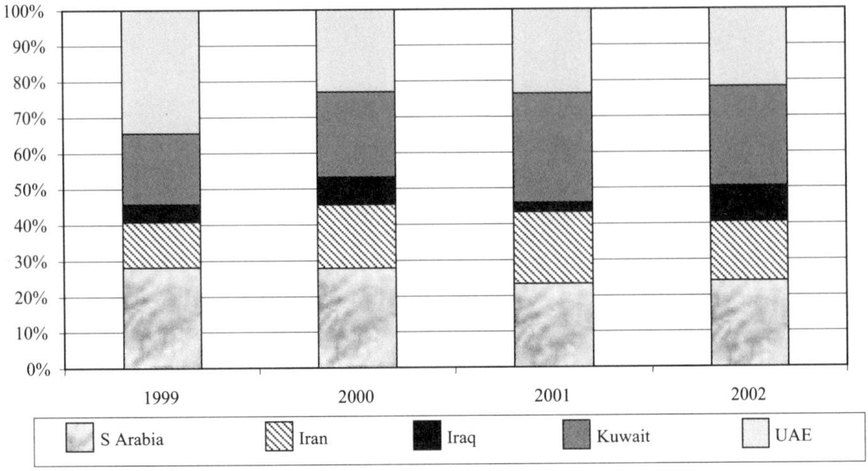

Note: Excludes approximately 0.6 mbpd of Reliance imports

Source: Fesharaki Associates Consulting and Technical Services (FACTS) database and analysis.

With a stagnant level of domestic production of oil, the country has to rely on increasing volumes of imported oil. This trend is likely to continue as the country is embarking on further refining additions. We project that by 2008 India will need to import over 2 mbpd of crude with most of this volume coming from the Gulf producers.

Figure 7.19
India's Crude Balance

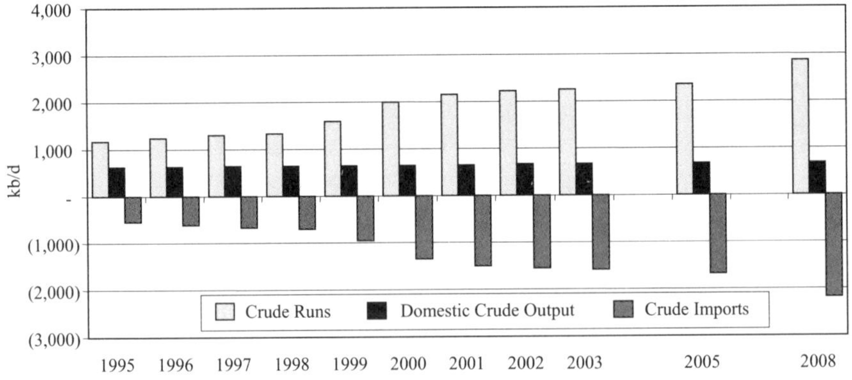

Source: Fesharaki Associates Consulting and Technical Services (FACTS) database and analysis.

[184]

ME and AP Balances: Implications for Refining Profitability

The Asia–Pacific (AP) region added more than 2 mbpd in refining capacity between 1998 and 2000. This combined with the relatively slower pace of Asian oil products growth in the same period had a tremendous impact on the regional oil product balance (Figure 7.20).

Figure 7.20
Increases in Asian Refining Capacity and its Impact
on Regional Product Balance: Net Imports/(Net Exports)

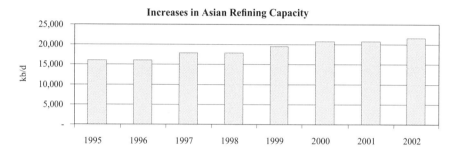

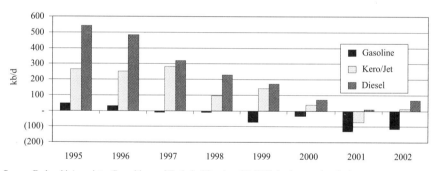

Source: Fesharaki Associates Consulting and Technical Services (FACTS) database and analysis.

As shown above, in 1995, Asia was a net importer of over 500 kbpd of diesel but by the beginning of this decade the net imports of diesel had reduced to almost zero and the region became net exporter of kerosene/jet fuel and gasoline. Two of the region's largest importers of diesel, China and India, transformed to self-sufficiency and net exports respectively.

[185]

Around the same period (1995 to 2001) there were no major increases in exports from the Middle East (ME) producers. Regional refiners showed restraint and prevented the glut from becoming worse (Figure 7.21).

Figure 7.21
Growth in Middle East Net Product Exports

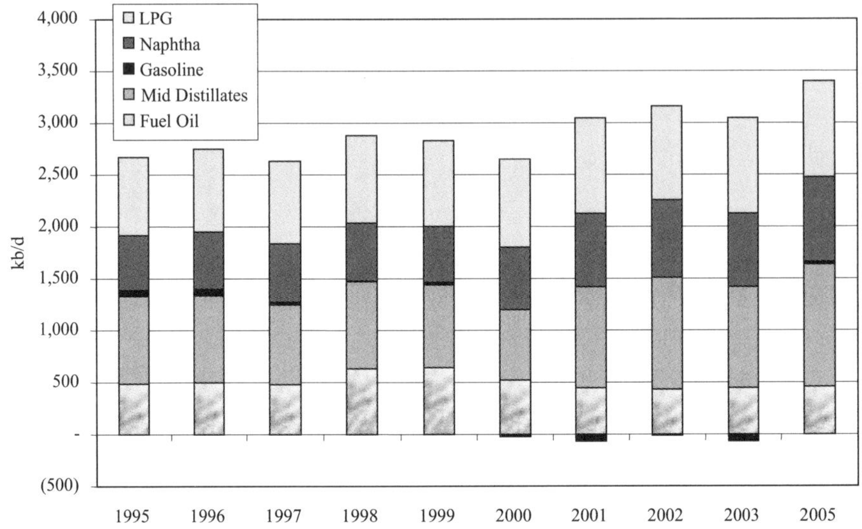

Source: Fesharaki Associates Consulting and Technical Services (FACTS) database and analysis.

However, the Middle East did experience substantial increases in condensate splitting. Between 1999 and 2003 some 670 kbpd of condensate splitting capacity came on stream. This wave of additions started in the UAE with the Emirates National Oil Company (ENOC) building 120 kbpd of capacity, followed quickly by ADNOC adding 280 kbpd, then Qatar adding 57 kbpd. Finally Saudi Arabia commissioned a massive 200 kbpd splitter in 2003. Increased condensate runs through these projects account for the steady increase in export availability of refined products through 2005. Besides refining output the data presented above also includes the output of field naphtha and LPG—the production of which is tied to the output of gas.

As noted earlier, LPG and naphtha demand will grow very rapidly. Still, our forecast indicates that LPG export volumes will rise. Naphtha exports will be more volatile, remaining above their 2000 levels yet with

[186]

considerable variability from year to year. A new feature will be the shift from gasoline net-import status to a slight net-export status by 2005—largely a product of higher crude and condensate runs and expansion of catalytic cracking and isomerization capacities. However, these exports are now forecast to be only in the vicinity of 26 kbpd, compared to current net imports we estimate at 69 kbpd. The largest export growth will be in middle distillates, where we forecast 2005 exports to approach 1.2 mbpd. As noted, the quality of certain exports may be very good—on a par with European, US, and Asian specifications. Moreover, fuel oil net exports are expected to decline during 2003–2008.

Figure 7.22
Middle East Exports/Asia-Pacific Net Imports (excluding LPG)

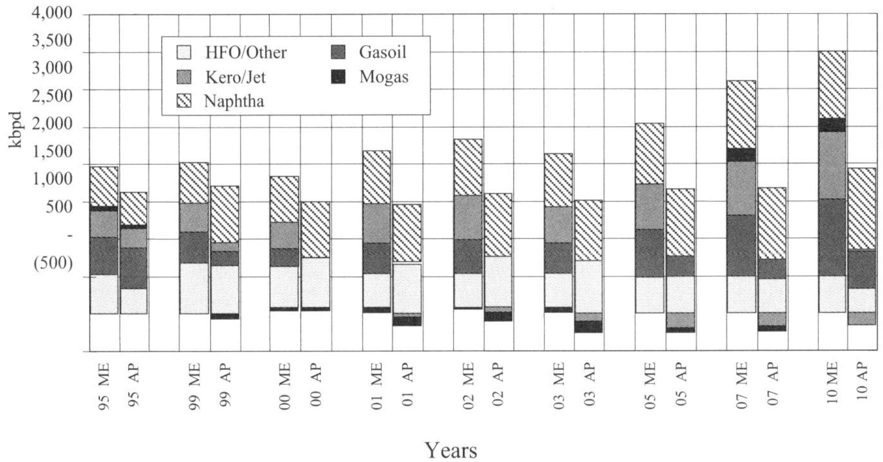

Source: Fesharaki Associates Consulting and Technical Services (FACTS) database and analysis.

In Figure 7.22, a comparison of the volume of products available for export from the Middle East (bars on the left hand side) and the volume of imports required by the Asia–Pacific countries (bars on the right hand side) yields an interesting pattern. Analysis of the relative surplus (from ME) and deficit (from AP) yields the following conclusions:

- For lighter products such as LPG and naphtha, the Asia–Pacific deficit will continue to be larger than ME export availability.
- For diesel, ME producers will have to continue placing substantial volumes of export to non–Asia Pacific destinations. Some 65% of the

[187]

diesel exports are estimated to be sold in Asia—the remaining volumes are absorbed by markets in Africa and South America.

- For some time in the future, Asia will continue to exhibit a surplus of gasoline. The region is indeed a net exporter of gasoline—most notable are the Indian exports of some 70 kbpd of gasoline to Iran.

- For several reasons Asia has a deficit in fuel oil—greater than what is available for exports from the Middle East. This has resulted in a relatively strong East of Suez fuel oil market and caused a regular flow of arbitrage barrels from N.W. Europe, S. America and the Baltic region into Asia.

These physical product balances in the Middle East-Asia Pacific market have a direct bearing on the region's refining profitability. Asian refining margins have indeed deteriorated from the level of 1995 (Figure 7.23). We anticipate a gradual recovery—though this projection is below our earlier estimates for future refining margins. The most important factor in the outlook for relatively lower refining margins in future are the plans of increases in India's refining capacity. It is also worth noting that any sustainable recovery in Asia's refining business depends strongly on the resumption of growth in oil products consumption in the region.

Figure 7.23
Past and Projected Gross Refining Margins: Dubai and Singapore Markets (US$ per barrel)

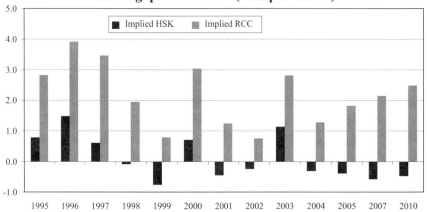

Notes: HSK: hydroskimming; RCC: residue catalytic cracking. Cracking yield is based on RCC.
Nominal $ upto 2002 (actual prices); 2003 $ thereafter.
Source: Fesharaki Associates Consulting and Technical Services (FACTS) database and analysis.

Asian Market Transformation: Gulf Challenges and Opportunities

The Gulf has and will continue to be the natural source of crude oil and refined products for the Asia–Pacific region. Therefore the recent developments in the Asian oil market have impacted the Gulf producers. Three areas where producers in the Gulf have been impacted are identified below:

- Asian product surplus
- Changing product specifications in Asia
- Deregulation of domestic prices leading to increased price sensitivity in key Asian markets.

As discussed previously, the rapid additions in Asian refining capacity and the relatively lower growth rate of oil consumption transformed the big importers into major exporters. Further complicating the equation is the development of product specifications in the Asian countries. Over the last five years several Asian countries made a leap forward in adopting stricter product specifications. Table 7.2 shows that Australia moved from diesel with 0.5 per cent of sulfur by weight (%S) in 1998 to 0.05%S diesel in 2003. Similarly, China moved from 0.5%S to 0.2%S diesel in the same period and India jumped from the same level to 0.1/0.05%S. A similar transition is observed in some of the other markets. The transition continues as Australia, Japan, South Korea and Taiwan are planning to move to 50 ppm (0.005%S) diesel over the next 2–3 years. What do these changes mean for the Gulf countries? There are essentially two implications:

- Some of the products being manufactured by the Gulf refiners are no longer suitable for several markets in the Asia–Pacific region. This is particularly notable in the case of diesel and to a lesser extent motor gasoline. The scenario has created a sense of urgency on the part of Gulf refiners to expedite upgrading and treating facilities so they can meet stricter product specifications both in the domestic and export markets.
- Another potential impact is that if product specifications are adopted before Asian refineries develop the capability to meet these requirements, then an increased volume of sweeter crude (mostly West African) will have to be utilized. This however will be a temporary phase as most of the Asian refineries are gearing up to manufacture tighter specification products utilizing Gulf crude.

[189]

Table 7.2
Transition of Automotive Diesel Oil Specification*
in Asia (1998-2006)

	10000	5000	3000	2000	1000	500	350	50	ppm
	1	0.5	0.3	0.2	0.1	0.05	0.035	0.005	%S
Australia								→	Jan-06
China						→			
India							→		
Indonesia		●							
Japan								→	
Malaysia						→			
New Zealand						→			
Pakistan		→							
Philippines						→			
Singapore					→				
South Korea								→	Jan-06
Taiwan							→		Jan-07
Thailand					→				

Note: *% sulfur by weight

▨ Current Range

⟶ Transition from 1998 to 2006

Source: Fesharaki Associates Consulting and Technical Services (FACTS) database and analysis.

Finally it is important to note that most of the major oil markets in Asia have either completed deregulation procedures or are in the process of implementing them. Deregulation does not necessarily mean complete opening up in all cases. For instance, although the oil markets of Japan and South Korea are completely deregulated in theory there are some key factors that bar the entry of new players in the sector. Similarly China, India and Taiwan have embarked on a process of opening up their petroleum sectors. However, refiners continue to receive substantial protection. Currently the markets of Australia, Thailand, Philippines and Singapore have been completely deregulated.

Although the extent and form of deregulation varies from country to country, there is one common factor—deregulation almost always results in decontrolling of the domestic prices of petroleum products. Two prominent examples are those of China and South Korea (see Figures 7.24 and 7.25). Also relevant is India, where prices of refined products have been allowed to align with international market prices from April 2002.

[190]

Table 7.3
Overview of Trends in Market and Price Deregulation
in the Asia–Pacific Region

	First Moves Toward Deregulation	Major Deregulation	Full or Near Complete Deregulation
China	1998	Dec. 2001	impediments remain
India	–	Apr. 1, 2002	impediments remain
Japan	1986	1996-97	end of 2001 onwards
South Korea	1991-96	Jan. 1997	1999 onwards
Australia	–	–	2000 onwards
Malaysia	still regulated	–	–
Philippines	1996	1998	1998 onwards
Taiwan	1987	1996-99	Dec. 2001 onwards
Thailand	1987	1991	1991 onwards

Note: Based on approximate dates and selected Asia–Pacific nations

Source: Fesharaki Associates Consulting and Technical Services (FACTS) database and analysis.

Figure 7.24
Crude vs Product Price in China
(January 1997–July 2002)

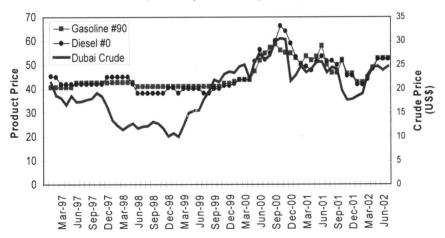

Source: Fesharaki Associates Consulting and Technical Services (FACTS) database and analysis.

[191]

Figure 7.25
Crude vs Product Price in Korea (January 1990–June 2002)

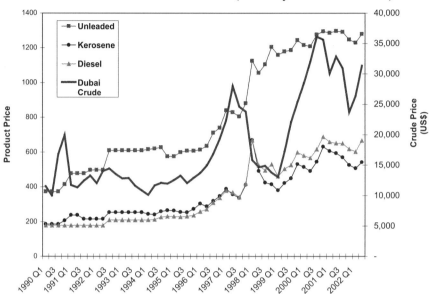

Source: Fesharaki Associates Consulting and Technical Services (FACTS) database and analysis.

What does this mean for the producers who supply oil to these markets? It is important to realize that consumers in these markets who were traditionally used to stable and generally lower domestic prices of petroleum products will now become more sensitive to prices in the international market. The consumers in these markets are therefore more likely to make a switch to cheaper non-oil alternatives wherever possible.

Deregulation often involves privatization—selling off government-held companies. This often opens the door for outsiders to invest in the oil sector, as was the case in South Korea and Philippines. In South Korea, privatization led to the investment by IPIC in the Hyundai refinery and Saudi Aramco in S-Oil. Similarly, Aramco invested in Petron, once the Philippines market opened up.

Currently the oil markets of China and India are undergoing deregulation and have therefore provided opportunities for investment by Gulf companies. Saudi investment in Fujian refinery is one such example, which will allow the company to lock-in significant volumes of the crude in the Chinese market. Major opportunities exist in India though the pace of deregulation and sell-off has been disappointingly slow. The government launched plans for selling its share in the Hindustan Petroleum Corporation Limited (HPCL), one of the country's largest downstream companies, which owns refineries and retail sites. Saudi Aramco and Kuwait Petroleum Company have shown interest in this sell-off. The prize of course is the Indian domestic market with its immense growth potential.

Another case is that of Pakistan, where the Ministry of Privatization is overseeing the process of selling Pakistan State Oil (PSO), the downstream oil marketing company with almost 70% of the retail market share. Again, the prize is the automotive fuels and lubricants market with their high potential. Two of the three front-runners in the purchase of PSO are Gulf companies—Kuwait Petroleum Company and the Saudi group Midrock.

The list of potential opportunities for the Gulf companies does not end here. Major openings in refining and retail might emerge as Indonesia moves ahead with deregulation and opening up of its oil sector. Currently, below 5% of the retail sites are owned by Pertamina and deregulation at the retail end can make the market available to both domestic firms as well as international players. Similarly, there are ample opportunities for investing in the refining infrastructure of the country. Investment in existing refineries can alleviate the burden of rising product imports.

This is not an exhaustive list. Asian countries continue to evolve and grow thereby creating both challenges and opportunities for the Gulf region as their biggest supplier.

Concluding Remarks

The Gulf region is currently the largest supplier of crude and refined products to Asia, while Asia is the largest market for Gulf oil. This relationship is poised to grow further as Asia grows increasingly dependent on imports—most of which will be sourced from the Gulf. This is corroborated by the fact that all of the new refining capacity coming up in Asia is configured around medium-heavy gravity and sour crude. Furthermore, the existing refineries are also gearing up to a similar crude slate.

As Asian markets deregulate, both challenges and opportunities are created for the national oil companies of the Middle East. Opportunities arise in the form of potential investment in the key growth markets of the region: China, India, and Indonesia. Challenges include the heightened sensitivity of oil prices in the Asian countries and changing product specifications.

In the meantime, there has been a two-way flow of investments between the two regions. Gulf oil companies have invested in Asia's downstream oil sector and the Asian oil companies have been investing in Gulf's upstream sector. This will further reinforce the buyer-seller relationship between the two regions in the years to come.

Despite the aggressive nature of the national oil companies of India and China, the Middle East will continue to be dominated by the influence of the national oil companies and Western companies for the foreseeable future. However, the participation of the Asian giant companies would affect the playing field and perhaps force Western companies to offer better terms to the Gulf countries than they might otherwise have done.

DIVERSIFICATION
OF ENERGY SUPPLY

8

Oil and Gas Prospects in the Atlantic Basin: Expanding Oil Production from West-Central Africa to Latin America

Christophe de Margerie

This chapter will focus on oil and gas prospects in West-Central Africa and the Atlantic Basin and their likely impact on the Middle East. The Atlantic Basin is, in a sense, a new supplier. However, to call it a wholly new supplier is rather misleading since the region has been producing oil for several years and is now producing gas as well. Without jumping to conclusions, this may be regarded as a real success story and much of this success is due to the positive role played by OPEC.

Why is there such renewed interest in the Atlantic Basin? It must be remembered that the region has huge reserves, amounting to more than 180 billion barrels of oil, which is 17% of the world total. In terms of gas, the reserves are less important, accounting for around 13% of the world total. However, production in the Atlantic Basin is much more significant in terms of world share—35% for both oil and gas. There are not only existing reserves, but also a lot of potential for new production.

There are three main drivers here. First, there are considerable reserves in the ultra-deep offshore region, mostly in Brazil, in the Gulf of Guinea, the offshore areas of Venezuela, Trinidad, in the Gulf of Mexico, and also Norway. Second, there are large heavy-oil reserve prospects, mainly in Canada, Alaska and in Venezuela serving the same markets—meaning the United States and Europe. The third driver is LNG, which enhances the value of gas reserves that are hard to valorize without a local market. Several LNG projects are now under way, some new and some existing, the biggest of these being Nigeria LNG. This project took more than 30 years to become a reality but it is now in production. Apart from current projects in Trinidad and Tobago, as well as Norway, there are also many new projects such as the one in Angola.

With regard to deep-water reserves, there are massive recoverable reserves. The biggest of these are in the Gulf of Guinea, with further reserves also located off Brazil, in the Gulf of Mexico and off Norway. What is important here is that production in these areas is still growing, except perhaps, in the Gulf of Mexico. It is definitely growing in Brazil, growing substantially in Angola, and just starting in Nigeria, while the other areas are also very important. By 2005, deep-water production is expected to be more than 5 million barrels a day. This will account for a large share of world production. TOTAL is among the international companies working in the deep offshore region and is proud of its success in this field. The company received the Offshore Technology Conference (OTC) award for the Girassol project in 2003. Girassol is the first and so far the biggest project of its kind in Angola, producing more than 200,000 barrels per day in water that is more than 1,200 meters deep. Another successful project has been Canyon Express in the Gulf of Mexico, working at a water depth of 2,200 meters, which is still a record depth for installing such complex pipelines. TOTAL is now in a position to apply these new techniques and technologies in other countries.

The second driver is extra-heavy oil, with probable world reserves of around 400 billion barrels. There is much discussion about what should be classified as heavy oil, which is usually defined as around 18° or 15° API, though in the case of Venezuela, the oil is only 7° to 8° API. However API is not the only factor: in places such as Canada the oil is quite solid and cannot be extracted without injecting steam. If all these resources are included, there are very large reserves indeed, with an anticipated production of 1.5 million barrels per day by 2010. Today production is only 600,000 barrels a day but this is nevertheless a major success, with producers benefiting from the high price of oil. Heavy oil projects are much more profitable today than was expected at the outset. An example of success here is the Sincor project in Venezuela, where TOTAL is a 47% partner. In addition to its upstream side, Sincor involves a huge refining capacity and is producing high quality synthetic crude at 32° API which is very much appreciated in the US refining sector.

The third driver is LNG, which has made a strong start in the Atlantic Basin. The region began developing late, long after the Far East and the Middle East but is catching up very quickly. In the case of Nigeria, production has already reached 9 million tons of LNG per year with projects that will raise this to 12 million tons. Nigeria is already becoming one of the largest LNG producers and this is only the beginning. In future, production could rise to 30 million tons. The country has a big advantage compared to other producers—being close to international markets, the transportation cost remains low. TOTAL is increasingly involved in LNG projects as part of the Group's ongoing commitment to the future of gas. TOTAL is also present in Angola, which could one day be a major LNG producer with huge reserves.

Of course it is not enough to have resources. To be a successful LNG player, a country must be able to secure investment and be able to sell the gas. This is where international companies can play a facilitating role. In Nigeria, by the year 2007, TOTAL's share alone will stand at more than 3 million tons of LNG per year, and the company expects to sell this share of the production. Countries like Nigeria are usually eager to put new resources on stream. It must be remembered that these countries are extremely poor, with huge populations, and therefore, it is very important for them to develop their resources. To facilitate this, they have offered LNG projects to international oil companies on attractive terms and conducted careful negotiations. A favorable LNG environment has helped, because these companies are already in a position to market their LNG production. This is especially true in relation to the American and European markets where a number of new opportunities are expected to emerge. However pricing is crucial—everything depends on who is offering the best price.

In some cases – and Abu Dhabi provides an example – an LNG project emerges from the desire to valorize gas that is already being produced. In Abu Dhabi, a request from the government was the beginning of the ADGAS venture. The starting point was not just how to sell the gas but to consider all the possible options in relation to the gas.

Having discussed the three main drivers for oil and gas production in the Atlantic Basin, it is logical to consider the impact of the region. The impact of the Atlantic Basin on future world supply could well be quite important, but much depends also on Middle East and OPEC policy. Most Atlantic Basin countries, with the exception of Nigeria, are not members of OPEC but are benefiting from "OPEC protection." Hence, it is important to consider the size of the reserves in question. It is true that most reserves of oil and gas are in the Middle East. However, if gas alone is considered, it must be borne in mind that the gas reserves in the former Soviet republics are roughly the size of reserves in the Middle East. In the case of the Atlantic Basin, the oil and gas figures are far more modest. Gas accounts for a large share of reserves but the greatest potential is in deep offshore oil resources. The ultimate reserves could be in the range of 200 billion barrels. This represents a lot, even if it is "only 10% of world potential reserves." The same applies to heavy oil, which is likely to have a growing impact in the future. In this case, the reserve figures are 400 billion barrels, which amounts to a potential 20% in world terms, although heavy oil still needs considerable additional technology to reduce costs and increase the recovery factor. Here, the greatest impact on world supply should come from an improvement in the recovery factor, and it would not be surprising if in 5 years time, the reserve figure reaches 600 billion barrels. As regards LNG, there is still a difference between the regions west and east of the Suez, for one good reason—the price. East of the Suez, the price is declining as LNG is still not a commodity market. Regions west of the Suez account for 11% of the LNG market, but this share will rise to 30% by the year 2010. So this market is catching up and it is linked to the US market.

To summarize the impact of deep-water production, it should be noted that there have been sizeable discoveries, perhaps with limited potential. There is still a lot of potential production mainly from huge, existing discoveries and there are probably smaller discoveries yet to be made. In the world of the deep offshore, 200 million barrels of reserves would be considered as relatively small. Such a discovery onshore would be substantial but in the deep offshore, larger reserves are necessary to justify the higher cost of operations. The Gulf of Mexico example mentioned earlier may be recalled. However, discoveries of 1 billion plus or 2 billion barrels would certainly be significant. In this case, the challenges are to develop the necessary technology to operate at 3000 meters of water depth rather than 2000 meters.

In the case of heavy oil, for the short term, projects involve limited production and are still not always very economical. In this field, TOTAL, BP and other international oil companies are all trying to remain conservative in their approach, although it is also important to be effective.

As for LNG, liquefaction is one of the best ways to valorize gas, whether in the short term, medium term or long term. LNG production is becoming cheaper and cheaper, technology has been improving greatly and all these factors have resulted in cost reduction. In terms of forecasting, 2030 might seem rather far ahead, but not in the oil business. Ten years is a normal cycle for a project, so most companies like to ensure reserve life of about 10 years. The Middle East remains the most important player in terms of oil. The Atlantic Basin will grow slightly but growth will become flat after 2015. So around 2012 or 2017, the supply situation will change, with supply growth coming definitively from the Middle East. In terms of gas, the change will not be so obvious because of the reserves of gas in the Middle East. LNG is important, and oil companies need to maintain a presence in all areas to remain major players in this field. Gas has sustained production growth both for local needs and LNG which is becoming a sizeable market. However, the LNG market is expected to grow sufficiently to avoid competition between the different gas basins.

The strategy of the major oil companies is to further develop profitable business, to seek international diversification, to meet technological challenges and also to promote partnership with host countries. The future of the oil industry lies in the Middle East, and that explains why oil companies continue to maintain a major presence in the region.

9

Russian Hydrocarbons in the World Market: Prospects and Realities

Vitaly V. Naumkin

Russia possesses tremendous reserves of hydrocarbon supplies.[1] Its known oil reserves are estimated at 48.6 to 120 billion barrels. Russia's gas reserves (47 trillion cubic meters) constitute 29 percent of the world total, and Russia produces 26 percent (640 billion cubic meters in 2002) of the world output.[2] Russia's new Energy Strategy regards the fuel and energy industry as a driving force of the country's development and welcomes a dynamic oil and gas production growth. For the first time, the Russian government has admitted the need for building up oil and gas exports.

A New Strategy of Growth

The current Energy Strategy is Russia's third attempt to define objectives for a long-term development of its national fuel and energy industry. The First Energy Strategy that was approved in the Fall of 1995 encouraged a broader use of natural gas for fuel and envisioned a stronger development of the oil and gas sector but these plans have not been fulfilled.

The Second Energy Strategy that was approved in November 2000 considered energy supply as the first priority. In accordance with that strategy, oil production was to increase by 15 percent and gas production by 27 percent over 20 years. This Strategy was oriented towards limiting exports of hydrocarbons and building up exports of petroleum products instead.

A number of basic recommendations of the Second Energy Strategy were also left unfulfilled. Thus the main provisions approved by the Government were based on the need to urgently raise the state-regulated prices and tariffs for fuel and energy resources. A special role in this process was assigned to the year 2001. However, the decision to raise prices and tariffs for fuel and energy in line with the recommendations of the Strategy was never implemented. According to the Strategy, the prices of gas in 2001 were to increase roughly 1.5 times and that of electric power by 1.35 times. In fact all these indicators increased only by 18 and 30 percent respectively. However, this is linked to the investment activity of gas and energy companies, to consumer interest in an economical, thrifty use of energy resources and, indeed, to the replenishment of budgets of all levels.[3]

The recently approved Third Energy Strategy once again changed the direction in which the national fuel and energy industry should develop. The positive side of this Strategy is that it is not based on political consideration as the first and the second ones were—but primarily on economic realities. The Government acknowledged the fuel and energy industry as the main driver of economic growth. In practice, it means that government officials would no longer oppose higher growth rates of oil production.

Another positive side of the new Strategy is the recognition of the benefits of the export and transit of hydrocarbons to the Government. This acknowledgment removes political barriers from building up the export potential of the oil and gas industry.

The main provisions of Russia's Energy Strategy, as approved by the Russian Government, proceeded from the necessity of increasing the rental character of taxation. The priority of the rental component in taxation had been confirmed by the Russian President. However, the State Duma in 2001 passed a law based on a different approach. The task was to introduce differentiated rates of taxation depending on the mining and geological, geographical and economic conditions.

In the Russian parliament, the question of introducing a tax on mining operations caused a lot of argument. The Government proposed to fix it at 357 rubles (about $12) a ton, while the State Duma in August 2003 decreased it to 347 rubles. The proposed tax was to add about $3 billion to the Russian budget annually. On the whole, oilmen reacted calmly to the introduction of the tax, although they believe the taxation of their industry to be excessively burdensome. In an interview with the Tsentr TV channel, the then Yukos President Mikhail Khodorkovsky said that taxes made up 60 percent of the cost of gasoline on the Russian market.[4]

Despite the burden of taxation, Russian oil producers have been providing constant growth in oil production. The new Strategy encouraged them to do so, and to start buying and building refineries abroad in order to refine their own products. A Russian analyst has commented as follows:

> Over 2.5 years the Government has radically changed its understanding of an advisable level of Government control over the fuel and energy industry. Initially, the Government's goal was to hold the controlling interest, or at least "golden shares" virtually of all major energy and petroleum companies. Now the Government is seeking to have equity only in the areas constituting key companies of the industry system. These would primarily include transportation infrastructure.[5]

In the new Energy Strategy, potential development of the fuel industry is linked to potential domestic and foreign market demand for Russian energy. The importance of market analysis is for the first time recognized in such a document as the basis for Russian hydrocarbon exports.

Figure 9.1
Russian Oil and Condensate Production Forecast

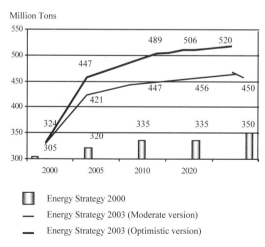

Source: Andrey Meshcherin, "Blagiye namereniyam" *Neftegazovaya Vertikal'*, No 9 (2003): 7.

By 2010, domestic consumption growth of fuel and energy resources is estimated to be 13 to 21 percent compared to 2000; by 2020, at 27 to 40 percent, the demand for motor fuel will grow 20 percent faster compared to a general level of energy consumption. The forecasts indicate that the share of natural gas in the national energy balance will go down from the existing 50 to 48 percent in 2010 and further down to 45-46 percent in 2020.[6]

The forecasts anticipate that the fastest growth of energy exports will be achieved by 2010—from 548 to 728–796 million conditional tons. After 2010 it may grow by another 3 to 7 percent.

Forecasts for the Growth of Oil Production and Exports

The Strategy anticipates that the highest rates of oil production growth will be experienced in 2003–2005, and by the end of that period will exceed the 2002 level by 11 to 18 percent (as shown in Figure 9.1). These rates will slow down over the subsequent five-year period, with the projected total growth amounting to an additional 3 to 6 percent.

Russia's fuel and energy industry is a dynamically developing sector of the Russian economy. It accounts for 15 percent of industrial output, about 40 percent of budget revenues and more than 40 percent of currency allocations. Oil extraction has been steadily growing since 1999 and in 2002 amounted to 366 million tons.

Over the recent years, many Russian oil companies have successfully modernized production, increased productivity and cut losses. In the words of Khodorkovsky, at the time when his group purchased Yukos, the prime cost of the oil that it was producing was $12 per barrel, whereas now it costs $1.5 per barrel.[7]

The new Strategy is to reestablish the role of Western Siberia as the main oil-producing region with a high potential. Oil production here is expected to grow until 2010–2015 up to a level of 290–315 million tons a year. Oil refining is also supposed to increase until 2005 by 12 percent compared to 2002 levels.

In 2003, Russia produced more than 8.2 mbpd of oil, or about 3 billion barrels a year (410 million tons). In the view of a Russian expert, Evgeniy Khartukov, on the basis of its known reserves, Russia can afford to increase its oil production up to 30 mbpd.[8] The President of Lukoil, Vagit Alekperov is sure that Russia will produce 9–10 mbpd in 2010.[9]

Europe in general and EU countries in particular are the main purchasers of Russian energy resources. In 2002, some 75 million tons of oil (50 percent of Russia's exports) were supplied to the EU alone and about 50 additional million tons to the remaining European countries. The EU countries' share of exports of Russian gas is even greater.

Russia still has a deficit of capacities for bringing oil to the world markets. Although the Transneft head, Semyon Vainstok tried to persuade Vladimir Putin in August 2003 that these capacities exceeded the volumes of exported oil, at the September Russo-American energy summit, he also confessed that Russia's deficit of export capacities constitutes roughly 40 million tons (about 280 million barrels) a year.[10] In order to eliminate this deficit, Transneft is planning to increase the capacity of the Baltic Pipeline System (BPS) now equal to 18 million tons (about 126 million barrels) to 62 million tons (about 434 million barrels). By spring 2004 the capacity of the BPS, according to company data, would have reached 42 million tons, while an additional 20 million tons will subsequently be pumped along the same pipeline (its diameter allows this to be done) after some more pumping plants have been built.

Besides, Transneft is carrying on a dialogue with Ukraine, expecting to convince its leadership to agree to the routing of oil via the pipeline Odessa-Brody in the opposite direction. In this case, Russia will receive an additional 9 million tons of oil for export.

Russia's oilmen are divided on the issue of the capacity of the Murmansk Pipeline System (MPS) which is planned for construction. The transport experts believe that the planned capacity of 150 million tons may turn out to be overstated and the volumes of export will not suffice.

Where Will the Oil be Exported?

The countries of North America, Western Europe and the Asia-Pacific Region (APR) are the largest oil consumers in the world today. Their oil refineries are mostly loaded to full capacity. Annually, the US yearly

[207]

refines more than 700 million tons of oil and Europe about 820 million tons, with roughly the same amount required by the APR.

Though the above countries are successfully developing their own oil production, they have to import large volumes of crude oil. Most exporters are operating in their markets and therefore every supplier has to face acute competition. Russia would have found it very hard to become a supplier in terms of stable demand, but in evaluating Russian prospects it must be remembered that oil consumption in these key markets will nevertheless grow eventually.

Besides, the majority of experts agree that the dependence of the US, the APR and Western Europe on oil imports will also gradually increase. So far they are receiving the main volumes from the countries of the Middle East. However, before getting to the refinery, Arab oil travels very long distances, and in some cases it will be possible to renegotiate its price. Furthermore, the diversification of energy sources is becoming a priority in modern times. Thus it makes sense to analyze Russia's chances of marketing its energy resources in novel outlets.

Over the last ten years the volume of US oil consumption has grown by roughly 100 million tons, or 750 million barrels. In the process, the production of US companies has been decreasing, with imports significantly increasing. At present, America's own production constitutes little more than 40 percent. By the most pessimistic forecasts, by 2010 oil consumption in the USA will reach one billion tons, but the nation's own production – due to a high prime cost – will most likely fall and imports will grow by roughly one percent a year. Summarizing these factors, Russian analysts predict that the new market players are quite able to shoulder the shipments of an additional 480–530 million tons of oil a year. It goes without saying that this can be done with the proviso that their produce will prove acceptable in terms of quantity and price.

It is believed that the Russian export blend Urals has considerable advantages over the oil supplied to the United States from South America, and therefore even at equal prices it can offer serious competition to the latter. However, if Russia manages to bring oil to American consumers through a cheaper route it would be possible for Urals to become a substitute for Arab oil as well.

[208]

Today the Russian mass media overestimates the importance of the first shipments of Russian oil to the United States. Although in the first six months of 2003 these shipments reached 1.2 million tons, they constitute less than one percent of the total volume of exports. The main obstacle is the high transportation costs.

The situation in Western Europe historically developed in a fashion similar to that of the US. The difference is that oil consumption in Western Europe is more stable and has been growing at a slower pace than in the United States. Western Europe's own production, as it is known, also makes up for 44 percent of its consumption, with imports from Middle Eastern countries accounting for 25 percent, imports from Russia being 18 percent and the remaining volume coming from North Africa.

As mentioned above, European and particularly EU countries are the main purchasers of Russian energy resources—in 2002, 75 million tons of oil (50% of Russian exports) were supplied to the EU, and around 50 million tons were additionally supplied to other European countries. The amount of Russian gas exported to the EU countries is even greater.

The forecasts relating to Western Europe's dependence on imports are similar: North Sea oil is the main source of raw material for European oil refineries, but most analysts tend to believe that production there has already peaked and will decrease henceforth.

Russian oil producers believe that it is possible to replace North Sea oil with Russian oil, but in so doing, one must consider the distinctive technological features of European oil refineries. Most of these are designed for refining light low-sulfur oil. Therefore those Russian companies that want to increase their full-fledged presence on the European market will somehow have to take part in the modernization of refineries, to allow them to be reoriented to the processing of a greater quantity of Urals.

This task is a rather complex one and refinery owners may regard such a proposition in various ways. While they understand perfectly the need to build new installations for the desulfurization of oil, they might expect different behavior from Russian companies. For instance, they might expect oil shipments with a greater price discount than usual. In any case, if a compromise solution is reached with oil refiners, Russia's share in the Western Europe market may rise to 25 percent until 2010.[11]

The APR markets of most interest to Russia are China, Japan and South Korea. China's dependence on imports is of relatively short duration. Its own production in 2003 covers roughly 70 percent of the total consumption, and China imports 30 percent of its oil. With the exception of 2 million tons supplied from Russia by contract with Yukos, this volume is provided by suppliers from the Middle East and Southeast Asia. However, China is a burgeoning market where the consumption of oil products is growing faster than its own extraction. Moreover, within the foreseeable future, the country's oil refining industry is expected to undergo reform. Almost 90 percent of the total volume of China's refining is so far concentrated in two state-owned companies and construction of new oil refineries may be required. Moreover, China is striving to diversify its suppliers and as its oil requirements increase, Russia could find a niche in the Chinese market, if it so desires.

In Japan and South Korea the situation is somewhat different. Global experts predict that the growth of oil consumption observed so far in these countries is bound to cease very shortly. Markets will stabilize and changes will become unlikely. The countries of the Middle East and Southeast Asia will most probably remain the principal providers.

Cooperation between Russia and the Asian region is viewed as a priority of external energy policy in the twenty-first century. Russia's interest in Asia as a new and promising avenue in external energy policy is conditioned by certain factors: Asia's geographical proximity to Russia's eastern regions (Siberia and the Far East), which possess substantial energy resources, as well as the region's predictably greater dependence on outside energy supplies.

The total consumption of oil in the Asian region may increase by 35 percent over 2000–2010. The share of intraregional deliveries will sink from 42 to 27 percent. The share of the Middle Eastern countries in meeting the total Asian demand for oil will rise from 52 to 65 percent, which will aggravate the problem of Asia's energy security and compel Asian governments, particularly those of Northeast Asia, to step up the search for new external sources of oil imports. Russia and the CIS states are regarded as the most significant and promising partners.

Before assessing Russian prospects as a whole, it must be noted that in addition to the traditional suppliers, the markets most lucrative for Russia are also of interest to the new players—Kazakhstan, Azerbaijan and Turkmenistan. Even by 2003 any reduction of exports to Europe by Russia was being fully compensated by their deliveries, and by 2005 they would be able to ensure a total of more than 50 million tons of oil per year. Their oil will be supplied first and foremost to the Mediterranean, but if the Baku-Ceyhan pipeline project is realized, Russian oil will have to compete with these sources in America as well.

Russia's chances of winning the emerging struggle are bright enough. A comparison of the oil prospecting and exploitation costs of Russia's best oil companies with those of the world leaders reveals that Russian companies are competitive in terms of the prime cost of oil. If these companies can find effective means of transportation and secure guarantees for the refinement of their oil, Russia's share in the world oil market will surely grow.

Gas Export from Russia

Gas production in Russia has stabilized at the level of 550-560 billion cubic meters. Gazprom alone in 2003 planned to produce 541 billion cubic meters, of which about 350 billion cubic meters was intended for consumption within the country. The main problem is the remoteness of gas production sites from the consumer and the correspondingly high costs of gas transportation. Alexander Solovyanov, a specialist from the Department of Prospective Development, Science and Ecology of Gazprom announced on October 1, 2003 that the company's annual losses resulting from gas transportation, production and storage constituted 8-9 billion cubic meters a year. Gazprom is systematically cutting the costs of gas pumping.

According to the forecasts by the Moscow-based Institute of World Economy and International Relations (IMEMO) the dynamics of gas exports from Russia will be as indicated in Figure 9.1.

Table 9.1
Russian Gas Exports

(compared to data for the 1990s, in billions of cubic meters)

	1990	1995	2000	2005	2010	2015	2020
Export to CIS countries	101	69	59.1	70-80	70-80	65-75	65-70
Export to other countries	112	122	133.5	175-180	175-195	195-205	200-210
Total	213	191	192.6	245-260	245-275	260-280	265-280

Source: Forecasts from the Institute of the World Economy and International Relations, Moscow.

At the same time, the estimated Russian gas production of 700 billion cubic meters by 2020, in the view of Leonid Michelson, Chairman of the Management Board of Novatek Joint-Stock Company,[12] means that Russia's share of world gas production will decrease from 29 to 15 percent, thus losing its significance on the international scene. If all obstacles preventing the expansion of Russian gas production are lifted, it will probably reach 850–900 billion cubic meters, out of which 200 to 250 billion cubic meters could be provided by independent gas producers.

Russian gas producers envisage a demand growth for gas in the Russian economy, as well as in the markets of Europe, the US and Asia. The United States is among the biggest gas consumers in the world (667.5 billion cubic meters in 2002, or 26.3% of the world consumption). In September 2003 Russian news agencies reported on the meeting between the US Energy Secretary Donald Evans and the Gazprom Board Chairman Alexei Miller in Washington. In this meeting, the US side expressed its interest in Russian gas supplies to the US market, and Gazprom considered cooperation with ConocoPhillips for the supply of LHG from Russia to the US.[13]

European natural resources are doomed to be depleted in the short term and therefore, will see a higher rate of gas consumption. Japan has already declared its willingness to increase the share of gas in its energy supply. Hence, Russian gas producers believe that the envisaged volume of 700 billion cubic meters will not be sufficient and should be enlarged, especially given the fact that Russia's share in the world markets will inevitably be occupied by its competitors. In their view, if the gas industry can undergo appropriate and much-needed evolutionary reform, then annual gas production can reach the aforementioned level of 850–900 billion cubic meters being provided from the following sources: 530 billion cubic meters from Gazprom; 180 billion cubic meters from independent gas producers of Western Siberia; and 110 billion cubic meters from the gas fields of Eastern Siberia and the Far East.[14]

At the same time, as Russian expert Yelena Telegina suggests,[15] in the foreseeable future the situation concerning gas supply to the APR may present the governments of Asian countries with the issue of ensuring the security of supplies. A steady increase in the figures of pure gas imports beyond 2000 is expected in Northeast Asia. In keeping with IEA forecasts, by 2010 up to 40 percent of gas consumed in the region will be supplied from outside. In this connection, the questions of energy supply and diversification of oil sources and gas supply to Asia are the possible connecting links with, and premises for, the development of cooperation between Russia and the APR countries, as well as for the implementation of projects for the export of Russia's energy resources to new markets in the east. Some experts estimate that, if the pipeline infrastructure is in place, the rate of profit in exporting gas to the rapidly growing markets of Asian countries may exceed 1.3–1.5 times the profitability of Europe's existing oversaturated natural gas market.

The Need for Investment

It should be noted that the situation in the Russian fuel and energy industry is not entirely as promising as it seems. The scope of geological survey work has sharply diminished. A danger exists that the old assets will collapse in an avalanche-like fashion and a great number of oil wells will be closed. The attraction of massive new investments may be the only way to solve this problem.

According to calculations made as far back as 1999 in the Russian Ministry of the Economy, around $200 billion would have to be invested for a dynamic development of the sector during 2000–2015. Nowadays, company-owned funds constitute roughly 90 percent of investment. Although the level of foreign investment attracted is steadily increasing, the absolute value of such investment is still negligible.

The main expectations are linked to European investors, primarily from the European Union (EU), which sees the import of energy as a question of vital importance. Nowadays the EU purchases more than 50 percent of consumable energy, including almost 80 percent of oil and 40 percent of gas. By 2020, this dependence is expected to increase to 70 percent, including up to 90 percent for oil and about 70 percent for gas. These dynamics will not be changed either by the liberalization of electric energy and gas markets currently underway in Europe, or by steps being taken towards energy conservation.

Meanwhile, sources of energy imports are few and far between. Half of the gas imported into the EU comes from the CIS countries (led by Russia) and another 25 percent from Algeria. More than 40 percent of oil is imported from the Middle East (Saudi Arabia and Iran), and 30 percent from North Africa (Libya). Considering the instability in the Middle East, increasing the volume of Russian shipments is a priority task for the EU.

The energy dialogue between Russia and the EU was initiated in October 2000. Its gist can be summed up in a simple phrase—oil for investment. The EU wishes to secure its future—with steady and predictable energy deliveries. Russia expects to obtain European investments and technologies. The greatest progress has been reached on questions involving trade in crude oil and natural gas. In particular, the EU has agreed to retain the mechanism of long-term contracts of gas shipment on a "take-or-pay" basis. A multibillion investment in gas pipelines is possible only if a long term market outlet is guaranteed. However, it is still not clear if long term contracts conform to European legislation. For instance, the Russian authorities are concerned over the EU's Gas Directive, which gives each EU country the right to limit the gas import from Russia within the limits of 30 percent of consumable volume. European Union policies appear to be contradictory. On the one hand, the EU invites Russia to increase the volume of deliveries and on the other it reserves the right to restrict these deliveries without any compensation.[16]

Discussions on attracting European investment to the Russian fuel and energy industry are running into greater difficulty. Needless to say, investment is a matter for private companies, and these issues have to be negotiated not with European officials but with European banks and energy companies. However, even European firms accustomed to geological and market risks are worried by the unstable legislative and fiscal regime in Russia. And they have reasons for such concern. For example, most of the joint stock companies that were active in the Russian oil business were swallowed up in the mid–1990s by big Russian companies, which often used not-quite-civilized methods and their political resources to achieve this goal. Meanwhile, the level of investment attracted by Russia's fuel and energy sector is fairly high, primarily due to serious underestimation. The capitalization of major world petroleum companies relative to oil reserves at their disposal constitutes $10–20 per barrel. In Russia, one barrel of reserves costs only $1–2. The same disparity exists with respect to the ratio between capitalization and oil production. For example, Lukoil should cost $140 billion, not $14 billion. The difference between these figures is explained by obsolete fixed assets and political instability, but the main issue is unsound economic legislation and a lack of transparency in management. All of these factors lead to a rise in "risk premiums" when planning investment projects.

It is evident that the investment climate in Russia has considerably improved in recent years. The expert assessments of rating agencies and the behavior of foreign investors attest to this fact. Whereas in the year 2000 foreign investments channeled into Russia's fuel industry amounted to $620 million, in 2001 they were more than $1 billion and in 2002 soared to $1.4 billion.[17] However, it should be noted that a conspicuous portion of these investments represents Russian capital returning from abroad.

Apart from export duties, Russia can potentially receive much more important benefits from the export of energy resources. These include massive investments; the renovation of productive capacities in the fuel and energy industry; the "self-reforming" of petroleum companies in the direction of civilized methods of doing business; and a beneficial effect for the economy as a whole. European governments and companies, having invested money and political capital, might expect stable and increasing

[215]

shipments of energy, favorable development of the Russian economy, income growth among the Russian population and, accordingly, growth in consumer demand for European goods. Only time will tell whether the European Union can be convinced of the advantage of such a bargain. As D. Victor and N. Victor have commented:

> Investors face obstacles everywhere in the Russian oil business, not only in developing new oil fields and pipelines (known as "greenfield" investment), but also for "brownfield" buyers of existing operations. In the early 1990s, British Petroleum, one of the first major foreign players in Russia, invested about half a billion dollars in Sidanco and nearly lost the whole sum when the Russian firm plunged into a Byzantine bankruptcy. Under Putin the tide seems to be turning. Confidence in Russian institutions is rising, and official statistics (though notoriously unreliable on the subject) suggest that the outflow of money from Russia has slowed. However, suspicions of insider dealing and other deterrents to investors remain. For instance, when the Russian government auctioned its stake in Slavneft in December 2002, every potential foreign bidder was discouraged from participating in the process. The auction itself lasted only four minutes; one team submitted three of the four bids, and the winning bid was barely above the reserve price. The low values that open markets assign to Russian oil companies measure the enormous difficulties that lie ahead in building appropriate corporate institutions and assuring investors of the safety of their stakes. According to a recent study by PriceWaterhouseCoopers, Western oil assets changed hands in the late 1990s for about $5 per barrel; Russian assets, on the other hand, traded as less than 20 cents per barrel.[18]

Nonetheless, investments in the Russian fuel and energy sector are in gradually growing.

The Dynamic Process of Enlargement

The year 2003 saw the conclusion of a deal for a merger of oil and gas companies: British Petroleum (now BP) and TNK (Tyumen Oil Company and Sidanco), the largest in Russia's history. Speaking to journalists, the Chairman of the Board of Directors of the multinational giant Alfa Group, Mikhail Fridman stated that "all juridical and financial transactions have already been completed," and that the company would be engaged in forming an efficient managing team and formulating corporate culture. However,

TNK-BP in 2003 already ranked tenth in the world in size among oil and gas companies, extracting more than 1.2 million barrels of oil a day. By May 2004, when Russia's Slavneft would be included in the deal, the daily extraction is supposed to grow by another 160 thousand barrels. Mikhail Fridman stresses that the TNK-BP company is Russian-British only in terms of its shareholder profile. "By its assets the company is Russian," he explained, "90 percent of our assets is in Russia, the rest is in the CIS countries." According to him, the company will work in accordance with Russian legislation and pay its taxes into the Russian treasury.

Both Russian and British shareholders of TNK-BP spoke with enthusiasm about the deadlines for the completion of the merger: in their opinion, the period of 6-7 months from the announcement of the merger to the launching of the new company is a very short term. Indeed, for such an unprecedented deal half a year is not so much, especially if one is to consider that in early summer it "got stuck" for several reasons: questions regarding the sum of payments to the Russian side were not resolved, it was unclear what to do with Slavneft and a petition for the approval of the merger was not even submitted to the Ministry on Anti-Monopoly Policy (MAP) until July 10, 2003. Indeed, the MAP pronounced a positive verdict only at the end of August 2003, after approving the merger of Yukos and Sibneft. According to Fridman, the money gained from the bargain would be invested mainly in the oil business. Furthermore, each of the TNK shareholders has his own interests in different fields: "for Alfa Group these are telecommunications and finances, for our partners, the aluminum industry and power engineering. Besides, there are plans for expansion both in Russia and abroad."[19]

The question concerning the half of Slavneft that was bought by TNK has been resolved in the best way possible for it. The initial terms for the merger were as follows: BP was to pay $3 billion to the TNK shareholders for a 50 percent share in TNK-BP, after which, in the course of three years, it was to make an annual payment of $1.25 billion in the form of ordinary BP shares priced in accordance with their market value as of the date of payment. After TNK acquired a 50 percent share holding of Slavneft, BP reduced the sum of initial payment by $600 million, refusing to include these assets into the bargain. However, the Russian side apparently managed to persuade the Britons of the economic effectiveness of the acquisition, and BP agreed to accept Slavneft as an addition to TNK—of course, not free of charge.

Incidentally, the leaders of the TNK-BP merger will have to resolve another problem in the near future, that of minority shareholders who are numerous due to the company's holding structure. These shareholders can make all kinds of demands and claims in connection with the deal that has been struck. The TNK-BP leadership is ready for this. "It has to be understood that the new company is a holding that incorporates dozens of associated companies, and in each of these there are minority shareholders," says Viktor Vekselberg, TNK-BP's Managing Director for Production. "We are certainly expecting certain problems." However, the company owners intend to cope with this problem. In addition, up to 40 percent of the company's income will be channeled into dividend payments to its shareholders.

The Costs of the Energy Boom

Moises Naim, Vice President of the World Bank and Editor-in-Chief of *Foreign Policy* magazine said in one of his recent interviews that Russia was fast becoming "an oil country" having its very strange peculiarities and, more particularly, an incorrect currency exchange rate. In Naim's opinion, the exchange rate in "oil countries" is subordinate to the tasks of the oil sector and therefore retards the development of other sectors:

> Oil destroys the country's policy and the people's expectations. It undermines the state's ability to properly distribute public wealth, leads to a concentration of power in the hands of the few, and emasculates democracy.[20]

Naim has noted only one of the many negative economic, social and political consequences of the ever greater orientation of the Russian economy to the export of hydrocarbons. Even if we do not refer to the macro-level, in the oil and gas sphere itself, certain phenomena have been observed that cause anxiety among Russian analysts.

Thus it should be pointed out that in view of the high price level of oil, the value of the shares of many Russian oil companies has been overstated. Experts believe that a smooth reduction of prices will cause their cost to decrease. Analysts of the Troyka Dialog Company have calculated how far the high oil prices distort the cost of the oil companies' shares. According to the company data, Lukoil and Yukos in 2003 were overstated by 4 percent, Sibneft by 11 percent and Tatneft by 35 percent. In general, spokesmen for the oil companies preferred not to comment on these figures. However, the spokesman for Tatneft alone confessed to *Finansovye Izvestia* that the value of the company may indeed have been overstated.[21]

A reduction in the share quotation of many companies in the oil and gas sector can be very significant. It is no accident that Troyka Dialog has already reduced its recommendations relating to the majority of the top oil companies, advising the shareholders of Yukos, Lukoil, Sibneft and Surgutneftegaz to abandon their shares more actively. The main reason for this is the overdependence on world oil prices, which, as most predictions indicate, are likely to fall. According to information from Troyka Dialog, the composite index of these four securities has risen by more than 50 percent since the beginning of the year, and the share quotations have exceeded their true cost. However, in the future there are no reasons for a rise in cost. A change in oil prices by $1 leads to a change in the net profit of Lukoil by 17 percent and Yukos by 8 percent. Troyka had forecast a considerable reduction in oil prices after 2003, falling to $22 as early as 2004 and to the level of $18-20 a barrel in 2005.

Analysts at Troyka Dialog believe that the potential for growth has been exhausted, and this means that bullish speculation is impossible. The shares will continue to rise only if the oil prices stay high.

Analysts of other investment companies have a more optimistic view. An analyst of the Broker Credit Service company stated:

> We shall change the recommendations on Tatneft, considering that the company has made public its plans for increasing its output by one percent, cutting costs and reducing non-specialized assets. On all shares the recommendation is "to hold." I have noticed that the recommendations of investment companies either completely coincide or differ in a fundamental way.[22]

Independent analysts' approaches also differ. Some investment companies prefer to compute a price reference point for shares, while others prefer to also calculate a true price.

Meanwhile, it is clearly not worth relying on the oil price alone in forecasts of share cost. It is also worth recalling that a significant drop in oil prices was predicted for this year yet, in effect, the prices skyrocketed.

"Russian companies will feel well even if prices of oil are not high, as they are oriented towards the growth of export deliveries," a Russian analyst contends. "The main thing is for the market to be able to digest these large volumes of output."[23] The shares of Russian companies will retain their attractiveness for a long time to come. Moreover, the oil market opportunities may remain favorable, and in that case, those who have sold their shares will incur heavy losses as a result.

Allied Competitors

A threat of competition from the gas producers of Central Asia on the internal market and potentially in the external market also, is a new factor in the development of Russia's gas industry. For objective reasons, the country will be forced to import gas from the Central Asian republics. A lot depends on the volume and character of the utilization of gas transported into Russia. Since the relative export gas potential (compared to internal consumption) of Central Asian countries is greater than that of Russia, and also considering its gas weakness, one may expect persistent pressure on their part. The Russian expert Yelena Telegina believes that attracting the potential of Central Asian countries while ceding to them a share of export markets in Europe will allow Gazprom to sell – without substantial investment – about 100 billion cubic meters of foreign gas a year towards 2010 and about 150 billion cubic meters towards 2015.[24]

In this connection the idea of establishing "a gas alliance" of CIS countries is taking on great significance. In January 2002, after two years of ongoing informal consultations, Russia put forward a proposal to form an alliance of four gas-producing countries (Russia, Turkmenistan, Kazakhstan and Uzbekistan) with a possible participation of the states in whose territory export pipelines to Europe are located. This group is dominated by Russia whose share amounts to 85 percent of the combined natural gas output of "the Four."

Such an alliance might ensure the formation of a single balance of production and consumption of natural gas, an effective control over the volumes and routes of shipments of all the exporters of Central Asian gas, single tariffs for pumping gas, a single price policy and a single channel for gas export via the available Gazprom pipeline system.

Given the proper organization of work, the consolidation of the gas potentials of "the Four" is of advantage to Russia economically, at least in the short and medium term. The EU envisages carrying out a liberalization of the gas market fully at the expense of external exporters (including Russia) whose share of incomes in the price structure may drop by 12.64 percent. The fall of export profitability for Gazprom can also be aggravated by the reduction of disparity between internal and external selling prices. However, a positive element is that Gazprom will spend less when using transit services in the EU.

The Caspian Sea region, where the economic and political interests of both regional and third countries clash, is a zone of particular geopolitical significance for Russia. The key issues of Caspian energy cooperation are transit and transportation of oil and gas resources to market outlets. The alignment of forces in the region will in many ways depend on the resolution of these issues. Russia's economic interests in the Caspian may be secured by realizing the projects of the Caspian Pipeline Consortium, Blue Stream and others. On the question of the transportation of Caspian hydrocarbons, Russia proceeds not only from a desire to avoid changing the geopolitical line up in the region, but also from the necessity of maintaining stability in the world markets of oil and gas in the interests of the producers and consumers of these resources.

Incidentally, in 1999 the CIS countries – the second ranking buyer of Russia's energy resources – were paying only $70 per ton of Russian oil (while the EU was paying $110) and $50 per 1,000 cubic meters of gas (while the EU was paying $65). In the short term, Kazakhstan – one of the CIS states – may become an important supplier of energy resources. As of today, the former USSR's share of European oil imports constitutes roughly 37 percent. Taking into account the projects for Russian oil to gain entry into the US and Chinese markets, this share will most likely grow thanks to the exports of Kazakhstan's raw materials. The Russian companies will apparently increase the shipments of oil products, though not necessarily from Russian oil refineries. In this sense, the mastering of the United Economic Space (UES) by Russian business is proceeding at full speed.

The Problem of Tariffs

Russia's internal interests concerning tariffs for electric energy and gas consist in avoiding serious conflict between the exporters of metals and fertilizers on the one hand, and the exporters of net energy and the budget on the other. The contemporary system of pricing in the gas sector is based on the fact that the entire Russian gas infrastructure had been set up during the 1970s–1980s at the expense of the state and to the detriment of other social factors. In order to create an export sector, the money was "withdrawn" from other industries and from the consumer sector. The Soviet Union annually invested around $10–12 billion into the gas industry. The apparent cheapness of tariffs today is due to disregarding the cost of infrastructure construction in those times. It may be conditionally said that the cheap gas inside the country is not only the result of Russia's rich natural resources, but also a "gift" from the inhabitants of the erstwhile USSR since the industry's infrastructure had been built on their latent savings.[25]

The European Commission has made certain demands precisely in this domain during the negotiations on joining the WTO. The EU's position has been expressed by Trade Commissioner Pascal Lamy:

> The question of dual pricing of energy products is the key one for the EU. The cost of energy in Russia has been artificially understated. The cost of natural gas constitutes only one-sixth of the world price. As a result, low prices lead to the annual subsidizing of Russian industry to the tune of about $5 billion. Producers can export their goods at unjustifiably low prices. This question is too important for the EU to be ignored.[26]

To all appearances, the European Union wants power-consuming Russian commodities to be priced higher. The press reported unofficial data

[222]

to the effect that the aim of negotiations on the EU side was the price of $45–60 per thousand cubic meters for the Russian industry. As a result, Russian energy firms would have gained more income for investment into export projects, while competition for the European metallurgical and chemical industry would have been reduced.

A jump in Russian gas tariffs, first of all, would have come as a one-time price shock inside an economy in which it is extremely important to cut down the level of inflation in the next few years. Second, the necessity for industry to cross-subsidize the Russian private consumer due to colossal social inequality must be taken into account. It must be noted that the disparity between the level of GDP per capita in the EU and Russia ($21,000 versus $2,500 at current prices) is too great to be simply ignored in the context of the European economic space. Finally, of importance to Russia are the liberalization processes of the internal gas and electric energy market that will lead to the natural rise in tariffs, possibly up to $40 as against the current figure of $21 as cited in an unpublished report of the World Bank on this issue.

For long-term planning there must be answers to a whole range of political questions. It is important to know how a consortium in Ukraine will work and whether it can rebuild the pipes within reasonable timeframes. Should the Baltic pipeline be laid in a way to bypass all countries, which will lead to an increase in the project's initial cost but will allow territorial tariffs to be cut down? Will the petroleum and other companies secure acceptable financial terms for producing gas within Russia in the process of gas industry reform? US experience, for instance, shows that for a rational long-term use of energy resources it is advisable to reclaim small and medium-sized deposits. New gas concessions of the oil companies or small deposits developed by independent companies might help to regulate the country's gas balance in the future and unburden export routes. The same goal is also objectively served by the program of constructing an atomic power station, which reduces the future demand for gas in the European part of Russia.

The question of what share of the internal gas consumption the EU is ready to admit from a single source is a separate problem. Officially there are no restrictions, but 30 percent has been recommended, especially in connection with the great dependence of future EU members on Russian gas. Nowadays Russia delivers 36 percent of gas to Greater Europe (31 percent to Great Britain, 16 percent to Norway, and in decreasing order, to Algeria, the Netherlands and Nigeria), with the EU internal output not likely to exceed 300 billion cubic meters. With a view to retaining its share (of the order of 30 percent) in the expanding European market, Russia has to increase deliveries from 130 billion cubic meters to 200–210 billion cubic meters in 2010. This makes it necessary to build about three strands of pipelines (30 billion cubic meters each) and increase output to the level needed to ensure these deliveries in addition to catering for the gradual revival of demand in Russia and the CIS. In this case, the possibility of simultaneous entry to other export markets remains unclear.

New Horizons

On October 3, 2003, inaugurating the World Economic Forum in Moscow, Russian President Vladimir Putin promised foreign investors stability in the economy and continuity in policy. The Ministry of Economic Development had calculated that in 2003 the growth of foreign direct investment in Russia amounted to 50 percent in comparison with investments during the same period in 2002.

Especially noticeable is the rise in the investment activity of Royal Dutch/Shell Group, which in 2004–2009 intends to bring the volume of its Russian investments up to $8 billion, a figure 8 times more than the present volume.[27] They will make up 20 percent of Shell's investment portfolio. Back in May 2003, the company announced its plans on the second phase of the Sakhalin II project, for which the investment would total $10 billion (Shell's share being 55 percent). According to Valery Nesterov, an analyst of Troyka Dialog, another one or two billion would be the volume of investment in the group of Salym deposits. As early as August 16, 2003 the Royal Dutch/Shell Group declared that it approved the budget for the development of the Salym group of deposits in Western Siberia to the tune of more than $1 billion. The oil extraction of the West Salym deposit is expected to start by the end of 2005 and its maximum level – 120 thousand barrels per day – will be reached in 2009.

However, Shell's plans in 2003 were still open to question. The Nature Ministry suspended the economic activity of the Salym Petroleum Development company, a joint venture with the involvement of Shell. Although on September 30, 2003 the Moscow Arbitration Court allowed a claim of Salym Petroleum Development and declared the Nature Ministry's injunction to be invalid, the conflict was far from being over as the Ministry was not going to relinquish its claims on Salym Petroleum Development.

Reports on the revision of the size of Russian oil reserves have revived interest in its market. At the World Economic Forum in 2003, the then Yukos President Mikhail Khodorkovsky declared that these reserves had been understated and that in fact they amounted to not less than 150 billion barrels.

Russia is continually seeking to increase energy shipments to the Asian markets. During meetings with the ministers of ASEAN countries in the format "ASEAN plus Russia" in June 2003, Russia's Foreign Minister Igor Ivanov reiterated Moscow's previous proposal to supply energy resources to the APR countries and thereby contribute to safeguarding the region's energy security.

In late 2003, President Putin declared for the first time that Russia might switch to the euro in settlements for energy with European consumers.[28] It is clear that this measure, if implemented, would prove advantageous to European countries. In the event that in the near future the world oil market is divided into two zones, those of the dollar and the euro, the dollar zone would still prevail, since the United States would remain the greatest oil importer.

Especially attractive for Asian consumers of energy resources are the deposits in Eastern Siberia, which, according to Russia's Energy Minister Igor Yusufov, are comparable to the resources of Western Siberia. The problem so far lies in infrastructure.

The government during the course of 2003 was faced with a serious dilemma of where to supply the oil from Angarsk. Yukos was the first to propose a variant export route to the Chinese town of Daqing. "At an earlier stage Russia declared its support for the project, but gave no government guarantees," Yusufov explains. Afterwards a project based on export to Nakhodka was proposed by Transneft. Interest in this project was expressed not only by the Russian officials attracted by the idea of free export from Nakhodka in many directions, but also the Japanese, who want to reduce their dependence on Middle Eastern oil. In May 2003, the Russian government even approved a unified framework route of the Angarsk–Nakhodka pipeline with a branch to Daqing, but it had not been decided which sector of the route must be built first. "The government has still no such exact, clear understanding," Igor Yusufov confessed. The issue here is not only about the difficult ecological aspects of these projects. According to the minister, it is impossible to build two segments of the route at once. Angarsk–Daqing is rated at exporting 30 million tons of oil a year and Angarsk–Nakhodka is rated at 50 million tons, but 80 million tons are not available for the export of oil in this direction as yet.[29]

While the Chinese government was unsuccessfully trying to get an answer to the question of whether Russia would fulfill the intergovernmental agreement where the Angarsk–Daqing variant was mentioned, the Japanese were not sitting idly by. "Two months ago we set up a joint Russo-Japanese energy commission, and now I have an official proposal from the Japanese government to participate in the project in all its aspects," stated Igor Yusufov.[30] In his words, the Japanese were ready not only to finance the construction of the pipeline costing $5 billion, but also to earmark $2 billion for the additional prospecting of deposits in Eastern Siberia, which are to provide oil for this pipeline. The Energy Ministry experts believe that exactly this sum is necessary to bring the oil deposits of Eastern Siberia to the level of Western Siberia. In 2003 the government began negotiating the terms on which such investments may be accepted.

Gazprom is nurturing far-reaching plans of increasing gas exports. Information leaked from Western sources that Gazprom and the Italian company ENI had decided to revise the fundamental terms of contracts on Russian gas deliveries caught the market by surprise. The two sides decided to exclude from these contracts a provision that banned sales to third parties. This, in turn, would allow ENI to resell the gas being bought from Gazprom to any third partner—in Italy and beyond. Earlier, ENI was obliged to pay for all the gas being bought from Gazprom in full, without reselling options, regardless of whether the company would later be able to sell the purchased gas on the Italian market.[31]

A similar problem was hotly debated at the Russo-Turkish negotiations. After the construction of the Blue Stream gas pipeline costing $3.4 billion, it transpires that Turkey, currently in the throes of economic difficulties, does not need the Russian gas in the volumes and at the price agreed in the Blue Stream project. However, by the terms of the contract, the BOTAS oil company was obliged to pay for the entire volume of shipments at the agreed price.

In return for compromise on Gazprom's part, ENI undertook to expand the transport facilities for the import of Russian gas to Italy via Austria. ENI would also cancel its veto on the conclusion of bilateral contracts between other Italian firms and Gazprom.

Within the European Union, all these events were regarded as a "tectonic upheaval in the mind of the Russians." For Gazprom had always acted in Europe as the supporter of long-term (for 15–25 years), rigid, "enclosed" contracts, basing this on the need to receive a guaranteed profit, out of which it finances the development of deposits in Russia that are difficult to access. What was also borne in mind was the extreme indiscipline of "cheap" internal Russian consumers in payments for gas supplies.

However, the situation in the EU energy markets is changing. First of all, for eight out of ten countries that have become new EU members (the exceptions being Cyprus and Malta) Gazprom has been the main gas supplier since Soviet times. There is no serious alternative to this supply in the near future. Second, Gazprom, despite chronic internal non-payments on the part of consumers, has managed to increase its gas output. Its exporting capacities are also growing in connection with gas transit from Central Asia (where Russia is buying gas two and a half times cheaper than it sells in Western Europe). Since early 2003, Gazprom has augmented shipments to Europe by another 18 billion cubic meters compared to the year 2002.

It looks as though the EU has already "reconciled itself" to its "dependence" on Russian gas. In the view of many Russian observers, the EU's former dream of minimizing dependence on a single supplier (to no more than 30 percent), is already forgotten.

Even Britain is holding talks on the possibility of importing Russian gas via the Baltic Sea and Germany. This project involves the financing of the construction of a pipeline by the German Ruhrgas, which owns 6.6 percent of Gazprom's shares. The question of German government support for this particular project featured on the agenda of the summit meeting between President Vladimir Putin and Chancellor Gerhard Schroeder in Yekaterinburg, held on October 8, 2003. A few days earlier, a similar contract was discussed in Moscow by Pierre Gadonneix, the President of Gaz de France.

The position of oil and gas companies in Russia remains solid and stable. However, pressure on the government continues to be exerted by a number of political forces, so as to make it curtail the super profits of fuel and raw-material companies. According to the forecasts of the Central Economic Mathematical Institute of the Russian Academy of Sciences, the super profit in the petroleum industry for 2003 will constitute $27.6 billion and in the gas industry will amount to $10.4 billion. The main portion of the super profit – about 75–80 percent – is export-generated. In the opinion of Sergei Glazyev, the State Duma Deputy, a portion of the super profit must go to the state budget through the imposition of the rent tax. Another proposed variant is to transfer a definite percentage of the super profit to the citizens' individual bank accounts. Such calls multiplied during the election campaign of 2003.

However, the well-entrenched positions of Russia's oil and gas companies will hardly be shattered and the government places its confidence in the growth of energy exports and on Russia's entry into new markets. Only a drastic fall in oil prices caused by a reemergence of Iraq as a major world oil producer can diminish Russia's chances of turning these plans into reality.

Russian Energy Trends: A Postscript

Between late 2003, when this paper was presented at the energy conference in Abu Dhabi, and mid–2005 when this volume went to the press, the main assessments and forecasts made have been borne out and proven by data characterizing the current Russian market and energy resources, while the trends noted at the time of the conference also remain valid.

[228]

However, some conference observations and assumptions need to be corrected. Reality sometimes surpasses the boldest predictions and sometimes turns out to be quite different from what analysts envisage. Who could have expected that Yukos, one of the largest and most prosperous Russian oil companies, would be close to collapse, while its managers, including Russia's wealthiest man, Mikhail Khodorkovsky, would end up behind bars? Who could have predicted the fantastic soaring of world oil prices that has taken place in the past months? In this present context, forecasts made by "pessimists" like the Russian analysts from Troyka-Dialog company ($18-20 a barrel) seem quite ridiculous. It would be worthwhile to give a general idea of the situation regarding Russia's hydrocarbons when viewed from an early 2005 perspective.

First of all, it should be remarked that the Russian government is oriented to the growth of energy resource production for export to a degree even greater than that envisaged by the forecasts of 2003. Today, Russia has already outstripped Saudi Arabia, having occupied the first place among petroleum producers in the world and has every opportunity to reach an output level of 10.8 mbpd as early as 2007. The high world prices of oil have allowed Russia to accumulate additional monetary resources in the Stabilization Fund, sustain high economic growth rates and pay off its debts to foreign creditors in advance.

During the last one and a half years, Russia has manifested a tendency for the state to impose a more stringent control over business in the fuel and energy sector. The Russian authorities are regarding the "Yukos case" as a purely criminal one, devoid of any political motivation whatsoever. Strenuous efforts were exerted to persuade foreign investors not to perceive it as a precedent motivated by political reasons that might cloud their business prospects in Russia.

Yukos' main extracting asset, Yuganskneftegaz company, has been purchased by Rosneft, a company which is 100 percent state-owned (its president being Sergei Bogdanchikov).

In 2004, the Russian authorities carried out a series of tax inspections of all big companies active in the Russian market. Many were presented with tax bills amounting to tens of millions of dollars.

In April 2005, TNK-BP, which was set up in 2003 through the merger of BP's Russian oil assets with those of Alfa Group (led by Mikhail Fridman), Access Industries and Renova Group (led by Viktor Vekselberg), announced that it received from the Federal Tax Service a notice relating to the second tax inspection for 2001, which charged the company 22 billion rubles in tax payments. Some analysts believed from the outset that the claim would be settled and that the sole aim of the authorities was to show that claims were being lodged not with Yukos alone.[32]

The Federal Antimonopoly Service (FAS) tightened control over all oil company activities. It has charged a number of companies with arranging deals to influence markets and prices. In particular, in March 2005 it was reported that Lukoil (led by Vagit Alekperov) and Sibneft (led by Roman Abramovich) might be fined for a cartel agreement in the regions.[33]

The sale of Yuganskneftegaz has not led to Yukos' bankruptcy as yet. It has become known that for the purchase of Yuganskneftegaz the state company Rosneft attracted a credit, including 6 billion dollars borrowed from Chinese banks by Vneshekonombank. This attested not only to state interest in increasing its presence in the oil and gas sector, but also to China's growing interest in Russian oil.

At the same time, the state planned to effect in 2005, a transfer of 100 percent of Rosneft's stock to the balance sheet of another state firm, Rosneftegas. The latter, in turn, would become a target for an exchange of assets with Gazprom with a view to bringing the state's controlling interest in the gas monopoly to 51 percent.[34]

Various arrangements for the merger of Rosneft and Gazprom by summer 2005 were examined, which certain analysts saw as indications of hidden rivalry among the different interest groups in the ruling elite.

A proposal by Russia's Ministry for Natural Resources not to allow foreign companies to develop "strategic deposits," during the discussion of the draft of a new law on mineral resources in parliament, caused anxiety among foreign investors. Russia's Minister for Natural Resources Yuri Trutnev declared that nothing more would be entered into the list of strategic deposits, as no unexplored and undeveloped strategic deposits would remain by that time. (As of 2005, the list contained just six deposits ready to be developed). The total financing needed to develop all the resources is in the order of 2.5 trillion rubles (about 90 billion dollars).[35]

In April 2005, the Kremlin made two statements aimed at calming foreign investors who had been frightened by the authorities' increased pressure on business. The first statement concerned the number of such deposits. As Russian President Vladimir Putin's assistant stated after the President's meeting with BP head John Brown on April 22, 2005: "There will be six or seven such deposits in the country, while others number hundreds and thousands." The second statement was that the licences already issued would not be revoked, as the law has no retroactive force.[36]

The meeting by BP head John Brown with President Vladimir Putin was of great significance for the United Kingdom, which since 2003 has already invested 5.3 billion dollars in joint business ventures with the Russians and intends to develop it further by acquiring new oilfields.[37]

The pipeline network remains a weak point in the program of Russian hydrocarbon exports. According to the director of one such enterprise, 70 percent of the oil pipeline's tubing has been in operation for more than 20 years, with the total wear rate more than 40 percent. In addition, in the unified gas distribution network, about 70 percent of the tubing has been in operation for more than 10 years.[38]

As matters stand in 2005, summing up Russia's efforts to develop its oil exports and oil transit from the CIS states via the Russian pipeline network one may identify four main directions:

- The Western direction, along which oil reaches the European states via Ukraine and Belarus.
- The Northern direction, the main segment of which is the Baltic Pipeline System (chiefly intended for bringing oil from the Timano-Pechora oil and gas province).
- The Southern direction, with traditional oil transportation to the ports of Novorossiisk, and also passing the Straits of the Bosporus and the Dardanelles.
- The Eastern direction, with oil supply to Japan and further to the states of Southeast Asia, as well as to the People's Republic of China (PRC).

[231]

As mentioned in the conference presentation, the TNK-BP company has been the initiator of Russian oil deliveries via the Ukrainian pipeline Odessa–Brody, which remained dry during 2002–2004, in the reverse direction (Brody–Odessa). Since September 2004, the pipeline has been working in this regime, but with the new government coming to power in Ukraine, the prospects of these deliveries being continued have become uncertain.

The increased activity of the fuel and energy business in Russia gives rise to the presumption that the bold plans for oil and gas exports to the United States are apparently bound to come true. It is known that US specialists are calculating the cost of options for oil imports by sea from the northern Russian deposits. Experts believe that the projects for gas supplies to the United States from the Russian offshore fields in the Barents Sea, which may be developed by cooperating with Norway, are quite realistic. The questions of energy cooperation have become part and parcel of Russo-American interstate negotiations, including at the top level. Efforts have been exerted to expedite the plans for the construction of the Murmansk Pipeline System, in which the US side is evincing interest.

Over the last year and a half, Russia has stepped up efforts to ensure its outlet to the oil markets of the Asia–Pacific Region. Oil deliveries to the PRC are made by rail, but the volume of deliveries is somewhat less compared to what Yukos had been planning earlier (the oil is supplied by Rosneft, Lukoil and Sibneft). The Russian government has decided to accelerate the development of the project for the construction of a pipeline from Eastern Siberia to the Pacific, along which oil could be delivered to all the potential Asian customers. The Ministry for Industry and Trade believes the question of developing the oil resources of Eastern Siberia and creating a pipeline network for exporting them to the east to be of paramount importance. As is known, China in 2004 accounted for 23 percent of the total growth of world demand for oil.[39]

Dynamic changes in the Russian gas market have continued. The new policy of Gazprom, which allowed West European partners to re-export its gas has been confirmed. Thus, the last restrictions on contracts with the largest importer of Russian gas – the German E.ON Ruhrgas – were lifted in 2005.[40]

In 2004, Gazprom and Royal Dutch/Shell started talks on an asset swap. The Russian monopoly sought to gain a share in the Sakhalin II project and Shell wanted a share in the projects for gas production from new deposits, with a view to replenishing its hydrocarbon reserves. An option under discussion was to give 50 percent participation in the project for the development of the Zapolyarni deposit in exchange for a 20–22 percent share in Sakhalin Energy (the operator of the Sakhalin II project, 55 percent of which belongs to Shell, 25 percent to Mitsui and 20 percent to Mitsubishi). By April 2005, Gazprom and Royal Dutch/Shell had either reached an understanding on this issue (as some media reports claimed) or were at a very advanced stage of negotiations.[41] Gazprom expected that a share in Sakhalin II would ensure its access to the markets of the countries of the Asia–Pacific Region. Thus this deal on the Russian side is also dictated by the desire to gain new markets and increase exports.

Besides, an agreement on an asset swap was signed between Gazprom and the German BASF company. Speaking at a press conference in Hanover on April 11, 2005, Vladimir Putin emphasized that the question in fact was about allowing foreign partners access to gas production:

> The German partners have 49 percent in the pipe. Gazprom and BASF gain a possibility of jointly taking part in gas distribution. And they will work in third countries, including Northern Europe.[42]

Thus Gazprom has chosen its strategic partner for the construction of the first leg of the North European pipeline that will run along the bed of the Baltic Sea from the Russian city of Vyborg to the German city of Greifswald. This project has been under discussion since 1997 to create an alternative route for gas supplies to Germany, Britain and the Scandinavian states.

In 2005, Gazprom's Chief Executive Alexei Miller launched a sensational initiative to revoke the regulation of pipeline rates for industry from 2006. In the process, company spokesmen have noted that the realization of this proposal will not necessarily lead to a price rise for gas, since the mechanism of exchange trade will be used and the stock exchange is not under the monopolist's control.[43] Gazprom's initiative largely reflected the pressure exerted on Russia by its Western partners in connection with its intentions to join the WTO, with the objective of liberalizing the gas market. Some Russian energy specialists viewed Gazprom's proposal with caution, while supporting it in principle. Boris Titov, head of the Coordinator of the Gas Market (CGM), an association comprising both producers and government officials, favored a gradual transition to a free-price system and exchange trade, saying that CGM had worked out a program for the adaptation period of transition to a free gas market, which was signed by Gazprom, RAO UES (Unified Energy Systems), metallurgists and oilers.[44] The head of RAO UES, Anatoly Chubais, also expressed an opinion that "it is absolutely wrong to free prices, given a monopoly supplier."[45] It is clear that everything will depend on the direction in which the reform of the Russian gas sector will proceed.

While stepping up gas exports, Russia envisages that by 2007 it can bring the Blue Stream pipeline to Turkey upto the planned production capacity (16 billion cubic meters a year) and by 2010 build a gas-transport system Yamal-West extending 5,350 km with a pipeline capacity of up to 65 billion cubic meters a year. It is proposed to start the construction of a North European pipeline for delivering gas across the Baltic Sea to the German coast (the 1,200 kilometer-long pipeline is planned to be laid along the seabed).

Currently under consideration are the projects for gas exports to the PRC, South Korea and Japan. The Chinese market is especially attractive for Russian producers. According to the Director-General of RUSIA Petroleum, Valeri Pak, three schemes of possible pipeline directions are being examined. However, all the options presuppose gas delivery from Eastern Siberia into a unified gas supply system (UGSS). The first option envisages gas deliveries from the Kovykta and Chayanda fields to China and Korea. The Sakhalin fields, according to this option, are called upon to satisfy the internal market of regions experiencing energy shortages—the Khabarovsk krai and the Maritime Territory, and also to ensure the supply of compressed natural gas (CNG). The second option provides for the supply of Kovykta gas only to local markets and the UGSS. Sakhalin in this case will be a raw material base for the deliveries of CNG as well as heating-system gas to Korea, while the Chayanda field is viewed as a facility for gas deliveries to China. According to the third option, Kovykta gas would be supplied to the UGSS and the Chayanda field would be left undeveloped until 2030, whereas Sakhalin would provide gas to all the markets of the Asia-Pacific Region.[46] Russia's gas operators also believe that it is rational to use the resource base of Sakhalin for the deliveries of compressed gas to the markets of Japan, Taiwan, the United States, Korea and China.

Gazprom has so far regarded the following option as the principal one: to use the gas of the Kovykta field for gasification of the southern part of Eastern Siberia (the Irkutsk oblast and the Krasnoyarsk krai) and then to supply it to the UGSS, that is, to the West. It is also contemplating the question of constructing a pipeline from the Chayanda field for delivery to the Asia–Pacific Region. Gazprom has also not excluded the possibility of branching the pipeline to Northeast China. In other words, the debates on the development of the gas resources of Eastern Siberia and routes for transporting gas to the east were far from over in mid–2005.

The balance sheet of the months that have elapsed since the energy conference enables us to conclude that Russia is gradually being transformed into one of the leading suppliers of hydrocarbons to the world markets and this trend will most probably be sustained.

GULF OIL: OUTLOOK AND OPTIONS

10

Gulf Oil in a New Map of World Oil Supplies: Long Term Prospects in the Changing Market Environment

Robert E. Mabro CBE

Wars are always associated with dreams. Launching a war always requires public support and effective motivation for the young men and women who will be exposed to the risks of death and injury. This drives governments to foster certain dreams, for example, claiming that the war will usher in a better world buttressed by the structures of a new international order. Of course, governments would acknowledge that destruction and casualties were inevitable, but that modern military technology would mercifully ensure that this would be very limited, almost insignificant. Governments would promise peace, security and greater prosperity as well as freedom to nations hitherto shackled by nasty dictatorships.

These are all great and inspiring visions, sometimes partially realized, sometimes vanishing rapidly like mirages in the desert or dreams that dissipate with the coming of dawn.

The Iraq War of 2003 was sold on a number of different grounds to the world at large—a world in which the sceptics outnumbered supporters. At one time or another, the US and UK governments indicated that some or all the following reasons had prompted them to launch a war:

- Iraq kept stocks of weapons of mass destruction and was engaged in programs for their production.
- Iraq had links with Al Qaida, thus making the invasion part and parcel of the wider war against terrorism. (This argument was advanced by the

US while the UK indicated that there was no evidence of an alliance between Iraq and Al Qaida.)

- Iraq failed to implement binding UN resolutions. This behavior brought the international order and the United Nations in particular, into disrepute.
- Saddam Hussein was a dictator who inflicted horrible sufferings upon his people. (Regime change was an emphatic US argument, which was adopted late in the day by the UK government.)
- Iraq had started war with Iran and invaded Kuwait, all in the space of 10 years, and continued to support the Palestinian *intifada,* thus posing a danger to regional stability.

The big dreams associated with these motives for the invasion of Iraq were as follows:

- The war would improve world security owing to the elimination of weapons of mass destruction.
- Another major benefit would be to weaken, if not to win a victory over terrorism.
- The international order would be restored to the advantage of world peace.
- The Iraqi people would be freed from the evils of a dictatorship, and democracy would emerge and blossom in Iraq, and through a domino effect, in the whole Middle East region.
- Free from the threat of Iraqi aggression, the Middle East region would enjoy great stability.

It appears that the first dream was based on the elimination of a non-existent threat. Weapons of mass destruction were not found despite an intensive search (being so well hidden perhaps as to make it also difficult for the Iraqi army to use!). It is also doubtful whether Libya, the first piece of the domino set to wobble is equipped with anything that represents a serious threat.

The second dream has turned sour because the war opened the Iraqi borders to suicide bombers and other fighters. Instead of eliminating a link with Al Qaida which apparently did not exist, the war created a situation favorable to terrorists as predicted by President Hosni Mubarak of Egypt and many others.

Has the international order been restored or disrupted? In fact, the war created a rift between some major European countries and the United States, posed problems for the European Union (EU) and the North Atlantic Treaty Organization (NATO) and gravely undermined the authority of the United Nations. Clearly, the third dream was far from being translated into reality.

It can certainly be said that Iraq was freed from an ugly dictatorship. However, the blossoming of a democracy, the necessary insurance against the eventual emergence of some new dictator, is obviously more difficult to achieve. A powerful army can bring about the demise of a political regime through sheer force. The designing of a social contract based on the consensus of a number of groups with different religious, tribal or political allegiance, various ethnic origins and divergent interests is a job for skilled politicians with a profound understanding of the country. People with such skills are in scarce supply. The serious risk is that the removal of the dictatorship, a positive measure in itself, would be followed later, either tomorrow or in ten years time, by a civil war or the emergence of another dictator. This risk arises not because the removal of a dictatorship is undesirable but because no plans were made to handle effectively the political, economic and social situation that was bound to develop after the invasion.

Finally, the dream of greater stability seems a bit far fetched. Much depends, in fact, on the meaning of stability. Stability arising from the fears that the US may now inspire as the sole world superpower cannot, and will not be durable. Sustainable stability is the outcome of free decisions and free compromises made by all the parties concerned in the region.

In my view, the war in Iraq had little to do with its stated objectives and their associated dreams. The reason is that governments are not in the business of realizing dreams, which are generated merely to gain support for policies that are not immediately attractive to public opinion. Rather, governments are in the business of making policy in response to political factors and events—international and domestic. The War in Iraq was intended by the neo-conservative wing of the Republican Party long before

[241]

the current US administration won the election in 2000; and Paul O'Neil, the former US Secretary of the Treasury has more recently revealed that it was an early priority of President Bush's government. The driving force was the view that the United States needed to assert its dominance in the international realm (as President Reagan tried to do), and to reveal with some resounding action that its new status as the sole global superpower is a reality, not just a perception.

Iraq was the ideal candidate to become the object of a hostile action that would send a clear signal to Russia, China, Europe, Iran and the Arab world that superpower might is the prerogative of the US alone. All these powers have strategic, economic or broad political interests in the region. From the US perspective, Iraq had the advantage over North Korea of not wielding nuclear weapons; over Iran by being a smaller, more manageable size; and over both of them by being an Arab country (so that an association of ideas with terrorism can easily spring into uncritical minds). Moreover, Iraq had a much despised and indeed despicable dictator; it had a history of aggression against neighbors; it had flouted UN resolutions; and it happens to have an unrivalled strategic location and borders with six countries: Iran, Turkey, Syria, Jordan, Kuwait and Saudi Arabia.

The tragic events of 9/11 provided a trigger. These outrages deeply traumatized the United States, which had escaped attacks on its mainland during the two World Wars. Americans went to bed one night feeling perfectly secure, only to painfully discover their shocking vulnerability the next morning. The government had to engage in some action to prove to their people that their country is very powerful and can confront any enemy, anywhere in the world. Such an action would restore confidence and soothe the hurt caused by that sudden feeling of vulnerability.

These were the fundamental motives for war. Yet wars involve a host of secondary considerations that give rise to many particular dreams. Various groups, national or foreign, corporations and even individuals, all with different economic or political interests will hope that the hostilities and the ensuing peace will bring about opportunities to pursue and perhaps fulfil their own objectives. Since the main focus of this chapter relates to oil, attention will be focused on dreams fostered by various lobbies concerned with the strategic dimensions of this important source of energy.

[242]

First of all, let me state that oil was not the *determining* cause of the war. Here, I define "cause" in the "Occam's razor" sense[1] that is best illustrated by this question: "Would the war have taken place if Iraq had no oil?" My answer to this question is a simple "Yes." This does not mean that oil was not one of the considerations present in the minds of the US decision-makers. While the government might give various reasons for deciding to go to war, the fact that Iraq is an important oil-exporting country is a bonus.

The US interest in securing an additional source of oil seems obvious at first sight. The United States now imports about 10 million barrels per day (mbpd) of oil, a volume that covers more than half its daily consumption. As oil consumption is expected to expand in the foreseeable future, often by a greater amount than domestic production, imports will also grow. It must be recalled that the United States consumes some 25% of the world oil production, and imports about 27% of oil in international trade. These facts alone explain that the United States naturally worries about its oil dependence and wishes to diversify its supply sources as much as possible. This is perfectly understandable and perfectly legitimate.

Since Iraq has very significant geophysical oil reserves, and its production, which rarely exceeded 3.5 million barrels per day can be expanded to 6.0 million barrels per day with appropriate investments, it follows that Iraq can play an important role in the world petroleum market in future. The development of Iraq's oil resources is a rational way to enhance the diversification of import sources for the United States, and indeed other countries—a desirable objective.

Had oil been the main or sole US objective, there would have been no case for a war on Iraq. The lifting of sanctions on oil investments in Iraq would have achieved this objective without much ado. A large number of foreign oil companies were engaged in negotiations with the previous Iraqi authorities during the sanction period. They were all ready to sign production-sharing agreements as soon as the sanctions are lifted. Lukoil went as far as signing a full contract. In any case, the United States was importing Iraqi oil, in a perfectly legal way, during the sanction period. At one time the import volume from Iraq was close to 1 million barrels per day. If diversification is the name of the game, significant diversification involving Iraq as a supply source had clearly been achieved even before the invasion, and more emphatically without any recourse to war.

[243]

Yet, the war was associated with dreams about oil. The dream entertained by a number of US strategic lobbies was to draw a *new map of world oil.* The idea was not new. In fact, in one form or another, it had some antecedents. The earlier concept originated in Venezuela some fifteen or twenty years ago. It envisaged the promotion of a situation in which the United States would only import oil from oil exporters in the American continent, mainly Venezuela, Mexico, Canada, Ecuador and Colombia. The concept was labelled 'hemispherical self-sufficiency.' It had no economic rationale, despite the fact that transport costs of oil to the US ports is lower from many Latin American countries and Canada than it is from the Middle East, because competition tends to equalize prices on a cost, insurance and freight (CIF) basis. In other words, the difference in transport costs is absorbed by the exporting countries, and is not paid by the importers. The idea of "hemispherical self-sufficency" was adopted eagerly by "arabophobe" commentators who even dreamt of an oil world consisting of three main regions: a self-sufficient Western Hemisphere, a Europe supplied by the expanding North Sea and Africa with limited dependence on the Gulf, and an Asia wedded to the Gulf in oil trade.

It is unclear whether hemispherical self-sufficiency was achievable when the idea first emerged. What is clear, however, is that it cannot be achieved today because the volume of oil imported by the United States exceeds significantly the export volume available from other American countries.

The main attraction of this concept for US strategic lobbies is that it encourages the switching of import dependence from an *unreliable* Middle East to *reliable* American countries. The idea now is to replace Saudi Arabia by other sources of oil imports to the United States. Recently, some lobbies have focused on Russia and the Caspian countries as candidates to replace Saudi Arabia on the international trade map of oil. Other strategists added West Africa to the list of newcomers with allegedly huge potential for oil export growth. The focus there is on Nigeria, Angola, Equatorial Guinea, Sao Tome y Principe and some others.

The idea that this mix of countries is more reliable as a supply source than Saudi Arabia and other Gulf countries is debatable. Political unrest can mar the stability of one or more African nation, or any Central Asian

Republic. Ironically, the supply interruptions of December 2002 and early 2003 occurred in Venezuela, the bulwark behind the hemispherical self-sufficiency theory, and also in Nigeria, one of the countries on which politically motivated and unrealistic strategists now want to depend.

The invasion of Iraq fostered the dream that Saudi Arabia could be replaced in the world petroleum map by another Gulf country. Indeed, Iraq has massive oil reserves that are insufficiently exploited. A democratic, pro-Western Iraq blossoming economically under a liberal regime could invite foreign oil companies under favorable conditions to invest in exploration, development and production of hydrocarbons. Oil production would then rise by 2008 to 5.0 million barrels per day, or perhaps 6.0 million barrels per day, or even to 7.0 million barrels per day.

It is not evident that the war will lead to the emergence of a peaceful, stable, pro-Western, democratic and economically liberal Iraq in the near future. It is not certain either that a nationalist government that may establish itself in Iraq after a long period of turmoil will offer production-sharing contracts to foreign oil companies on very soft terms. To be sure, the doors of the oil upstream sector will be open to private investors but on terms that reflect the advantages enjoyed by Iraq in terms of low exploration risks, huge reserves and low production costs. It is important to keep in mind the fact that Iraq, having suffered a long period of hardship and destruction through three wars and 12 years of sanctions, will always be concerned with the maximization of its oil revenues. This need may force Baghdad to cooperate on certain occasions with OPEC and other oil-exporters with output restrictions that aim to shore up prices.

Apart from all this, the idea that Saudi Arabia's role in the world oil market can be taken over by another country is based on a misunderstanding of what the country's role entails. This role has three elements, the first of these being volume. Saudi Arabia currently supplies about 12% of the world oil consumption. To replace the country on this front requires finding additional supplies of 10 million barrels per day now and around 16-18 million barrels per day in 2020. With a big stretch of the imagination, it might be just possible to do without a large part of the Saudi oil supplies some time towards the end of this decade, but certainly not for a very long time.

The second feature of Saudi Arabia's role is that it is the only country in the world that holds a significant volume of surplus capacity—probably 3 million barrels per day. This enabled Saudi Arabia to compensate for reductions in oil production resulting from the Iraq-Iran War of 1980–1988, the Iraqi invasion of Kuwait in 1990 and the Iraq War of 2003. Neither Iraq, nor Russia nor any other country can afford to invest huge sums merely to create idle oil production capacity. No other country would build a total production capacity of 12-14 million barrels per day, which would make it tolerable to hold 2-3 million barrels per day of idle plant capacity for emergencies.

The third feature of the Saudi oil industry – which it shares with Kuwait and to some extent with Abu Dhabi – is an ability to reduce production significantly without causing much damage to the behavior and recovery of its huge oil fields. Again, this is not an advantage enjoyed by Russia, the Caspian countries or the West African producers. However, Iraq may display some flexibility in this aspect sometime in the future.

All three features in combination create the necessary conditions for the performance of the swing producer role. In that sense, Saudi Arabia is irreplaceable and the idea that some other country can perform this role is patently wrong. The idea that Saudi Arabia's role is unnecessary or of no real value is also dangerous to entertain. The world petroleum market needs a buffer that is available at short notice during emergencies.

There are those who display great optimism about increases in oil production that are likely to occur during the rest of this decade. There is an optimistic forecast for every oil-exporting country based on investment plans, statements from officialdom or from private oil companies eager to impress financial analysts or based on scenarios developed by consultants or international organizations. Taking oil production in 2003 as a base, the postulated increases in oil production to 2010 are as indicated in Table 10.1.

The grand total of these postulated increases is of the order of 17-18 mbpd. This optimistic supply scenario suggests there will be a huge supply surplus over demand, assuming that oil demand will increase by 1.5–1.8 mbpd per year during the years 2004 to 2010, which would total 10.5–12.6 mbpd by the end of this period.

Table 10.1

Oil Production by Region/Country: Postulated Increases to 2010

(Base year = 2003; Units = mbpd)

Country/Region	Increase (mbpd)
Iraq	3.0-4.0 mbpd
Russia	2.5 mbpd
Caspian	2.0 mbpd
West Africa (including Nigeria)	3.5 mbpd
Deep Offshore (USA, Brazil etc)	1.0 mbpd
Venezuela	1.5 mbpd
Canada	1.0 mbpd
Algeria	0.5 mbpd
Libya	0.5 mbpd
Iran	1.0 mbpd
Kuwait	0.5 mbpd
UAE	0.3 mbpd

Source: Author's own forecast of high supply case.

The world petroleum market cannot absorb the 6-7 mbpd, which is not required for consumption at prevailing prices. This volume would remain in excess of the consumption demand at the collapsed prices that this potential surplus will bring about.

The inevitable conclusion is that oil prices will collapse long before this production surplus materializes. In fact, price movements in the oil market respond to anticipation, long before the expected event actually occurs. Traders bid prices down (or up) as soon as they come to believe that a surplus (or a shortage) may emerge. The early price collapse, due to anticipation, will also have an adverse impact on the investment projects on which further production increases depend. Both national and private international oil companies will suffer from very significant reductions in their cash flows. Capital expenditure budgets would then be slashed. After a time lag, the response to low prices is a reduction in supplies.

[247]

There is no doubt that a very chaotic and disturbing situation will arise as soon as the production surplus reaches 1.0 or 1.5 mbpd. The mechanism leading to a downward price spiral was revealed by the events of 1998 and can be described as follows. It all begins with a front-end price that declines faster than the fall in the prices of subsequent futures months. This eventually changes the term structure of prices from backwardation to contango. As soon as the contango displays a positive price differential between the first and second futures month, which more than compensates for the cost of oil storage, traders can make an immediate profit by buying physical oil, adding it to inventories, and selling it at the higher futures price a month ahead. When inventories build up, traders bid down prices since higher inventories cast a shadow on the market through overhanging supplies. This creates a vicious cycle of lower prices associated with a contango, higher inventories, further lowering of prices and still higher inventories. This cycle eventually comes to a halt when the storage costs exceed the positive differentials in the term structure of prices. By that time, however, oil prices would have probably fallen to very low levels as they did in 1998.

An assessment of the likelihood of the 'optimistic supply scenario' – which should be really labelled the 'market disaster scenario' in light of our analysis – must take into account a number of factors and constraints that its proponents seem to ignore.

There are political obstacles to the implementation of investment plans in oil-exporting countries, as indeed elsewhere. One may ask, for example, when will Iraq enjoy the political stability that enables a steady flow of efficient investment projects to proceed? When will Iran or Venezuela find it politically possible to enter into agreements for developments in the oil upstream sector with foreign investors on terms that are mutually acceptable? How should the future political stability of Nigeria and Angola be rated? Is it really possible to predict correctly political developments in Russia and the Caspian countries? Problems of political stability are not unique to the Middle East as one may be led to believe from the general commentaries on the oil situation.

An appraisal of the supply scenario must also involve questions relating to geology and economics. For example, is it certain that the oilfields on which such significant production increases depend will deliver as expected? A large proportion of the funds required to yield a net output increase may have to be spent on measures to counteract the natural production decline of old fields.

The financing requirements of ambitious investment plans may exceed the resources available to national oil companies, and in some cases to the private international corporations. National oil companies are always starved of funds by hungry governments faced by ever-increasing expenditure needs to meet the demands of a growing population. For example, the budgetary problems faced by Petróleos Mexicanos (PEMEX), Petróleos de Venezuela, SA (PDVSA), and the Nigerian national oil companies are well known. Private oil companies also face pressures from their shareholders who want capital invested to yield high rates of return and sometimes request that funds are returned to them through back purchases of equity. As a result, capital expenditure budgets may be smaller than necessary to finance ambitious investment plans.

From this list of possible obstacles to the fulfilment of the 'optimistic supply scenario' it should not be inferred that the world petroleum market will not suffer from an excess supply situation at some point during this decade. The point is that the volume of possible excess supplies will be much smaller than implied by the scenario. Yet, this small imbalance can have a devastating impact on prices because what appears to be small *on average* can be significant *at the margin,* and in economics it is the margin that rules.

Oil developments over the next 20 or 30 years may involve three phases:

- a period of surplus production, small but troublesome, some time during this decade
- a gradual tightening of the oil market towards the end of the next decade
- a drive in research and development for new transport fuels and engines gaining strong momentum in the 2020s.

These are the broad features of the scenario. However, the unfolding of this cycle will not be smooth and uneventful. Price volatility is the main characteristic of the path followed by the oil market. Much can happen along the way, from accidents, political events, financial or economic shocks, to policy changes, all of which are generally unpredictable and likely to have an impact on prices and perhaps on supply and demand.

A world petroleum market in turmoil (assuming such an occurrence for the moment) may elicit more successful attempts at cooperation between oil-exporting countries than in the past. They may even persuade the major oil-importing countries of the Organization for Economic Cooperation and Development (OECD), which are witnessing steadily increasing import dependence, to agree on some international scheme of market stabilization. However, these are only hopes and history does not provide us with much cause for optimism.

The urgent task for the Gulf states is to address the two major issues currently confronting them:

- the instability of their oil revenues in the short and medium term
- the long term risk of an economic demise of oil.

The first issue calls for financial policies that balance budgets over a cycle so that public expenditures are not increased when revenues are temporarily buoyant and not decreased when they are temporarily depressed. It also calls for a much greater governmental attention to matters of oil policy. Ministries and national oil companies, almost everywhere, require an injection of talent in order to ensure that the world oil situation is well appraised continually and that the behavior of the market is well understood. Furthermore, oil is not only a matter for geologists, engineers and economists. It involves diplomacy, complex issues of international relations and it relates to many vital interests of the exporting country. Oil expertise should be prominent in the field of finance and foreign affairs, and in the planning and industry ministries, national assemblies, universities and the media. Unfortunately, this is far from being the case.

The long-term issue – the risks attached to the possible economic demise of oil – raises the question of economic development. Although much has been achieved in the past 20 or 30 years, particularly in the development of infrastructure, heavy industry, services, health and social welfare, an enormous task lies ahead.

Economic development is not only about natural resources but also about human resources and human capital. The task is to form generations

[250]

of men and women who are able to think analytically and critically. They should be encouraged to unleash their creative talents. The economic development task begins in kindergartens, schools and universities. It begins with a reform of syllabuses and of teaching methods. It also requires labor market policies that provide the right incentives for the jobs and skills on which economic development critically depends.

These tasks cannot be performed over a short period of time. They have to be approached gradually, and one has to take into account that gestation periods can be very long. Oil countries may have a breathing space of some 30 years. This is barely sufficient to accomplish the required tasks and to ensure continuing prosperity even after the oil era.

11

Energy Policy Planning for the Future: Strategic Options for Decision Makers in the Gulf

Vahan Zanoyan

Although the main focus of this chapter is on strategic options for energy policy-makers in the Gulf, it is appropriate to first outline some of the main features of the current global environment. After highlighting those issues in a broad way, attention will be shifted to the Gulf to discuss the main drivers of energy policy, pinpoint energy and economic development issues, indicate how the two are related and also sketch the potential role of the national oil companies.

The Global Environment: 2002–2005

United States

Any talk about the current global environment ought to begin with the United States, and an analysis of its role. Although it is possible to discuss United States foreign policy drivers at great length, only the main points will be highlighted.

In the last two years, the US has adopted new strategic priorities marked by an enormous obsession with security and driven primarily by a military doctrine. This policy is having a major global impact. The unilateralists are in power though they are somewhat on the defensive in the aftermath of the war in Iraq and are consequently under severe pressure to make policy adjustments. The military sphere of foreign policy dominates both the diplomatic and economic spheres. There is no such thing as real diplomacy anymore. It is American internationalism that dominates, the basic presumption being that if it is good for the US, it is good for the rest of the world, and that the US leads while the rest of the world follows. A combination of idealism and American nationalism drives the process. In this context, idealism takes the form of an almost infinite optimism that the US can change the world and that military power is meant to be used to transform systems, not just to address specific threats. American nationalism is based on the conviction that the United States is a unique nation in human history and therefore, what is good for the US is good for the rest of the world and ought to be imposed.

In the post-September 11 environment, there has been significant erosion of the strategic importance of the Gulf region in the eyes of Washington. This erosion has nothing to do with oil reserves. Officials in Washington realize that September 11 did not change below-the-ground realities and oil reserves are still where they were. However, the above-the-ground situation has changed to such an extent that the strategic importance of the Gulf can no longer be secured just by oil production.

What do these idealists and nationalists want? In the short-term, they want first and foremost to keep their jobs, hopefully even after the 2004 US Presidential elections. They want to win the peace in Iraq, which is not a situation from which they can just turn around and leave like they have done in other places. They want to save face with the Roadmap for Middle East peace even if they do not preserve the Roadmap itself. They also want to increase pressure on Iran. In the longer-term, the idealists hope that this entire region can be transformed into democratic, docile, capitalistic countries, all living in harmony and in peace with Israel and with the West. Their dream is to repeat the experience of Poland, which almost overnight became a democracy and a capitalist country adopting the values of the West. That is the vision that they hoped for.

This policy drive from Washington is the active ingredient in global affairs and most governments are trying to respond to this policy. However, responding to this or any other American foreign policy initiative is not cost-free—it comes at a price. If the response means opposing those initiatives, it entails certain costs. If the response means cooperating with the US, this also entails costs of a different kind.

However, the American campaign has peaked. First, there is no clear solution to US economic constraints. American soldiers are dying in Iraq every day. It is not possible for the US alone to underwrite all the investments necessary to rehabilitate Iraq and, therefore, the push toward internationalization is already happening. The purely unilateralist approach cannot be used to tackle some of the world problems beyond Iraq, such as North Korea, China and other perceived or real threats.

Europe

Europe could potentially play the role of a global mediator but is very reluctant to lead for many reasons. First, the European Union is divided within itself and there is no real unanimity when it comes to foreign policy objectives and priorities. Second, the EU is busy absorbing new members, which is a major preoccupation. Third, there are fundamental distractions caused by the internal contradictions of the European Monetary Union (EMU). Fourth, the United Kingdom is split, and this is a very important factor to be taken into account. The United Kingdom suffers from an almost schizophrenic divide, with the country torn between the urge to support and align itself with US security interests and, on the other hand, its urge towards more European multilateralism.

Asia

In Asia, the operating phrase is "reform and more reform." Reform in Asia covers a wide range of policy agendas and differs in scope from country to country. Japan is still unable to carry out fundamental reform for several reasons, many of which stem from structural and demographic factors. China is reforming very rapidly, but there are still some very serious problems, such as unemployment, regional disparities within the country and very weak financial systems. India is also undergoing reform and has gained in key sectors. However, it suffers for the most part from very poor infrastructure and some structural budget deficits. Southeast Asia has not yet recovered its earlier economic pace and is desperately searching for a new growth model.

Latin America

Latin America is also facing severe structural difficulties. The failure of growth and the collapse of incomes led to a major call for redistribution of income and wealth. As a result, new populist and leftist tendencies have emerged in Latin America. Brazil and the policy initiatives of President Lula da Silva are generally seen as the model, but deep divisions remain.

Russia and Central Asia

Russia and Central Asia are getting richer as oil exports increase, but there is no evidence of parallel reforms at the economic level. However, an improvement in financial conditions alone is inadequate to rehabilitate those economies. An increase in oil revenue without real economic development simply sets them on the path of becoming *rentier* states which, for some at least, appears to be the main objective. Meanwhile, Russia is deeply engaged in a masterful balancing act of its geopolitical and economic interests *vis-a-vis* the US, Europe, the Middle East and Asia.

The Middle East

The Middle East is largely preoccupied with damage control, with very few new constructive initiatives. The "Riyadh Entente"—a short-cut phrase to describe the mid-1990s reconciliation or rapprochement between Saudi Arabia and Iran, the integration of the Syrian and Egyptian stands primarily in reaction to the collapse of the Oslo accords and to the *intifada*, and to the different unfinished businesses in the Middle East, such as Iraq—is the only meaningful surviving reality. The Riyadh Entente is more critical than ever, given the latest regional developments, but the process is itself under some strain. However, damage control remains the most important characteristic in the region, and will be reverted to shortly.

Other Global Trends

The rest of the world is not idly watching US foreign policy initiatives. Regional blocs are being formed to solve local economic problems and there are other alliances like the Riyadh Entente in the Middle East. Similar measures are being taken in Latin America, Asia, and Europe, which are in large part designed to counter or oppose American initiatives. The developing world is desperately seeking a new model that offers growth with equity. The prime example of this is Latin America, although it can also be seen elsewhere. There is a faltering of consensus on globalization, which is mostly propelled by the security-driven foreign policy initiatives of the United States. In the more globalized environment that prevailed in past years, there was more interdependence and probably greater economic cooperation. Today, the American attitude may be summed up as follows: 'Go fix it yourself. We don't do economics. We don't do diplomacy. We are here primarily for security purposes.' The overall impact of this US attitude is higher security risk and country risk for international companies seeking investment opportunities abroad.

The Global Energy Sector

Defending crude oil prices will become increasingly difficult further into the future. OPEC, partly because of superb supply management skills and partly because of luck in recent years, has managed extremely well so far. In the six months prior to October 2003, OPEC faced about 2 million barrels per day of supply disruptions from Venezuela, Nigeria and Iraq. However, higher price levels are increasingly difficult to defend. This is simply a matter of market dynamics. Most areas of the world either have already opened up or are currently opening up to upstream oil investment with the exception of certain countries here in the Middle East and Mexico. Christophe de Margerie has already covered the emerging gas crunch in China as well as in the United States and Europe, which has given a major impetus to LNG and long-haul pipeline construction. International oil companies are looking for new investment targets, especially the oil giants, who bear the enormous burden of replacing production every year. Some of the big companies have to book over a billion barrels every year just to replace production. As their traditional producing areas become more mature, this requires increasingly higher capital commitments and faces higher technical risks.

[257]

At the same time, one of the least publicized developments in the global energy sector is the evolving role of national oil companies (NOCs) in some producing countries. NOCs need to adapt to the changing demands and expectations of their shareholders (i.e., the states to which they belong) from the hydrocarbon sector. The governments, in turn, adjust their expectations and demands from the hydrocarbon sector according to the pressures imposed on them from both domestic economic and financial necessities and from changing international conditions. In the light of geopolitical shifts and the new security-driven militarism of the US discussed earlier, many governments in the Middle East are reconsidering their economic and strategic options. Add to this the decades of economic stagnation in the region, and the glaring need for a new hydrocarbon policy becomes clear. Similar shifts are taking place in the Caspian, Asia, North Africa, and West Africa. These shifts are bound to have a profound impact on the organization and mandate of the NOCs of these countries.

Energy Policy in the Gulf: The Main Drivers

Against this background, some policy drivers in the Gulf region may be examined. Traditionally, in the last 20 to 25 years, the hydrocarbon sector has played two basic roles for the major producers—first, as an exogenous "cash cow" that provides all the revenue needs of the state, and second, in some cases, as an instrument of foreign policy. It is exogenous because it has no real, operational links with the rest of the economy. The only thing that comes back to the economy through the finance ministry is the oil and gas revenues. However, in terms of the production itself, it has no real linkages. It is a "cash cow" because it is the only source in this part of the world to finance all government activities, and it is an instrument of foreign policy because it has become the key source of strategic significance for the producers.

However, in my view, these two roles are no longer adequate. The exogeneity is no longer affordable, because of the high cost of keeping the oil and gas sector exogenous to the rest of the economy. This aspect will be detailed later. The "cash cow" role is no longer adequate, but not because of any deficiency in cash generation. It has become inadequate to address the real economic problems in this part of the world, unless it translates into actual economic development rather than just financial well-being. As an instrument of foreign policy, the function is no longer effective simply because it is no longer an adequate means to secure the strategic importance of this region and other factors need to be considered.

What is the preoccupation of major exporters today? The primary aim is short-term financial survival. This translates into a focus on short-term revenue needs; a perennial shift between price defense and market share defense; the on-again, off-again campaigns to lure non-OPEC producers into cooperation and the medium-term inconsistency of price targets. Those who have observed OPEC would have seen such situations happening over the past decades. It is typical in that it follows the cyclical side of the market itself. The medium-term inconsistency of price targets arises because the higher they are, the more unsustainable they are.

Taking into account the first set of points related to securing the present, and adding the financial requirements of these countries in the short-term, together constitutes the key driver of the price defense and market share defense strategy. This has been the major preoccupation of the governments, whether in or out of OPEC, and this part of the issue is being addressed adequately. The decision-makers in the region have done extremely well and they have improved their grasp of the tools of what may be called supply response to existing market conditions. The term often used to describe this is "market management," but supply management describes what OPEC does much better. Market management would mean something far more sophisticated in terms of trying to affect the longer-term demand level, which they do not undertake. These issues, which dominate the agendas of most of the oil and gas ministries of these countries, fail to address the true strategic issues.

What then are the strategic issues for major oil exporting countries? These may be regarded from two distinct perspectives: First, securing the present—i.e., maintaining the status quo. This, in turn, has two parts: first, prolonging the importance of oil as a source of energy and second, prolonging the importance of the producers as a source of oil. If an oil producing country can manage these two aspects, then its importance can be secured. This has been the main focus of policy-makers and therefore the record here is very good.

However, very little thought has been given to the second major strategic issue, which is securing the future. Securing the future also involves two elements. First, it is necessary to substantially reduce dependence on oil revenues in this part of the world. This is an oft-repeated point and although several five-year plans have announced it as an objective, it does not seem to have been implemented seriously anywhere. Second, investing in the global energy sector of the future, and not just extracting hydrocarbon resources from the ground and handing it over to the market.

As stressed earlier, the challenge of reducing dependence on oil revenues has not been met. This challenge has three parts:

- Macroeconomic reform
- Planning for energy-intensive economic development
- Efficient energy clusters.

The first part, macroeconomic reform, has received considerable lip service but very little serious treatment. The second part is energy-intensive economic development, which will be discussed briefly, and the third part relates to efficient energy clusters, which is also addressed in some detail.

The second dimension of securing the future concerns investment in the global energy business of the future. The global energy industry has evolved considerably in the past two decades. New technologies have been developed that have transformed the supply side of the business, and could be on the verge of transforming the demand side as well. This process is driven by the large multinational oil and gas companies, and the main producing countries and their NOCs are not significant players in these trends. The national oil companies can play an important role as the only viable vehicle for gaining relevance in the global energy business. The national oil companies are the main operating link between the producing countries and the international oil companies. They need not be involved in either the policy aspects or the regulatory aspects of the relationship between these countries and the international oil companies that invest there. However, at the operating level, they do constitute a link and they remain partners with these companies.

Energy and Economic Development

The exogeneity of the oil and gas sectors entails huge opportunity costs for the Gulf economies. There is vast economic development potential in the energy sector that remains unrealized in most areas of the Middle East. Aside from generating export earning, energy resources can serve the following purposes:

- help to develop local economies
- create economies of scale and synergies across different sectors of the economy
- help diversify export earnings away from crude oil and natural gas
- create opportunities and inducements for the private sector to repatriate capital and invest in these economies
- alleviate unemployment pressures
- attract considerable foreign investment and technology
- provide vast new opportunities for training
- open new export markets and create new business relationships and strategic alliances.

To some extent, Saudi Arabia has tried to take advantage of this potential through various downstream gas projects but much of the potential remains unrealized. Chronic unemployment and economic stagnation in the last two decades in this part of the world make the situation no longer affordable. Natural gas itself can fuel a wide range of industrial and other economic activities, from petrochemicals, fertilizers, water desalination, power generation, aluminum, steel, residential developments or even the modern day business services sector, all of which are extremely energy intensive.

Aside from energy-intensive industrial development, there is a vast potential in establishing real economic linkages between the energy sector – oil and gas production – and other sectors, which have not been realized. The amount of oil and gas production in this region should be supporting a very diverse range of secondary and tertiary service industries. Excellent examples exist – such as Houston, Calgary, Stavanger in Norway and Aberdeen – that demonstrate this potential and clearly indicate the type and

[261]

scope of secondary and tertiary economic activities that can be developed revolving around a certain amount of oil and gas production.

Energy-intensive economic development is essentially a light-to-heavy industrialization program that aims to create new economic activity centers using natural gas as feedstock. It is mostly gas-based because gas offers many more options to add value than oil. The leading question should be: what else can be done with gas other than just exporting it for hard currency? There is much that can be achieved. An entire heavy or light industrialization plan can be fueled by it. An entire business services sector can also be established through it. There are many interesting examples but it involves very important coordination between different ministries, such as the ministries of industry, oil, finance and trade.

Figure 11.1
The Efficient Energy Cluster

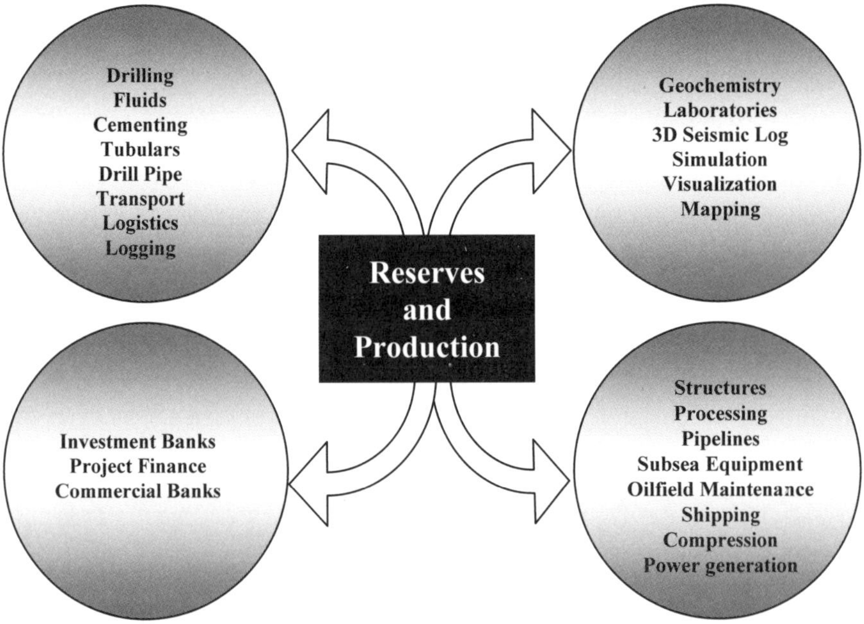

The value of the economic linkages between oil and gas production and the rest of the economy can best be demonstrated through the examples of energy clusters. A sizeable volume of oil and gas production, if organized in a certain way, can support a very wide range of different economic activities, industries and services. Figure 11.1 above demonstrates some of the economic activities that can be supported through oil and gas production.

The top ten service companies in the United States and Europe are companies that service the oil and gas sectors around the world. According to AME Info and Datastream, as per the July 2002 figures, the market cap of these companies is bigger than that of the top ten among the Arabian 100 companies combined (Figure 11.2). So, this is not a small business.

Figure 11.2
Western Service Sector Companies Versus the Arabian 100

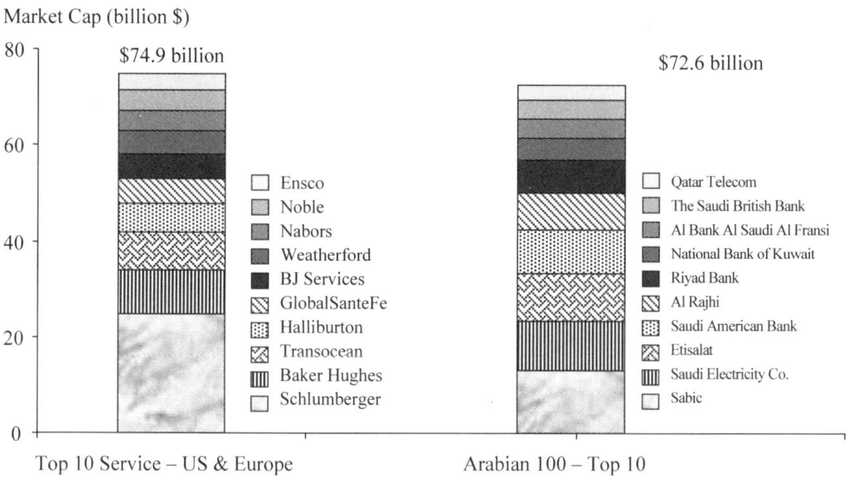

Market Cap (billion $)

$74.9 billion

$72.6 billion

Ensco	Qatar Telecom
Noble	The Saudi British Bank
Nabors	Al Bank Al Saudi Al Fransi
Weatherford	National Bank of Kuwait
BJ Services	Riyad Bank
GlobalSanteFe	Al Rajhi
Halliburton	Saudi American Bank
Transocean	Etisalat
Baker Hughes	Saudi Electricity Co.
Schlumberger	Sabic

Top 10 Service – US & Europe   Arabian 100 – Top 10

Source: ameinfo.com/fn and Datastream. Market cap figures are at end July 2002.

The Houston Business Database lists over 100 regional and international energy service companies with Houston exposure that provide over 20,000 jobs in this field.

What does it take to have a little Houston or an Aberdeen in a place like the Gulf? First, there must be more than just one or two buyers of these services. Second, there must be a real market for these services. These conditions are not currently met, since in each country there is just one big monopoly—the NOC, as the single buyer of the services. The UAE could be an exception, since there are a number of companies producing. It is necessary to have more decentralized oil and gas sector activity, and more outsourcing to encourage the supply of these services.

[263]

Certain regulatory measures are also needed to allow for the emergence of a competitive private sector that can serve the needs of the big national oil companies as well as the international oil companies. This also requires regional cooperation and coordination, both at the governmental level and by the private sector, to provide an expanded marketplace of both buyers and providers of energy-related services.

Much of this may seem impossible but it can be done, and it has been done. This region has to start thinking outside the box and believe that just because something has not been done in the last thirty years it does not mean that it cannot be done. Cynicism is easy, but finding a real solution to solve problems is more meaningful, and that is the difficult part.

The Role of the National Oil Companies

Where do national oil companies come in? It is possible for national oil companies to fit in the various policy initiatives prescribed above. However, the way that NOCs are currently structured, organized and empowered by their respective governments does not allow the emergence of efficient energy clusters in this part of the world. This is not the fault of the NOCs. It is what they have been designed to be and do by their shareholders.

However, the world is changing and as the governments, which are the shareholders of these national oil companies, face different domestic and global economic and political circumstances, they are driven to review the role of their NOCs and their hydrocarbon sectors in relation to national priorities. Some of the typical questions that many NOCs and their governments are currently asking include:

- What should be the role of a national oil company in the development and management of a country's hydrocarbon resources?
- Should it continue to serve the interests of its shareholders by remaining just an extension of the government bureaucracy, or should it evolve into something else?
- As an oil company, should it stick purely to operations or should it be involved in the policy side of the hydrocarbon resource development process?

[264]

- Does the traditional relationship between national oil companies and governments encourage and promote competitive performance by the national oil companies?
- Does the government really want the national oil company to be competitive, or does it just want it to extract the hydrocarbon and pass on the revenue to the finance ministry?
- Are NOCs realizing the full potential benefits of their alliances with international oil and gas companies?

The question of whether producing countries are optimizing the value of their strategic alliances with international oil and gas companies is an important one. When IOCs seek entry into a producing country, they want access to reserves, probably on preferential terms. Yet, what is it that the producing country wants from them? That is often not clear. In fact many national oil companies are not sure how to answer this question. Will the IOCs seeking entry into their country prove to be their competitors or their partners? Do they bring with them capital, technology and access to markets and management skills in such a way that these will actually be beneficial to the NOCs? Should the NOCs strive to benefit in broader ways than these from their partnerships with IOCs? These are critical questions, and the answers are different for each NOC.

One of the complex issues that every oil producing country faces sooner or later is defining the role of its NOC vis-à-vis other agencies or ministries of the state. At the surface, this seems a simple task. The government's role should be clear—it owns the resource below the ground, sets the broad national priorities in the governance and development of the country's hydrocarbon resources, formulates the hydrocarbon sector laws and policies, and creates the necessary regulatory bodies and regulatory environment conducive for the efficient functioning of the companies. On the other hand, the role of the national oil company is to take the below-ground resources and turn them into commercial assets. The NOC generates growth and adds value while operating and managing the assets owned by the state. It also serves as the main operating link with international oil companies.

In practice, however, things are not this simple or straightforward. Sometimes NOCs grow into vast establishments with a life of their own, and they become a political force in their own right. For a long time, Petroleos de Venezuela acted in such a manner and was stronger than the oil ministry in Venezuela. The government finally realized that this situation could not continue. Some national oil companies act as independent agencies doing regulation, even though this represents a direct conflict of interest for them. Very few national oil companies focus strictly on operations, which is what they are supposed to do.

Figure 11.3
Defining the Roles

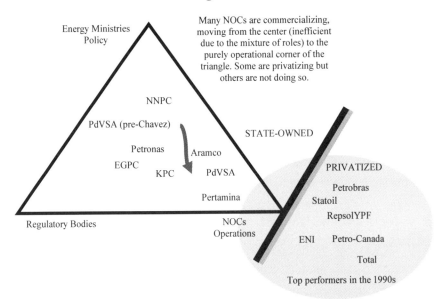

The functions and relative roles of various government agencies involved in the hydrocarbon sector are not static, but change and evolve over time. Figure 11.3 depicts the 3 key functions involved in the governance of a hydrocarbon sector:

- Policy—in principle, the mandate of the oil ministry
- Regulation—in principle, the mandate of independent regulatory agencies
- Operations—in principle, the mandate of the NOC.

However, very few NOCs operate strictly in the "operations" corner. Most interfere in policy or regulation or both. The positioning of various NOCs within the triangle in Figure 11.3 reveals how much "multi-tasking" these organizations carry out, and in some cases, indicates how their role has changed over time.

In many ways, the key commercial and competitive issues faced by national oil companies are the same as international oil companies but they face different challenges. Here are some critical questions that shed light on the nature of the challenges: How can NOCs commercialize without having the ruthless discipline imposed on IOCs by the market? Is it possible to be guided by the same financial performance measures as IOCs without being privatized? Should an NOC go international? Does a national oil company keep its status as "national" if it invests internationally, and how does such a situation work? How can an NOC create indigenous gas demand within the country? The full optimization of strategic alliances with international oil companies mentioned earlier involves monetizing natural gas. Most national oil companies are very oil-focused and they do not have a lot of gas experience. Partner selection through strategic matching and alignment of interests is yet another issue. This is also an issue for international oil companies but in a different context. Product export is an interesting issue because in many big markets, specifications and regulations are changing so rapidly that it requires substantial investments in the downstream sectors to meet the product specifications, and many national oil companies are reluctant to invest. The key ingredients of a commercialized national oil company's competitiveness apply also to international oil companies. These relate to corporate culture, corporate governance, business environment, skills and capabilities.

The main problem is that in many of the producing countries, the qualities and standards that national oil companies could develop are not consistent with what their shareholders expect them to achieve. That is the difference in the governance of an IOC and that of an NOC. The shareholders demand these qualities from an international oil company, but they do not demand the same from a national oil company. The NOCs are organized to optimize political objectives, not efficiency. That is the main

[267]

reason why it becomes more difficult for a national oil company to meet the best in class performance standards.

Concluding Remarks

In conclusion, there are few points to be underscored. Even though the Gulf region remains the only strategic supplier of crude oil to the global market, that feature alone no longer guarantees its strategic significance to the rest of the world. It needs to focus on other aspects. No country in this region can afford any longer to treat its hydrocarbon resources as an exogenous cash cow, and must develop the vast economic development potential of energy. The focus should shift from merely developing gas or oil resources to developing the economy using these resources, and that reasoning has not yet entered into the strategic planning of policymakers here. There are substantial gains to be made from more cooperation and integration within the region in energy production and distribution. Cooperation between different national oil companies is important for the region, but this is not happening to the extent necessary. Today, gas cannot be exported from Qatar to Kuwait. There may be all kinds of reasons for this, but this is a ridiculous situation. There is much to be gained from greater cooperation and integration. Finally, it is time to review the role of national oil companies. This may not always lead to big changes, or even to small changes. However, it is worthwhile to have a thorough reassessment of the role of NOCs in the development and governance of their country's hydrocarbon resources.

CONTRIBUTORS

FATIH BIROL is Chief Economist and Head of the Economic Analysis Division of the Paris-based International Energy Agency. He is also responsible for briefing the Executive Office and Governing Board of the IEA on the economic impact of energy market and industry developments. He is organizer and director of the *World Energy Outlook* series, the IEA's flagship publication. The *World Energy Outlook* series is widely recognized as an authoritative source for world energy information and long-term energy projections. Input for this series comes from more than twenty IEA analysts and other senior energy experts drawn from around the world.

A Turkish citizen, Dr. Birol was born in Ankara in 1958. He earned a B.Sc degree in power engineering from the Technical University of Istanbul. He received his M.Sc and Ph.D in energy economics from the Technical University of Vienna. He worked for six years in the secretariat of the Organization of Petroleum Exporting Countries (OPEC) in Vienna, before joining the IEA in 1995. Apart from his principal job, Dr. Birol teaches energy economics at universities in Austria and Germany. He regularly contributes articles to technical journals on international energy analysis and policy and delivers a number of speeches around the world each year.

CHRISTOPHE DE MARGERIE has spent most of his career with the TOTAL group of companies. In 1974, he joined the Corporate Finance Division of the TOTAL group where he was successively in charge of the Budget Department and the Affiliates Department, and became Group Treasurer in 1987. In May 1990, he joined TOTAL Trading and Middle East as Senior Vice President of Finance. Two years later, he was appointed Executive Vice President of TOTAL Trading and Middle East, heading the Middle East Division, and became a Member of the Group Management Committee. In June 1995, he was named President of TOTAL Middle East. He was appointed Executive Vice President of TotalFina, President of the Exploration and Production Division and Member of the Group Executive Committee in May 1999, and became Executive Vice President of the Exploration and Production Division of TotalFinaElf four months later. In January 2002 he became President of the Exploration and Production Division of TotalFinaElf (renamed TOTAL since May 2003). Mr. Christophe de Margerie graduated from the Ecole Superieure de Commerce de Paris.

DOROTHEA H. EL MALLAKH has been the Executive Director of the International Research Center for Energy and Economic Development (ICEED) since 1987, having served earlier as Executive Administrator, Treasurer and Board Member of the Center from its establishment in 1973. She was first Associate Editor of *The Journal of Energy and Development* (1975–1987) and continues to hold the position of Managing Editor. Dr. El Mallakh has been an Adjunct Professor in the Department of Mineral Economics, Colorado School of Mines (where she remains a Board Member of the university's cooperative program with the French Petroleum Institute); a member of the Board of Editors of *Energy Policy* (1992–2002); Secretary and Vice President for International Affairs of the International Association for Energy Economics (1988–1992); as well as Vice President for Conferences and Board Member of the US Association for Energy Economics (1993–1996).

Dr. El Mallakh, who holds a Ph.D. from the University of Colorado at Boulder, is co-author, co-editor or contributor to the following publications: *Energy Watchers I through X* (Boulder, CO: ICEED, 1990-1999); "Middle East Oil Resource Policies," in Elise Boulding (ed.) *Building Peace in the Middle East: Challenges for States and Civil Society* (Boulder, CO: Lynne Rienner Publishers, 1994); J.R. Hayes (ed.) *The Genius of Arab Civilization* (New York University Press, 1975; MIT Press, 1978 Arabic edition and 1983/1988 paperback editions; New York University Press, third edition); *Saudi Arabia: Energy, Developmental Planning, and Industrialization* (D.C. Heath & Company, 1982); *Energy Options and Conservation* (ICEED, 1978); *The Slovak Autonomy Movement, 1935-1939* (Columbia University Press, 1979); and articles in such publications as *Al-Petrol* (Cairo), and

Current History. Dr. El Mallakh has presented a number of papers at international energy conferences.

FEREIDUN FESHARAKI is the President and Founder of Fesharaki Associates Consulting and Technical Services (FACTS, Inc.). He gained his Ph.D. in Economics from the University of Surrey, later completing a Visiting Fellowship at Harvard University's Center for Middle Eastern Studies. In the late 1970s, he attended the OPEC Ministerial Conferences as Energy Adviser to the Prime Minister of Iran. He joined the East-West Center in 1979, where he heads energy-related research. His area of specialization is oil and gas market analysis and the downstream petroleum sector, especially in the Asia–Pacific region and the Middle East. His pioneering oil and gas market studies of the Asia-Pacific/Middle East regions have received wide recognition.

Dr. Fesharaki has authored or edited over twenty-three books and monographs and written more than 70 papers. He has served on the editorial boards of several journals including *Energy Economics, Energy Policy; Journal of Energy Finance and Development; Energy: The International Journal;* and *Hydrocarbon Asia.* In 1993, Dr. Fesharaki served as the President of the International Association for Energy Economics (IAEE). In 1989, he was elected a Member of the Council on Foreign Relations. Since 1991, he has been a member of the International Advisory Board of Nippon Oil. Dr. Fesharaki is also a member of the Pacific Council on International Policy. In 1995, he was elected as a Senior Fellow of the US Association for Energy Economics for distinguished services in the field of energy economics. In 1998, Dr. Fesharaki joined the Board of Directors of the American-Iranian Council and in 2002, he was appointed a Senior Associate of the Center for Strategic and International Studies (CSIS) in Washington, DC.

HERMAN T. FRANSSEN is the President of International Energy Associates, Inc. The Group provides energy economic analysis, global and regional market assessments, project evaluation and risk analysis. Dr. Franssen was Senior Economic Advisor to the Minister of Petroleum and Minerals of the Sultanate of Oman from 1985 to 1996. In 1986, Dr. Franssen was the first senior Western advisor admitted to an OPEC ministerial meeting. He was instrumental in establishing IPEC, the group of Independent Petroleum Exporting Countries two years later. From 1980 to 1985, Dr. Franssen was Chief Economist at the International Energy Agency (IEA) of the OECD in Paris. He co-authored and edited several studies at the IEA and took principal responsibility for the first major *World Energy Outlook* published in 1983. Dr. Franssen was Director of the Office of International Market Analysis of the US Department of Energy (1978–1980), and was a Specialist in Energy and Science Policy at the Congressional Research Service of the US Library of Congress from 1974 to 1978.

Dr. Franssen has written for several energy publications and participated in major US and international energy conferences. He also serves as Director of Petroleum Economics, Ltd. (PEL) in London. A member of the International Energy Advisory Board, he is also a Senior Advisor to the Energy Intelligence Group in New York and Washington, DC. Dr. Franssen is a Senior Associate both at the Center for Strategic and International Studies (CSIS) in Washington, DC, and the Centre for Global Energy Studies (CGES) in London. He is an Associate at Middle East Consultants in London and is also an Editorial Board Member of the *Journal of Energy and Economic Development*, University of Colorado. Dr. Franssen holds a B.A. in International Economics and Political Science from Macalester College, St. Paul, Minnesota and M.A., M.A.L.D. and Ph.D. degrees in International Economics from The Fletcher School of Law and Diplomacy, Medford, Massachusetts.

ROBERT E. MABRO CBE is Director Emeritus of the Oxford Institute for Energy Studies, and Fellow of St Antony's College, Oxford. He gained his degree in civil engineering from Alexandria University and worked as a civil engineer in Egypt for a short period. From 1962 to 1964 he studied philosophy in France, and in 1966 he obtained an M.Sc in Economics with distinction from London University. His academic career began at the School of Oriental and African Studies (SOAS) at London University, where he specialized in Middle East economic developments. In 1969 he joined Oxford University as Senior Research Officer in the Economics of the Middle East. His first oil publication was a monograph (co-authored with the late Elizabeth Monroe) entitled *Oil Producers and Consumers: Conflict or Cooperation* (New York, NY: 1974). In 1976, with the Right Honorable Aubrey Jones, PC he founded the Oxford Energy Policy Club at St Antony's College. Later, he founded and became the first Director of the Oxford Energy Seminar, held annually at St Catherine's College. This was followed by the establishment of the Oxford Institute for Energy Studies, an educational charity devoted to research on the economics, politics and international relations of energy. Among his publications are thirteen books and monographs, as well as several articles and papers. Among his more recent books is *Oil Markets and Prices: The Brent Market and the Formation of World Oil Prices,* co-authored with Paul Horsnell.

Mr. Mabro is the recipient of several awards and honors, including the International Association for Energy Economics 1990 Award for Outstanding Contributions to the Profession of Energy Economics and to its Literature. In December 1995 Her Majesty Queen Elizabeth II named Mr. Mabro as a Commander of the Order of the British Empire (CBE) in the New Year Honors List. In 1997 the President of Mexico presented him with the medal of the Mexican Order of Aguila Azteca and in 2000 the President of Venezuela awarded him the Francisco Miranda medal. In 2001 Mr. Mabro received the French title of Officier des Palmes Academiques.

VITALY V. NAUMKIN is President of the International Center for Strategic and Political Studies in Moscow (since 1991). He was Visiting Professor at the Department of Political Science at the University of California at Berkeley during 2003. He has been Editor-in-Chief of *Vostok-Orients*, the journal of the Russian Academy of Sciences since 1998, and has also been Head of the Middle Eastern Department of the Institute of Oriental Studies at the Russian Academy of Sciences since 1984. Dr. Naumkin is currently an expert on the Security Council of Russia. He has served as a Member of the Council for Foreign Policy of Russia under the Minister of

Foreign Affairs and as an Advisor to the Supreme Council/Federal Assembly. From 1989 to 1994, Dr. Naumkin was Deputy Director of the Institute of Oriental Studies at the Russian Academy of Sciences. During 1980 to 1984, he was a Professor at Moscow State University, where he had earlier been a senior researcher for eight years. Dr. Naumkin served in Russian diplomatic missions abroad from 1972 to 1977.

Dr. Naumkin is the author of several books and articles on international relations, strategic studies, oil politics, Islamic studies, history and contemporary studies of the Middle East, Central Asia and the Caucasus. His publications have appeared in Russian, German, English, Arabic and French. He has lectured at many universities and research centers in the USA, UK, France, Italy, Egypt and Turkey. He earned his Ph.D. degree in 1972 from Moscow State University and speaks Arabic, French, English and Russian.

RICHARD PANIGUIAN joined British Petroleum (now BP) in 1971 after graduating in Middle Eastern Languages and Politics. After a brief spell in London, Mr. Paniguian spent three years in Dubai and Oman in BP's oil marketing business. Sponsored by BP, he studied at the INSEAD Business School at Fontainebleu, where he obtained his MBA in 1976. Two years in planning were followed by a posting to Iran as Commercial Representative during 1979 and 1980. In 1981 he returned to London to become Manager of Oil Trading, moving on in 1984 to become Vice President of International Trading in New York. In 1987, he moved back to London to become Head of Capital Markets in BP Finance, before being appointed President of BP Turkey in 1989. In 1992, he was posted to Brussels as Director of Human Resources, before taking up the position of Chief Executive of BP Shipping in early 1995. He also served as President of the Chamber of Shipping from 2001 to 2002.

Mr. Paniguian is the Group Vice President for Russia, CIS, Caspian, Middle East and Africa. In this position, he is responsible for BP's growth strategy in these regions and all aspects of reputation and corporate governance. Having been associated with the Middle East for a number of years in various capacities, Mr. Paniguian also provides guidance and advice to the Group on all business and political issues associated with this key region.

PAUL STEVENS is Professor of Petroleum Policy and Economics at the Centre for Energy, Petroleum and Mineral Law and Policy (CEPMLP), University of Dundee, Scotland. He provides consultancy services for many companies and governments. Dr. Stevens was educated as an economist and specialist on the Middle East at Cambridge and the School of Oriental and African Studies (SOAS). He taught at the University of Surrey (1979–1993) and at the American University of Beirut (1973–1979), interspersed with two years as an oil consultant. He has published extensively on energy economics, international petroleum and economic development issues and the Gulf political economy and also participates regularly in conferences and lectures on these subjects.

Dr. Stevens has authored several articles in energy journals. Some of his publications include: "Resource Impact: Curse or Blessing?   A Literature Survey" in the *Journal of Energy Literature* (vol. ix, no. 1, June 2003); "Economists and the Oil Industry: Facts Versus Analysis, The Case of Vertical Integration" in L.C. Hunt (ed.), *Energy in a Competitive World* (2003); "Micro-Managing Global Oil Markets: Is it Getting More Difficult?" in *Journal of Energy and Development* (vol. 26, no. 2, 2002); "Pipelines or Pipe Dreams? Lessons from the History of Arab Transit Pipelines," in the *Middle East Journal* (Spring 2000); "Introduction— Strategic Positioning in the Oil Industry: Trends and Options" in Paul Stevens (ed.) *Strategic Positioning in the Oil Industry: Trends and Options* (Abu Dhabi: ECSSR, 1998); "Energy Privatization: Sensitivities and Realities" in *The Journal of Energy and Development* (vol. 23, no. 1, 1997); "Increasing Global Dependence on Gulf Oil—This Year, Next Year, Sometime, Never?" in *Energy Policy* (vol. 25, no. 2, 1997); and "Oil Prices: The Start of an Era" in *Energy Policy* (vol. 24, no. 3, 1996).

HASSAAN VAHIDY worked with Fesharaki Associates Consulting and Technical Services Inc. (FACTS) for a period of 4 years. Working initially as a Senior Consultant at the company's Hawaii office, he later headed consulting and research for the firm from Singapore, focusing on the downstream oil and gas industry in the Middle East and Asia Pacific. His primary areas of research are oil and gas demand forecasting, refinery process analysis and economics as well as deregulation and privatization policy. He has led and participated in several projects pertaining to the economic viability of investments in the region's oil and gas sector. He holds an MA degree in Economics from the University of Hawaii. Mr. Vahidy has also served with Royal Dutch/Shell in Pakistan, where he was involved in implementation and management of business process control systems. He is currently working with ChevronTexaco in Singapore.

WALTER VAN DE VIJVER was Group Managing Director of the Royal Dutch/Shell Group of Companies and CEO of Shell Exploration and Production until his resignation in 2004. His career with Royal Dutch/ Shell Group began in 1979 and included assignments in Qatar, Oman, the United States, United Kingdom and the Netherlands. He started his career in Shell as a Field Engineer and held several positions in the Group's Exploration and Production business. In 1993 he was appointed General Manager of the Brent Business Unit in Shell UK Exploration and Production, where he initiated and implemented the massive Brent Redevelopment Project.

In 1997, he became Chief Executive of Shell International Gas and Shell Coal International in London. In August 1998, he moved to Houston to take up the position of President and Chief Executive Officer of Shell Exploration and Production Company. He led the restructuring and repositioning of the Exploration and Production and Gas and Power businesses in the United States. Since July 2001, he has held the position of CEO of Exploration and Production. Mr. Van de Vijver holds an M.Sc degree in civil engineering from the Delft University of Technology.

THOMAS E. WALLIN has worked at the Energy Intelligence Group for over 20 years in various key positions. He is currently President and Chief Operating Officer, having been appointed in March 1999. Previously, he was Group Editor with responsibility for all editorial operations, including new products. He also served as Editor of the *Petroleum Intelligence Weekly* and was the company's London Bureau Chief from 1983 to 1986. As a reporter and an editor, he covered an extremely broad range of international oil and gas issues over the years, with particular emphasis on oil markets, production, pricing strategies and industry analysis. He is the author of a number of special reports including: *The International Crude Oil Market Handbook; The Complete Guide to Oil Price Swaps and Derivatives;* and *West Siberia: The Key to Russia's Oil and Gas Future.*

Mr. Wallin started his career as an editor and analyst, working at the Council on Foreign Relations in New York. He also served briefly as an officer in the United States Foreign Service. He gained a Master's degree in International Economics from Columbia University's School of Public and International Affairs and received a Bachelor's degree from Vassar College, majoring in History.

VAHAN ZANOYAN is President and Chief Executive Officer of PFC Energy. With over 25 years of experience in analyzing energy markets, he is an expert on the production and pricing strategies of oil and gas producing countries, and the geopolitical forces affecting the global energy industry. More recently, Mr. Zanoyan has focused on business development strategies in the Middle East and North Africa, as well as on the challenges faced by national companies in their relationships with host governments and international oil companies.

Prior to joining PFC Energy, Mr. Zanoyan was Managing Director at Wharton Econometric Forecasting Associates, where he founded the Middle East Economic Service and served as the company's expert on oil markets. He was also responsible for all economic consulting services covering other areas of the world. Mr. Zanoyan holds graduate degrees in Economics from the University of Pennsylvania and The American University in Beirut. He received his B.A. in Political Science from the American University in Beirut.

Keynote Address

1. See http://www.eia.doe.gov/oiaf/aeo/conf/doman/NEMS%20talk%20 ieo2003%20wo%20talking%20points.ppt.

2. See http://www.newsgd.com/news/headlines/200307310001.htm.

3. Lord Browne, Chief Executive, BP, Humboldt University, Berlin, April 29, 2002. See http://www.bp.com/centres/press/berlin/highlights/ index.asp.

Chapter 4

1. *Middle East Economic Survey* (MEES), October 13, 2003.

2. *Middle East Economic Survey* (MEES), October 13, 2003, D5.

3. The Organization of Petroleum Exporting Countries (OPEC) members include Algeria, Indonesia, Iran, Iraq, Kuwait, Libya, Nigeria, Qatar, Saudi Arabia, United Arab Emirates and Venezuela. The term OPEC-10 refers to all OPEC members minus Iraq.

4. The term OPEC-9 refers to all OPEC members minus Iraq and Venezuela.

Chapter 5

1. US Department of Energy, Energy Information Administration, International Energy Database, February 2003, available at http://iea. doe.gov/emeu/aer/pdf/pages/sec11-321.pdf (accessed on October 3, 2003).

2. Ibid.

3. *Oil & Gas Journal*, December 27, 1965, 82-83.

4. Ragaei El Mallakh, *Economic Development and Regional Cooperation: Kuwait* (Chicago, IL: University of Chicago Press, 1968), 31. Only three Gulf states were oil producers during the 1913–1933 period: Bahrain, Iran, and Iraq. Saudi production began in 1934, followed by Kuwait in 1946, and Qatar in 1950. The United Arab Emirates is a relative newcomer.

5. Saudi Arabia and Kuwait jointly administer the Neutral Zone and divide reserves and output on a 50–50 basis.

6. *International Petroleum Encyclopedia 2002* (Tulsa, OK: PennWell, 2002), 218. Crude oil reserves for the Soviet Union in 1970 were 77 billion barrels, 63 billion barrels a decade later, and only 24 billion barrels in 1990. This coincided with the lagging Soviet oil industry, which since then has seen an upward revision beginning in 1991 (of 57 billion barrels) to reach 59 billion barrels in 2001. Adnan Al-Janabi, a former Iraqi Oil Ministry official and former head of the Economics Department at OPEC, gives Iraqi reserves as follows: proven reserves of 112 billion barrrels, about 100 billion barrels of reserves "growth," and 150 billion barrels of probable reserves. He concludes, "This makes Iraq the least developed oil province in the world." See *Middle East Economic Survey*, August 11, 2003, D1.

7. US State Department estimates, *Middle East Economic Survey*, September 22, 2003, A13. Under Secretary for Economic Affairs Alan Larson put the average for Iraqi oil exports in 2004 at 1.5 mbpd and 2 mbpd in 2005 based on production of around 1.85 mbpd in 2004 and 2.35 mbpd in the following year. This is a markedly more conservative estimate than that announced in July 2003 of restoring Iraqi production capacity to 2.8 mbpd by April 2004.

8. Ibid.

9. *Middle East Economic Survey*, November 17, 2003, 1A.

10. The President of the United States, "The National Security Strategy of the United States of America," September 2002, page 1, available at:

http://www.whitehouse.gov/nsc/print/nssall.html, accessed on February 22, 2003.

11. *Middle East Economic Survey*, July 14, 2003, A3. The subsequent response to this assertion was negative in both political and legal terms. Thus, US policy retreated from the push for early and massive privatization of Iraqi state-owned enterprises and specifically the critical oil sector.

12. About two weeks after Bremer's comments, the United States dropped the idea of an Oil Advisory Board. *Middle East Economic Survey*, July 28, 2003, A15.

13. Edward L. Morse, "Is the Energy Map Next on the Neo-Conservative Cartography Agenda?" reprinted from the Oxford Energy Forum in *Middle East Economic Survey*, August 18, 2003, D1-D3. This assertion was buttressed by the response of the Deputy Secretary of Defense to a query as to why the United States had confronted Iraq but not North Korea, stating that one difference was that Iraq was "swimming" in oil. Morse goes on to assert that those who support this political ideology "want to undermine, if not destroy OPEC."

14. The President of the United States, "The National Security Strategy of the United States of America," September 2002, 13.

15. Several books dealing specifically with oil in international relations have been published, including David Harvey, *The New Imperialism* (Oxford: Oxford University Press, 2003) and Gawdat Bahgat, *American Oil Diplomacy in the Persian Gulf and the Caspian Sea* (Gainesville, FL: University Press of Florida, 2003). The privatization arguments can be found in publications from, for example, the American Enterprise Institute and The Heritage Foundation. A thought-provoking volume dealing with options for US foreign policy in general (so-called "hard" versus "soft" power) is Joseph Nye, *The Paradox of American Power* (New York, NY: Oxford University Press, 2002).

Chapter 6

1. OPEC-10 excludes Iraq.

2. There are two types of economic rent inherent in the international price of oil. One arises because even if the oil market were competitive, low cost producers would earn producers' surplus. The other arises because supply restrictions orchestrated by the oil majors in the 1950s and 1960s and OPEC thereafter, earn producers super normal profit.

3. Generally, most empirical studies put the short run own price elasticity of oil demand at around -0.2. Thus a 10 percent rise in price would reduce the quantity demanded by 2 percent.

4. USGS Fact Sheet FS-145-97.

5. David Deming, NCPA Policy Backgrounder 159, January 29, 2003 (http://www.ncpa.org/pub/bg/bg159).

6. Globally the average is around 33-35 percent.

7. The dramatic and unexpected increase in world oil demand in 2004 has meant that much of the analysis presented in this 2003 conference paper has been overtaken by events, particularly the assumption that the call on OPEC would be relatively flat.

8. The following data on capacity has been taken either from various issues of *Middle East Economic Survey* or from Peter Newman, *Implications for the Global Oil Industry,* Oxford Energy Forum, November 2003.

9. This is as opposed to a trading system which implies a permanent transfer of quota which would be politically unacceptable in most cases.

10. Some analysts are trying to argue that the price collapse of 1998 was a deliberate ploy by Saudi Arabia, which was engineered to bring recalcitrant OPEC members and greedy non-OPEC producers into line. This is extremely implausible. The decisions at Jakarta in November 1997 were a mistake. The only real debate is whether it was bad luck or bad judgement.

Chapter 9

1. This analytical survey uses the materials of Russia's Goskomstat (State Statistical Bureau), the analytical departments of energy companies, and the world and Russian press.

2. Based on data from Andrey Meshcherin, "Blagiye pozhelaniya" (Pious wishes), *Neftegazovaya Vertikal'* (Oil and Gas File), No. 9 (2003): 5–12.

3. See Alexei Mastepanov, "Kakaya energeticheskaya strategiya nuzhna Rossii?" (What energy strategy does Russia need?), *Neftegazovaya Vertikal'*, No. 17 (2002): 11.

4. Interview dated August 17, 2003.

5. Andrey Meshcherin, op. cit: 7.

6. Ibid.

7. Interview dated August 17, 2003.

8. Evgeniy Khartukov, "Yest' problemy, no oni razreshimy" (There are problems, but they can be solved), *Neftegazovaya Vertikal'* No. 7 (2003): 53.

9. Stanislav Roginskiy, "Nuzhny li my drug drugu?" (Do we need each other?), *Neftegazovaya Vertikal'* No.17 (2002), 22.

10. Maria Ignatova, "Uzkoe mesto" (Bottleneck), *Izvestia*, September 23, 2003.

11. *Neftegazovaya Vertikal'* No. 9, op. cit. (2003): 11.

12. Leonid Michelson, "Eksport gaza iz Rossii" (Gas export from Russia), *Neftegazovaya Vertikal'* No. 8 (2003): 30.

13. www.km.ru/view_print.asp, September 11, 2003.

14. Leonid Michelson, op. cit. 33.

15. Yelena Telegina, "Mirovoi energeticheskii rynok i geopoliticheskie interesy Rossii" (World energy market and Russia's geopolitical interests), *Mirovaya ekonomika i mezhdunarodnie otnosheniya*, No. 5 (2003): 62–63.

16. See N. Kaveshnikov, "Neft' v obmen na investitsii" (Oil for investment), *Deloviye lyudi,* September 2003: 11–13.

17. In accordance with the data provided by Goskomstat.

18. David G. Victor and Nadejda M. Victor, "Axis of Oil?" *Foreign Affairs,* March/April 2003, 55.

19. See Anna Skornyakova, "BP soglasilas' na Slavneft" (BP has agreed to Slavneft), *Nezavisimaya Gazeta,* September 2, 2003.

20. Moises Naim, "Neft' razrushaet politiku i ozhidaniya lyudei" (Oil destroys policy and people's expectations), *Nezavisimaya Gazeta,* September 25, 2003.

21. See survey in *Izvestia,* September 9, 2003.

22. *Izvestia,* September 9, 2003.

23. *Izvestia,* September 9, 2003.

24. Yelena Telegina, "Mirovoi energeticheskii rynok," op. cit., 62–63.

25. Here and in subsequent sections reference is made to the materials of a closed discussion in the journal *Rossiya v gliobal' noi politike,* prepared by L. Grigoryev and A. Chaplygina.

26. According to the data published in the newspaper *Kommersant-Daily* (translated from Russian).

27. Yekaterina Kravchenko, "Rossiya prityagivaet neftedollary" (Russia attracts petrodollars), *Izvestia,* September 25, 2003.

28. M. Ignatova, E. Kravchenko and A. Tikhonov, "Obmen valyuty" (Conversion of currency), *Izvestia,* October 13, 2003.

29. Maria Ignatova, "Neft' dyrochku naidyot" (Oil will find an outlet), *Izvestia,* September 25, 2003.

30. Ibid.

31. Georgi Bovt, "Protiv truby" (Against the pipeline), *Izvestia,* October 9, 2003.

32. Alexander Tutushkin, Yekaterina Derbilova and Svetlana Ivanova, "TNK-BP napugala rynok" (TNK-BP has frightened the market), *Vedomosti,* April 12, 2005.

33. Pyotr Orekhin, "Sibneft and Lukoil mogut razdelit' sud'bu Yukosa" (Sibneft and Lukoil may share Yukos' lot), *Nezavisimaya Gazeta*, March 18, 2005.

34. Fyodor Chaika, "Gosudarstvo privatiziruet Rosneft" (The state is privatizing Rosneft), *Izvestia*, April 19, 2005.

35. Igor Naumov, "Privatizatsionnie plany grandiozny tol'ko na bumage" (Privatization plans are grandiose only on paper), *Nezavisimaya Gazeta*, March 18, 2005.

36. http://www.rian.ru/economy/20050422/39728001/html.

37. Based on evidence of Russian information agencies.

38. Alexander Dolgopolsky, "Tekushchaya situatsiya" (The current situation), *Neftegazovaya Vertikal'*, No. 5 (2005): 35.

39. Alexei Kontorovich, Andrei Korzhubaev and Leonti Eder, "Neftyanoy rynok Kitaya" (China's oil market), *Neftegazovaya Vertikal'*, No. 5 (2005): 34.

40. Irina Reznik and Rodion Levinsky, "Gazprom blagoslovil reeksport" (Gazprom has blessed re-export), *Vedomosti*, April 4, 2005.

41. Pyotr Orekhin, "Gaz na gaz" (Gas for gas), *Nezavisimaya Gazeta*, April 11, 2005.

42. Andrei Kolesnikov, "Kak i s kem promyshlyal Vladimir Putin v Germanii" (How and with whom Vladimir Putin was doing business in Germany), *Kommersant*, April 12, 2005.

43. Pyotr Orekhin, "Gazprom otkazyvaetsya ot prava diktovat' tseny" (Gazprom relinquishes the right to dictate prices), *Nezavisimaya Gazeta*, March 24, 2005.

44. Yelena Tikhomirova, "Uroven' tsen mozhet byt' sovershenno nepredskazuemym" (The price level can be completely unpredictable), *Nezavisimaya Gazeta*, March 24, 2005.

45. Orekhin, "Gazprom otkazyvaetsya," op. cit.

46. "Vostoku Rossii nuzhny prioritety. Intervyu c Valeriem Pakom" (Russia's East needs priorities: An interview with Valeri Pak), *Neftegazovaya Vertikal'*, No. 5 (2005): 12.

Chapter 10

1. Occam's Razor is a method which eliminates one by one all the factors that are not necessary to explain a phenomenon. This method thus identifies the "sufficient" cause.

BIBLIOGRAPHY

Bahgat, Gawdat. *American Oil Diplomacy in the Persian Gulf and the Caspian Sea* (Gainesville, FL: University Press of Florida, 2003).

Bovt, Georgi. "Protiv truby" (Against the pipeline). *Izvestia*, October 9, 2003.

Chaika, Fyodor. "Gosudarstvo privatiziruet Rosneft'" (The state is privatizing Rosneft). *Izvestia*, April 19, 2005.

Data provided by Goskomstat (State Statistical Bureau), Russian Federation.

Data provided by *Kommersant-Daily* (translated from Russian).

Dolgopolsky, Alexander. "Tekushchaya situatsiya" (The current situation). *Neftegazovaya Vertikal'*, No. 5 (2005).

El Mallakh Ragaei. *Economic Development and Regional Cooperation: Kuwait* (Chicago, IL: University of Chicago Press, 1968).

Grigoryev L. and A. Chaplygina. Materials prepared for a closed discussion in the journal *Rossiya v gliobal'noi politike*.

Harvey, David. *The New Imperialism* (Oxford: Oxford University Press, 2003).

Ignatova, Maria. "Neft' dyrochku naidyot" (Oil will find an outlet). *Izvestia*, September 25, 2003.

Ignatova, Maria. "Uzkoe mesto" (Bottleneck). *Izvestia*, September 23, 2003.

International Petroleum Encyclopedia 2002 (Tulsa, OK: PennWell, 2002).

Interview with Mikhail Khodorkovsky broadcast by Tsentr TV, August 17, 2003.

Kaveshnikov N. "Neft' v obmen na investitsii" (Oil for investment). *Deloviye lyudi,* September 2003.

Khartukov, Evgeniy. "Yest' problemy, no oni razreshimy" (There are problems, but they can be solved). *Neftegazovaya Vertikal'*, No. 7 (2003).

Kolesnikov, Andrei. "Kak i s kem promyshlyal Vladimir Putin v Germanii" (How and with whom Vladimir Putin was doing business in Germany). *Kommersant*, April 12, 2005.

Kontorovich, Alexei, Andrei Korzhubaev and Leonti Eder, "Neftyanoy rynok Kitaya" (China's oil market). *Neftegazovaya Vertikal'*, No. 5 (2005).

Kravchenko, Yekaterina. "Rossiya prityagivaet neftedollary" (Russia attracts petrodollars). *Izvestia*, September 25, 2003.

Mastepanov, Alexei. "Kakaya energeticheskaya strategiya nuzhna Rossii?" (What energy strategy does Russia need?). *Neftegazovaya Vertikal'*, No. 17 (2002).

Meshcherin, Andrey. "Blagiye pozhelaniya" (Pious wishes). *Neftegazovaya Vertikal'* (Oil and Gas File), No. 9 (2003).

Michelson, Leonid. "Eksport gaza iz Rossii" (Gas export from Russia). *Neftegazovaya Vertikal'* No. 8 (2003).

Middle East Economic Survey (MEES), October 13, 2003.

Middle East Economic Survey, August 11, 2003, D1.

Middle East Economic Survey, July 14, 2003, A3.

Middle East Economic Survey, July 28, 2003, A15.

Middle East Economic Survey, November 17, 2003, 1A.

Middle East Economic Survey, September 22, 2003, A13.

Morse, Edward L. "Is the Energy Map Next on the Neo-Conservative Cartography Agenda?" reprinted from the Oxford Energy Forum in *Middle East Economic Survey*, August 18, 2003, D1-D3.

Naim, Moises. "Neft' razrushaet politiku i ozhidaniya lyudei" (Oil destroys policy and people's expectations). *Nezavisimaya Gazeta*, September 25, 2003.

Naumov, Igor. "Privatizatsionnie plany grandiozny tol'ko na bumage" (Privatization plans are grandiose only on paper). *Nezavisimaya Gazeta*, March 18, 2005.

Newman, Peter. "Implications for the Global Oil Industry." Oxford Energy Forum, November 2003.

Nye, Joseph. *The Paradox of American Power* (New York, NY: Oxford University Press, 2002).

Oil & Gas Journal, December 27, 1965.

Orekhin, Pyotr. "Gaz na gaz" (Gas for gas). *Nezavisimaya Gazeta*, April 11, 2005.

Orekhin, Pyotr. "Gazprom otkazyvaetsya ot prava diktovat' tseny" (Gazprom relinquishes the right to dictate prices). *Nezavisimaya Gazeta*, March 24, 2005.

Orekhin, Pyotr. "Sibneft and Lukoil mogut razdelit' sud'bu Yukosa" (Sibneft and Lukoil may share Yukos' lot). *Nezavisimaya Gazeta*, March 18, 2005.

Reznik, Irina and Rodion Levinsky. "Gazprom blagoslovil reeksport" (Gazprom has blessed re-export). *Vedomosti*, April 4, 2005.

Roginskiy, Stanislav. "Nuzhny li my drug drugu?" (Do we need each other?). *Neftegazovaya Vertikal'*, No.17 (2002).

Skornyakova, Anna. "BP soglasilas' na Slavneft" (BP has agreed to Slavneft). *Nezavisimaya Gazeta*, September 2, 2003.

Survey in *Izvestia*, September 9, 2003.

Telegina, Yelena. "Mirovoi energeticheskii rynok i geopoliticheskie interesy Rossii" (World energy market and Russia's geopolitical interests). *Mirovaya ekonomika i mezhdunarodnie otnosheniya*, No. 5 (2003).

The President of the United States. "The National Security Strategy of the United States of America." September 2002 (http://www.whitehouse.gov/nsc/print/nssall.html).

Tikhomirova, Yelena. "Uroven' tsen mozhet byt' sovershenno nepredskazuemym" (The price level can be completely unpredictable). *Nezavisimaya Gazeta*, March 24, 2005.

Tutushkin, Alexander, Yekaterina Derbilova and Svetlana Ivanova, "TNK-BP napugala rynok" (TNK-BP has frightened the market). *Vedomosti*, April 12, 2005.

US Department of Energy. Energy Information Administration. International Energy Database, February 2003 (http://iea.doe.gov/emeu/aer/pdf/pages/sec11-321.pdf).

Victor, David G. and Nadejda M. Victor, "Axis of Oil?" *Foreign Affairs*, March/April 2003.

"Vostoku Rossii nuzhny prioritety. Intervyu c Valeriem Pakom" (Russia's East needs priorities: An interview with Valeri Pak). *Neftegazovaya Vertikal'*, No. 5 (2005).

INDEX

[291]